HISTORY OF
WORLD SEAPOWER

HISTORY OF WORLD SEAPOWER

BERNARD BRETT

Photographic acknowledgments

Academia des Ciencias de Lisboa 46; Aerospatiale, France 239 bottom, BBC Hulton Library 16, 18, 21 top, 21 bottom, 108 bottom, 109; Bernard Brett Collection 6–7, 14, 47, 64–65, 232–233; Bibliothek fur Zeitgeschichte, Stuttgard 204, 205; Bridgeman Art Collection 32, 69, 95; British Aerospace 182, 184; British Museum 36; Bundersarchiv, Koblenz 154, 217; Cunard 104 top; Falklands Pictorial 144, 145, 147, 148, 214, 216; Fleet Air Arm Museum 179, 180, 185, 191; Fotomas 30, 42, 45 top, 55, 62, 68 bottom, 74, 79, 81 top, 97, 131; Grumman Aerospace 195, 230; Imperial War Museum 151 top, 152 top, 152 bottom, 153, 168, 222; Jorvik Viking Centre, York 41; Keystone 173, 174 top, 174 bottom, 207; Lockheed Corporation 252; Magdalene College, Cambridge 56–57; Mary Evans Picture Library 8, 12–13, 38–39, 48, 50, 54, 63, 66, 80, 81 bottom, 98, 99 top left, 99 top right, 104 bottom, 105 top, 105 bottom left, 105 bottom right, 106, 107 bottom, 110, 111 top, 111 bottom, 129, 134, 140, 141, 142, 156, 169, 171, 176; National Archives, Washington DC 82–83; National Maritime Museum, Greenwich 24–25, 51, 68 top, 72, 73, 76, 112; Public Records Office, London 150; Press Association, London 248; Robert Hunt Library 143, 146–147, 149, 151 bottom left, 189, 199, 202, 203, 208, 209 bottom, 210 top, 210 bottom, 215, 218, 223 top, 229, 231; Royal Air Force Museum 194; Royal Navy 241, 242, 247; Royal Navy Museum 31, 90, 92, 93, 94, 117, 126 bottom, 127, 128, 133, 136, 137, 138, 139, 161, 164 bottom, 166, 167, 172, 181, 183, 190; R. Nichol Collection 108 top, 139, 140, 186–187; Science Museum, London 45 bottom, 100, 101 top; Sheridan Photo Library 9, 10, 11 top, 11 bottom, 14 top, 17, 22, 26–27, 29, 33, 49, 53, 71, 75; Swedish Maritime Museum 77, 78 top, 78 bottom; The Research House 34, 102 top, 102–103, 103 top, 107 top, 182, 186, 197, 211, 219, 220; US Navy 83, 87, 114, 118, 119, 120, 121 top, 121 bottom, 122–123, 124, 125, 126 top, 131, 157, 159, 160, 163, 177, 178, 188 top, 188 bottom, 192–193, 198, 209 top, 224, 225, 226, 227, 228, 234, 235 top, 235 bottom, 237, 238, 239, 240, 243, 244, 245 top, 245 bottom, 246, 249, 250, 251; US Navy Historical Branch 82, 118, 164 top, 200–201

Front cover:	Top to bottom, left to right: Detail, *The Eve of the Coronation Review, 27 June 1911* by A.B. Cull (National Maritime Museum/Hamlyn Group Picture Library), *The Redoubtable* at Trafalgar by A.E. Mayer (Hamlyn Group Picture Library), Scene from Falklands War (Imperial War Museum), U.S.S. *New Jersey*, brought out for Vietnam, U.S.N. Skipjack with teardrop hull, (The Research House, London), The Battle of Salamis, 480 B.C. (The Mansell Collection, London)
Titlespread:	*The Pursuit of the Graf Spee* by Norman Wilkinson, 1939 (National Maritime Museum/Hamlyn Group Picture Library)
Back cover:	*The Battle of Trafalgar* by W.C. Clarkson, 1793–1867 (The Institute of Directors/Bridgeman Art Library, London)

**This edition produced exclusively for
W H Smith**

Published by
Deans International Publishing
52–54 Southwark Street, London SE1 1UA
A division of The Hamlyn Publishing Group Limited
London · New York · Sydney · Toronto

Copyright © The Hamlyn Publishing Group Limited 1985
ISBN 0 603 03723 2

Printed by Graficromo s.a., Cordoba, Spain

Contents

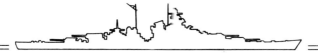

Oar Power

Since the beginning of time the oceans and seas which cover two-thirds of the earth's surface have presented man with a challenge. To the prehistoric tribes who built settlements along the water's edge it was, on the one hand, a valuable source of food, on the other, a force to be looked upon with awe, a mysterious element that was never still. Stretching further than the eye could see, subject to violent changes of mood, the waters were peopled with demons and monsters, and, later, as religion grew out of primitive animism and hunting magic, with gods and goddesses.

To the nomadic hunter-gatherer, rivers and lakes were serious barriers. Not being a natural swimmer like some other animals, man would have been confused by the sudden appearance of a stretch of water lying directly in his path. Faced with three alternatives – to retrace his steps, follow alongside the bank, or try to cross – man, being what he is, took up the challenge.

Our prehistoric forebear, who missed very little – his carefully observed drawings of animals bear witness to this – soon discovered that tree trunks and logs would float in water and would carry his weight

From an illustration of an Egyptian merchant ship, by the author.

A *contemporary interpretation of an ancient Egyptian ship.*

without sinking. An early chronicle credits Onous, a Phoenician, as the man who first thought of lopping the branches from a tree trunk and using it to keep him afloat while propelling himself through the water. But primitive man must have discovered this well before Sanchoniathon, a fellow Phoenician, wrote of it. From propelling an unstable log through the water, lying lengthwise and paddling with hands and feet, it was a short step to building more seaworthy craft with less likelihood of capsizing. Lashing several logs together to form a simple raft in time led to more advanced boat-building techniques, using whatever materials lay to hand: logs were hollowed out to become canoes; animal skins were inflated into water-wings or stretched over whicker frames; and reeds were bunched together to form buoyant raft-like boats. Curiously enough these early craft – the dugout canoe, coracle and

bari, and the kayak – have stood the test of time and are still in use in some parts of the world.

No one knows with any certainty who built the first ship, but the stone model of a sailing vessel, unearthed by Sir Flinders Petrie, the archeologist, at Fayim in Egypt, has been estimated to be 11,000 years old. Of more recent times, dating back to 4000 B.C., is an Egyptian vase decorated with a silhouette which is obviously a boat with a sail. Clearly the Egyptians used sailing ships for trade on the Nile, but these were river craft, not strongly enough constructed to venture out to sea. Later, despite their hatred of the sea, the Egyptians did build sea-going ships, clumsy vessels made from short, thick planks of 'sunt' – sycamore – held together with wooden pegs; these ships had neither ribs nor keel. The square sail, hoisted on a bipod mast only when a favourable wind blew up, was lowered to the deck when the ship was under oars, her main source of propulsion.

A papyrus of the Pharaoh Sneferu, dated around 2900 B.C., reveals that he commanded a fleet of 40 such ships to sail to Byblos in Phoenicia to trade for cedar wood, which could be cut into far longer planks. After due ceremony and religious incantations, they left the Nile Delta, and turning east into the Mediterranean, hugged the coast, never out of sight of land, during their voyage to Phoenicia. They were steered by six oars slung three each side of a sturdy platform mounted at the stern. Calling on the aid of the gods, they decorated the stern-posts and prows of their ships with the Sacred Ankh, or Symbol of Life and the Eye of Horus. Over the centuries, the eye became a popular symbol to paint on the prow of a ship and many of today's fishermen still use it on the front of their boats.

But the Egyptians were never a seafaring race, it was left to the neolithic inhabitants of Crete to establish the first great trading empire in the Mediterranean, destined to become the crossroads linking three continents. As early as 3000 B.C., sea-going vessels from this small island nestling in the sea, 200 miles from the North African coast, were exporting volcanic obsidian for edged tools and weapons to Egypt, and importing goods from Lipari, off Sicily. By 1200 B.C., Minoan merchants were carrying metalware, oil, almonds, wine and pottery from Crete to every port in the Mediterranean and had founded a colony on the coast of Palestine. Under the protection of Rhea, the Cretan mother-goddess, they ventured far beyond the sight of land, to dominate the sea trade of the eastern Mediterranean and Adriatic.

Unfortunately it is difficult to build up an accurate picture of their ships from the stylized impressions on their artifacts. These fanciful representations, drawn, engraved and carved by artists rather than seamen, offer the barest clues from which to construct a credible likeness. Steatite seal stones, unearthed by Sir Arthur Evans while excavating the palace of Knossos near Heraklion, the present-day capital of Crete, make it clear that some of their vessels were quite large, having one or two and, in some cases, even three masts. One such find is an ivory model of a sailing ship from the late Minoan period (1700–1500 B.C.), showing a cargo hold and cover. Another, an intaglio seal, depicts a single-masted ship carrying a horse, and in 1908, Professor Seager, an American ar-

cheologist, discovered, amongst other treasures, a heavy gold ring engraved with a ship leaving the shrine of Rhea. Following such slender clues, experts have been able to piece together a picture of the Minoan ship that became the prototype for all subsequent trading vessels of Classical times. These slow, ponderous vessels, up to 300 tons (305-tonnes) displacement, were driven by sail alone as large crews of oarsmen and the stores needed to feed them, took up far too much valuable cargo space.

By 800 B.C. the Greeks were becoming interested in sea commerce, founding overseas settlements and colonies that called for capacious trading vessels, but it was the Phoenicians who became the pioneers of the trade routes. Originating on the north coast of the Persian Gulf, the Phoenicians, or Sidonians as they later termed themselves, migrated to the eastern Mediterranean, where they founded the coastal cities of Tyre and Sidon. From there they launched out to set up colonies in the south of France and Spain, on the islands of Corsica and Sardinia and at Carthage. In time they became the greatest maritime trading power in the Mediterranean, pioneering the use of carefully charted trade routes, which took them as far north

A Minoan ship seal.

as Britain in search of tin from Cornwall and the Isles of Scilly. A hardy race of venturesome seafarers, accustomed to striking a hard bargain, they nevertheless hugged the coast wherever possible.

They built two types of merchant ship. The smaller, the 'gaulus', was used for coastal trading in and around the eastern Mediterranean and Aegean Sea. The larger 'hippo', or ship of Tarshish (a mysterious city, the exact location of which has never been determined), was an ocean-going vessel carrying a single square mainsail, laced to the cross yard of a central mast, with a steering oar mounted on each quarter. A deep-hulled ship, the length-to-beam ratio was 2.5 to 1; it was fully decked, with hatches for cargo and crew, although, according to a contemporary painting, cargo was sometimes carried above decks. They mounted wooden horses' heads on the stem-posts of their craft, and the upswept stern-posts were carved to re-semble fish-tails. It was in such ships as these that the Phoenicians sailed out into the Atlantic Ocean, south to the Canary Islands and north to southern Britain. There is also evidence to indicate, that, using a canal commenced during the reign of the Pharaoh Necho II, cut to link the mouth of the Nile with the Red Sea, they navigated the shores of the Indian Ocean in search of trade. A carving on a marble sarcophagus, discovered in the Old Harbour at Sidon in 1914, shows that the later Tarshish ships had an additional mast in the bows, which carried a small square sail laced to a single yard. Although this sail added little to the speed of the ship, it made it easier for her to steer a course.

The Phoenicians were a secretive people who kept their trade routes to themselves, spreading spine-chilling tales of sea monsters and supernatural demons of the deep in an attempt to discourage other mariners following after them. Jealous of the design

The battle between the 'Sea People' and the Egyptians, from the Medinet Habo reliefs.

of their vessels, they are known to be the first seamen to scuttle a ship rather than allow it to fall into the hands of an enemy to be copied. Eventually one of the ships of Carthage was washed up on the shores of Italy, an incident that was to put an end to 500 years of sea supremacy.

The Mediterranean Warship

The Athenian historian Thucydides speaks of King Minos of Crete as the first known king to build a strong navy and control the greater part of the Greek seas. It was natural that warships should evolve from the trading vessels. At first they were used to protect the slow, cumbersome traders from pirates, who from early times infested these seas, attracted by easy pickings and valuable cargoes. Later the warships became powerful fleets, able to support the invading armies of ambitious states seeking to dominate the eastern Mediterranean. The Minoan trader, gradually over the years, developed into a long, narrow, elegant galley, built for speed, with an upswept stern, a heavy, pointed bronze-plated ram at the bow and a narrow fighting platform running the full length of the

Top and above: Ships of the 16th century B.C., from a fresco at Santorini.

Below: A Phoenician warship from Sennacherib's campaign to Palestine, 702 B.C.

centre of the galley. The oared galley was to remain the principal fighting ship of the Mediterranean for the next 2,500 years. A large square sail which was slung horizontally was only hoisted to assist the rowers when the wind was in a favourable direction; it was unshipped and stowed when the ship went into action. Under its main means of propulsion, oar-power, the galley could reach a probable speed of 9 knots, covering long distances at a cruising speed of 4.5 knots, the rowers maintaining this for as long as 20 hours, fed at their benches with bread soaked in wine. When the flautist piped the beat up to ramming speed, it cut through the water at a good 12 knots, giving the vessel sufficient impetus to sink the ram deep into the hull of an enemy ship. Whenever possible the galleys were dragged ashore at night, stern first, to

An ancient Roman war trireme with ram.

10   20   30   40   50

S C A

allow a speedy launch in an emergency. Here they were propped up with poles or rocks. Crews lit their cooking fires and slept close to their ships, ready at an instant's warning to rush down the beach, leap aboard and stroke away to safety. When at sea they anchored for the night using a large pierced stone tied to a rope; the admiralty-type anchor was not introduced until about 600 B.C.

The Greek Trireme

The lack of records cloaks the trireme in mystery, although certain factors are clear – it was certainly rowed at three levels with one man to each oar. A chance comment by Thucydides confirms this, '. . . each sailor taking his oar, cushion and oar-strap . . .'. The early Greek trireme was propelled by 150 oarsmen, 50 to each bank;

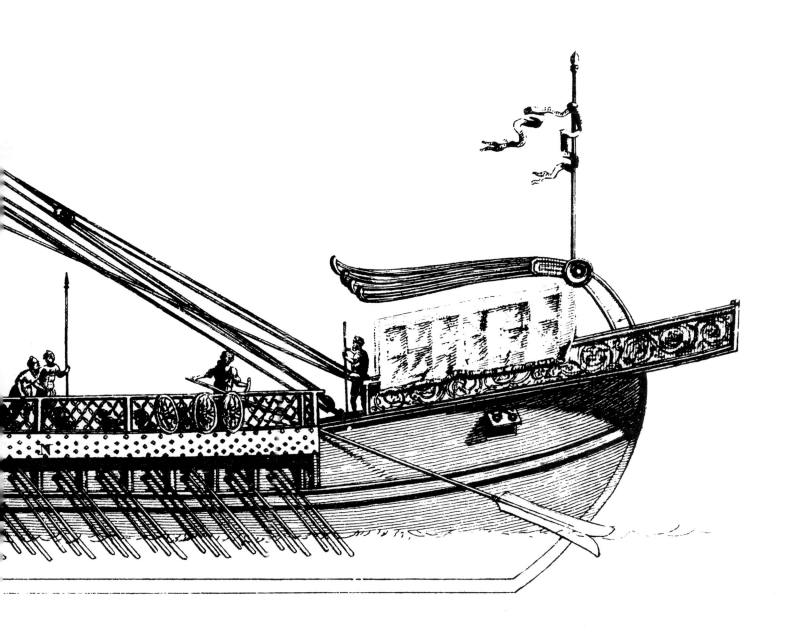

Top: The Argonauts, from an Attic plaque by the 7th-century B.C. painter Analatos.

Above: Interpretation of a Phoenician trading vessel, by the author.

the rest of her crew of 200 was made up of officers, petty officers, marines and archers. By the time of the Persian Wars, the numbers of oarsmen had increased to 170 who were drawn from the poorer citizens, but were not slaves. The 'thalamite', the lowest level, had 27 oarsmen each side, rowing through ports. They were close to the water, but with sufficient clearance for a small boat to creep beneath them. Ac-

cording to one chronicle this effective tactic was used by the Syracusians to attack Athenian rowers at their benches. The second bank of oars, the 'zigite', also had 27 oarsmen each side. The top bank, the 'thranite', had 31 oarsmen each side who rowed through an outrigger to give greater leverage.

The blades of the three oars, each at a different level, had no more than a square

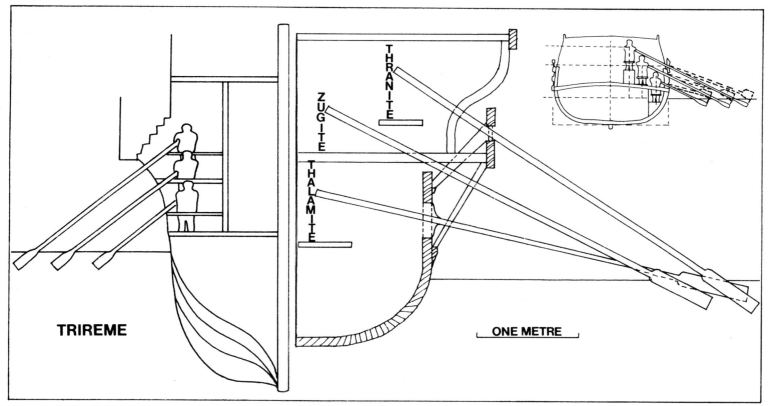

TRIREME

THRANITE

ZUGITE

THALAMITE

ONE METRE

yard in which to operate; this called for great rowing skills on the part of the oarsmen. Thucydides, an Athenian himself and no doubt biased, claimed that the skill of the Athenian oarsmen was the despair of their rivals at sea. It would seem that the Phoenicians were more skillful in open water, but the Athenians had the edge manoeuvring in their narrow home waters.

It was the Greeks, particularly the Athenians, who perfected the war galley. The ones used in the Trojan War, which took place about 1270 B.C., like those described by Homer in the *Iliad* and the *Odyssey*, were most likely of two types: the light, fast triakonter of 30 oars, 15 each side; and the heavier warship, the pentekonter of 50 oars, 25 each side, the oars set in a single bank. Thole pins, with leather loops to hold the oars, are often mentioned, so there can be little question that these galleys were rowed from benches, not paddled as canoes. (Furthermore, in the *Odyssey*, Homer refers to Odysseus dragging one of his drunken crew aboard, to leave him lying 'beneath the benches'.) The ships themselves were constructed of pine wood, their oars of polished fir. The mast, also of fir and slotted into a box attached to the ship's keel, could quickly be lowered before a battle, or taken ashore when the ship was not in use. Although Homer continuously mentions 'black ships', this almost certainly refers to the black tar or pitch, used to waterproof them below the waterline. Above the waterline, they were invariably painted in bright primary colours, vermilion being one of the

most popular hues. According to one record, an artist called Mimnes painted a snake along the hull of a ship in such a way that it appeared about to bite the helmsman.

As greater speeds were demanded of galleys, the danger of 'hogging' – the keel of the vessel arching through strain – and 'sagging' – a downward arching of the keel – made it dangerous to lengthen them to increase the number of oars in a single bank. The Phoenicians solved this problem by designing a ship with a double bank of oars. It was called the bireme and appeared towards the end of 700 B.C. It was about 80 ft (24 m) long with a 10-ft (3-m) beam and a narrow, railed fighting cat-walk running the full length of the ship. The bireme was taken an important step forward by the Greeks, sometime between 550 B.C. and 525 B.C., with the introduction of the trireme, the ultimate in Mediterranean war galleys. Its speed, manoeuvrability and ramming power immediately made all previous designs obsolete, in much the same way as the 'all big gun' battleship *Dreadnought*, commissioned at the turn of the 20th century, made all other types of ironclad obsolete.

The oars themselves, according to Athenian naval records, were between 13 ft 2 inches and 13 ft 10 inches (4.0 and 4.2 m) in length. The measurements of a ship shed, excavated at Piraeus, would seem to indicate a maximum dimension for triremes of 110 ft (33.5 m) in length, with an 18-ft (5.5-m) beam. As well as the 'trierach' or commander of the ship, each galley carried a pilot, ten hoplites or hea-

No one knows for sure the positions taken up by the rowers on a trireme; these are two of the more acceptable theories: left, Graser's and right, Lemaître's.

The Athenians leave Athens for Salamis, from a drawing by Pinelli.

vily armed foot-soldiers, four archers, 15 deck-hands to handle the sails and the working of the ship and a flautist to pipe the beat for the oarsmen. Many different rowing systems have been put forward, but in 'Frogs' (405 B.C.) Aristophanes suggests that the thalamite oarsman sat behind and below at least one of the other two, as he refers to a rower 'making wind into the face of the thalamite'.

This then was the vessel upon which the Athenian navy chiefly relied. The city had been slow to build a powerful fleet, but after suffering a humiliating defeat at the hands of Aegina, a small island peopled by pirates 20 miles (32 km) to the south of Athens, a powerful lobby was formed to demand an extensive shipbuilding programme. Yet the Aeginian threat was of small importance compared with the menace from Xerxes the Persian. At the height of his power, the Persian king's armies crossed the Hellespont in 492 B.C. and marched down the coast of Macedonia and Thrace. Supplies and equipment for these armies had to be transported by sea. A sudden storm off Mount Athos scattered his supply ships, and despite having the

waves whipped for having the temerity to disperse his fleet, Xerxes had to send back his troops for lack of supplies. After a second attempted invasion in 490 B.C. was repulsed by Milliades at the Battle of Marathon, the Greek Congress of States was confident that Xerxes would not return for a third attempt. Only Themistokles of Athens had doubts.

Themistokles was convinced that Xerxes would not let the matter rest there; infuriated by the two previous defeats suffered by his armies, the Persian would come again, but in even greater force. Time and time again the Athenian urged his fellow citizens to build up their navy, which at the time consisted of 40 ageing and outdated pentekonters. Never could the Congress of States beat the Persian hordes on land; its only hope lay in cutting off the enemy's food supply by destroying his fleet. Faced with starvation, he would be obliged to turn back. As archon – the archon, or regent was appointed by popular vote to lead Athens for one year – Themistokles had already persuaded the Athenian Assembly to build a strong naval base. By fortifying the peninsula of Piraeus and making use of its three natural harbours, the Athenians would be less vulnerable to a surprise attack. He commissioned moles to be built which narrowed the harbour entrances so that they could be closed with chains and stout walls were constructed connecting them with Athens. Previously the Athenians had hauled their ships to the open beaches of the Bay of Phalerum.

Unmoved by Themistokle's forceful arguments, the Assembly pleaded poverty as the excuse for not implementing his naval programme. Then in 483 B.C., the sensational discovery of a rich and totally unexpected silver lode in the state-owned mine at Laurium gave him his opportunity.

Estimated as being worth over 600,000 drachmas – 1 drachma a day was the income enjoyed by a middle-class family, 200 drachmas the accepted ransom for a captured man-at-arms – it was enough to cover the running expenses of the state and allow its citizens a flat-rate bonus of ten drachmas each. Seizing his opportunity, Themistokles pushed a Navy Bill through the Assembly, using the surplus silver to institute a shipbuilding programme. Although the timber felled to build the fleet denuded Attica of trees and led to soil erosion, by the middle of 480 B.C. Athens had the strongest navy in the Greek seas, more than all the other states combined.

Greek hoplites in battle.

She could then boast 200 superbly built and equipped triremes – long, low-lying galleys with powerful rams. The intervening years had been spent in bringing the crews up to strength and training them in sea warfare. The rowers practised manoeuvring into line ahead, line abreast and raising the beat with speed for ramming. Marines and archers perfected the use of their weapons on a rolling deck. The seamanship of the Athenians never measured up to that of the Phoenicians – who were at that time the mainstay of the Persian fleet – in open sea, but they were much the masters in their own narrow waters.

The Battle of Salamis

In 480 B.C. Themistokles was proved right. During the spring of that year, Xerxes assembled an invasion army in Asia Minor; approximately two million strong, it dwarfed to insignificance his two previous attempts. According to Herodotus, this army was supported by a fleet of 1,207 warships and 3,000 lesser ships carrying 200,000 men. The weather holding good, the Persian troops crossed the Bosphorus on two bridges of boats and followed the route of the former invaders down the coast of Macedonia. To avoid his fleet sharing the fate of the ships of the first expedition, which were wrecked off the treacherous coast below Mount Athos, Xerxes ordered a canal to be cut across the narrowest part of the peninsula, deep enough to take his largest ships. Relentlessly the Persian army pushed south. Leonides and his Spartans bought the Greeks time by their heroic stand at the pass of Thermopylae, but this did no more than slow down the juggernaut. Only when the Persians had plundered their way to within sight of Athens were the Greek forces fully mobilized and their ships manned. After bitter argument, and the violent opposition of Themistokles, the Athenians had reluctantly agreed to abandon their city in favour of making a stand at the narrow Isthmus of Corinth. Strongly fortified this would become the last line of defence against the Persian invaders. It took an oracle, forecast by Pythia, the priestess announcer of the will of Apollo at Delphi, to win the Athenians over to the plan.

An incident at the battle of Salamis.

'Safe shall the wooden wall continue for thee and thy children.
Wait not the tramp of the horse, nor the footmen mightily moving
Over the land, but turn your back to the foe and retire ye.
Yet shall a day arrive when ye shall meet him in battle
Holy Salamis, though shall destroy the offspring of women,
When men scatter the seed, or when they gather the harvest.'

On the strength of this nebulous prediction attributed to the god Apollo, the Athenians evacuated their city, crossing over to the island of Salamis. A small garrison, left behind to defend the Acropolis, held out for a fortnight, but was finally overrun and butchered to a man by the Persians. Helplessly the Athenians watched from the beaches of Salamis as their city went up in flames, their houses sacked, their temples desecrated. The sight of the immense Persian fleet rounding the southernmost tip of Attica and pulling their ships ashore at Phalerum, threw the southern Greeks into a panic. Fearful that a defeat at Salamis would cut them off from their homeland on the Peloponnese, they clamoured to withdraw the fleet to the Isthmus of Corinth. But the Athenians, who had no intention of leaving their relatives and fellow citizens to the mercy of Xerxes, insisted on facing the Persian fleet in the narrow straits of Salamis. Fortunately for the Greeks, the elements had again been unkind to the Persians – a hundred or so of their ships had been destroyed by gales or driven ashore by heavy seas. Nevertheless, nearly a thousand Persian galleys pulled into the Bay of Phalerum – seemingly impossible odds for the 380 ships assembled by the Greeks.

Although the Athenians had by far the largest fleet among the Greeks, the Spartan Eurybiades was, by reason of age, made commander-in-chief, but Themistokles, the Athenian admiral, had virtual tactical command. Seeing his allies beginning to waver, Themistokles, a wily politician as well as a fighting man, conceived a strategy. He had Sikkinos, his most trusted slave, rowed from Salamis across the straits to Phalerum, there to present himself before the Persian king. Sikkinos was to tell Xerxes that the Greeks intended escaping to the north under cover of darkness the following night. Furthermore, if Xerxes's fleet were boldly to attack the Greeks, Themistokles, realizing his cause was hopeless, would desert to the Persians, taking his 200 Athenian galleys with him.

Anxiously the Greek trierarchs huddled over their fires built alongside their triremes; sleep was out of the question since the admiral had told them of his plan. Would Xerxes be taken in? As the night wore on, the answer ran down the beaches from ship to ship – the Persian fleet was on the move. The news brought by Areistides the Just of Aegina had been confirmed by Panaitos of Tenos, a trierarch, who together with his crew had changed sides at the eleventh hour. One after the other, the Persian galleys paddled out of Phalerum to station themselves in three lines across the entrance to the Salamis straits: the top Phoenician fleet to the east of the Island of Pysttaleia (present day Lipsckoutali), the Ionians and other East Greeks to the left (these had joined the Persian cause as their islands had been overrun by the invaders). A hand-picked commando of 400 nobles and battle-seasoned infantry had been landed on the island to rescue any Persian survivors and slaughter any Greeks who sought refuge there. A powerful Egyptian squadron, a third of the Persian fleet, was sent racing up the west coast of Salamis to cut off any Greek ships attempting to escape past Megara in the north.

Themistokles looked to the north and south, dying fires marked the position of each trireme; it was still dark, but soon the sky would lighten in the east, heralding '. . . the fair, white horses of the day'. Around him, rank upon rank of Athenian marines crouched, hushed and expectant. 'All is at stake,' his voice carried across the beach, as he urged them to die rather than live as slaves under the Persian yoke. 'The very future of the Greek people lies in your hands.' The crews and rowers were already dragging the galleys through the sand to the water's edge. Soon they were afloat, the marines scrambling aboard as the banks of rowers began to paddle into deep water. The pipe of the flutes, eerie in the pre-dawn darkness, set the beat as the Greek galleys formed into line abreast, facing towards the mouth of the straits.

Dawn broke with the Persian fleet less than a mile ahead, the crews tired and jaded from paddling all night to keep station, the look-outs constantly alert, watching for the escaping Greeks. The Persian admirals had long since suspected a ruse, but even Ariabignes, the High Admiral, brother to Xerxes, had not dared to disobey the king's orders. At the first sight of the Greeks, the order to attack had run

Opposite top: 'The Battle of Salamis 480 B.C., by Kaufmann.

Opposite bottom: 'Conquerors of Salamis', by F. Cormon.

down the lines of the Persian fleet, water foamed round the blades of their oars as they dug in to reach ramming speed. The rhythmical singing of the dreadful Paian – 'O Saving Lord', the battle hymn of the Greeks – rolled across the water towards them. But the Greek centre was back-paddling, retreating into a deep crescent, drawing the Persians to the narrowest part of the channel. Forced to shorten line until they were only a few ships abreast, the Phoenician squadron found themselves crammed between Pysttaleia and the mainland. The Greek manoeuvre had been executed to coincide with the daily wind from the south, which always rose at the same hour and raised a heavy swell. As the Phoenicians struggled to keep a safe station, a great cry was heard from the Greek fleet, 'Men, how much further are you going to backwater?' Athenians swore it came from an 'apparition of a woman' – their goddess Pallas Athene. Trumpets blared along the Greek lines; the rowers thrust in their oars; and as the flautists raised the beat, the galleys gave a great leap forward, gathering speed to ram.

The astonished Phoenicians found themselves caught in a pincer movement, their heavy ships, buffeted by the wind and with oars entangled, were drawn to the centre of the channel unable to manoeuvre. The 30 ships of Aegina raced towards the Ionian squadron stationed in the narrows between Psyttaleia and the town of Salamis. Both fleets fought with their masts lowered, but the ships had been designed for quite different naval tactics. The Phoenicians, higher out of the water with massive upswept sterns, relied on archers and javelin throwers to soften up the enemy with a rain of arrows and darts prior to boarding him. The Greek galleys, on the other hand, were lower in the water, carried fewer fighting men – only ten marines and four archers – and relied almost entirely on ramming and sinking the enemy. Though slower and heavier than the Persian warships, they were more manoeuvrable in a choppy sea, and the bronze-shod ram, an extension of the keel, made a deadly naval weapon. Once the ram was deep in the hull of a foe, the rowers back-paddled, and, as the gaping hole began to fill with water and the enemy to sink, the Greek marines and archers took their toll. The poet Aeschylus, who took part as a marine in the Battle of Salamis, wrote that, 'the hoplites and archers did wonders and soon threw the enemy into confusion'.

Aeschylus goes on to give an eyewitness account of the battle, putting the words into the mouth of a Persian messenger who had carried the news of the defeat to the mother of Xerxes.

'The first rammer was a Greek
which sheared away a great Sidonian's
    crest;
then close, one on another, charged
    the rest.
At first the long-drawn Persian line
    was strong
and held; but in those narrows such a
    throng
was crowded, ship to ship could bring
    no aid.
Nay, with their own bronze-fanged
    beaks they made
destruction; a whole length of oars on
    beak
would shatter; and with purposed art
    the Greek
ringed us outside, and pressed, and
    struck;
and we –
our oarless hulls went over, till the sea
could scarce be seen, with wrecks and
    corpses spread.'
(from a translation by Gilbert Murray)

King Xerxes watched the battle from a throne set up on a promontory at the foot of Mount Aegaleos. Surrounded by scribes and secretaries, tablets at the ready, eager to record the prowess of each Persian captain, the king to his dismay saw the cream of his Phoenician squadron mauled by the Greeks. As the front rows ground to a halt, locked in combat with the Greeks, disabled or sinking, his following ships pressed on, ramming each other in a desperate attempt to manoeuvre. Marines and archers who threw themselves overboard to avoid going down with their ships, were clubbed to death by Greek hoplites manning small boats launched from Salamis, 'as men gaff tunnies or some shoal of fish'. Towards the end of the afternoon, Xerxes knew the battle was lost with most of his ships fleeing back to their base at Phalerum.

Among the Persian remnants that fought on was the galley of Artemesia, Amazon Queen of Caria. Audaciously flying a Greek banner, she rammed and sank the ship of King Clamasithymus, an old enemy of hers, although a Persian. The Greeks, believing her to be an enemy who had changed sides, allowed her to pass; only later did they realize that they had allowed

a prize of 10,000 drachmas, the reward for her capture, to slip through their fingers. Xerxes, also deceived, bitterly remarked, 'My men have become women and my women men'. A handful of Phoenician captains who complained to the king that the East Greeks had given them no support were less fortunate. Xerxes, seeing that the Ionians were still fighting on, ordered the Phoenicians to be beheaded '... to put an end to them playing the coward themselves then blaming their betters'. To add to the king's chagrin, a messenger arrived with news that his selected Persian commando unit on Psyttaleia had been cut to pieces by

Greek hoplites ferried across from Salamis. The following morning, after a night of thanksgiving and celebration, the Greeks pulled for Phalerum to finish off the Persian fleet, but the enemy had gone, ordered to return to Asia by Xerxes. It had been a great naval victory: the Persians had lost 200 ships, many more had been captured; the Greeks had lost only 40 ships. The destruction of the remainder of his fleet off Mycale in Asia Minor the following year, finally put an end to Xerxes's attempt to conquer Greece. Cut off from seaborne supplies, his army had no choice but to pull back in to Asia.

Warships on the Trajan Column in Rome.

Legions at Sea

For generations after the Battle of Salamis the Greeks were masters of the eastern Mediterranean, but other states were growing in power and were ready to threaten this supremacy. By reason of her dominating position on the north coast of Africa, Carthage, a Phoenician colony, was clearly destined to become a great sea power. She had sided with the Persians at the time of Salamis, attacking the Greek colonies in Sicily, and strangely enough, suffering a naval defeat at Himera on the northern coast on the very day that Xerxes's fleet was routed. Smarting under this setback, Carthage concentrated on building up her navy. However, many years were to pass before she was finally able to wrest the mastery of the Mediterranean from Athens. By then Greece had been weakened by internal squabbles, the invasions of Alexander the Great and the threat from Rome, now a major power.

Rome essentially, was a land power and although her invincible legions were extending her empire to both the east and the west, she fully realized the need for a strong fleet to control the seas if she were to continue to expand. At the time of the first Punic War in 264 B.C., Rome was forced to rely on outdated triremes manned by her Greek allies to oppose the mighty quinquiremes of Carthage. The quinquiremes completely dominated the western Mediterranean, shattering Roman sea communications and mounting attacks on the Italian coast itself – little wonder that the Carthaginians were able to boast that they had prevented the Romans bathing on their own Italian beaches. It was during such an attack on Sicily, in an attempt to force the coastal towns and ports to surrender, that one of Carthage's quinquiremes was wrecked on the Italian coast. It fell into the hands of the Romans virtually intact and they were quick to seize the opportunity to use it as a model. The Roman Senate decreed that a fleet of 100 such quinquiremes and 20 triremes should be built, using the skills of the Greek shipwrights who had settled in Italy.

Teams of rowers were trained on dummy rowing benches constructed ashore, ready to man the ships as they were launched. The consul Caius Duilius, who was given command of the embryo navy, soon discovered that training ashore was no match for experience at sea, and unless some new weapon were discovered, his fledgling sailors would be completely annihilated by the hardy Carthaginians. Invincible on land, the Romans, even at the height of their naval power, always remained soldiers at sea rather than sailors. Not for them the sudden charge to ram, the outflanking tactic, or the 'dickplous' – breaking through the enemy line to take him from the rear. Thus any new weapon for the Romans would need to exploit their prowess as hand-to-hand fighters – Caius Duilius came up with the grappling iron.

The war against Carthage was already four years old when, in 260 B.C., the Romans fought their first sea battle at Mylae on the north coast of Sicily. A Carthaginian fleet of 125 galleys, sighting a slightly superior force of Roman ships, immediately attacked. Thirty of their fastest galleys raced in for the initial assault, confident of an easy victory. To their astonishment, at the first impact hinged gangways, 36 ft (11 m) long and 4 ft (1.2 m) wide, dropped from the Roman ships. A spike at the end, known as the corvus, bit deeply into the decks and held the gangways firm. Taken completely by surprise, the Carthaginians were overwhelmed by the Roman marines, who swarmed across the gangways and made quick work of the action with their short swords. In this first Roman naval action, more than 40 of the enemy were sunk or captured. The remainder lost heart and fled for their home ports. By 67 B.C., the Roman navy had complete control of both the eastern and western Mediterranean, but it had its setbacks. In 249 B.C., the consul Appius Claudius Pulcher was defeated at Drepanum, losing 93 ships and 20,000 marines to the enemy. However, this was put down to the admiral going into action against the signs of an oracle. Informed that the sacred chickens were refusing to eat, he replied, 'Throw them into the sea, if they don't want to eat, they can drink, then.' This sacrilegious remark all but cost him his life; only the intervention of powerful relatives and friends allowed him to escape with a heavy fine. Hannon, a Carthaginian admiral defeated off Sicily, was less fortunate; on returning home, he was tried, condemned to death and crucified.

Later Mediterranean Galleys

The dominance of the heavy Roman warship, however, was coming to an end. Agrippa, a Roman admiral, demonstrated that fast, light craft could be just as

Overleaf: The Battle of Lepanto, 1571, from a painting of the Venetian School.

23

A mosaic of a lighthouse and ships at Ostia.

effective if handled intelligently. During the Battle of Actium in 31 B.C. between Octavian and Mark Antony (supported by his mistress, the Egyptian Queen Cleopatra) who were struggling for internal power, small light craft immobolized Mark Antony's heavier, slower ships by running alongside and shearing off their oars. Over the years the Roman galleys were provided with new forms of armament; catapults were fitted to the upper deck, some of which could hurl half a ton of stone or lead a distance of 600 or 700 yards (550 or 640 metres). Crude harpoons (heavy logs with iron beaks) when fired from a catapult proved as revolutionary as the grapnel had been. Greek fire, a mixture of naphtha, sulphur and pitch, blown through long copper tubes or thrown in the form of grenades, was used effectively to set enemy vessels ablaze. For the next 200 years, Roman galleys not only dominated the Mediterranean, but ventured beyond the Pillars of Hercules to invade the countries of the north, including Britain.

The many-oared galley continued to be the main type of warship used in the Mediterranean right up to the major naval engagement at Lepanto in 1571. Outside the Mediterranean, the galley made its final appearance during an even later naval engagement which took place in the Baltic in 1790, and there were still a few in service during the Russo-Swedish War of 1809. While still continuing to rely on oar-power assisted by auxiliary sails, the

galley underwent a number of radical changes over the centuries. By the beginning of the 12th century A.D., the trireme and more cumbersome quinquireme, had given way to the fast, heavily armed dromon. The dromon carried up to three masts with lateen sails. The lateen sail, of Arab origin and triangular in shape, was laced to a long sloping yard controlled by a system of blocks and tackles which allowed the vessel to sail against the wind. It was armed with 'ballistae', giant crossbows which projected heavy spears, and 'catapultae' which hurled stone balls. It also carried a Greek fire projector, positioned in the bows.

By the time of the Battle of Lepanto, the Venetian galleass had been introduced; it was the direct result of an attempt to combine the fire power of the sailing galleon with the manoeuvrability of an oared galley. A type of oared frigate, it was the first naval vessel to fire cannon through gun ports. The Venetian galleass used at Lepanto carried three lateen-rigged masts and rowed 26 oars each side, four men to each oar. They had eight broadside cannon, four each side, mounted on the upper deck above the rowers, two large guns mounted in the after castle and eight more in a circular turret at the prow. There was also the powerful iron-tipped ram. The role of the galleass was to lead the attack; two abreast they would pepper the enemy with cannon shot, slowing him down to allow the galleys to ram and board.

The Battle of Lepanto off the Gulf of Corinth opened at first light on 7 October 1571. The fleet of the Holy Alliance under the command of Don John of Austria, the 25-year-old natural son of the Emperor Charles V, was made up of 279 galleys and six Venetian galleasses and carried 29,000 men. The Holy Alliance, patiently formed by Pope Pius V, consisted of the ships of Spain, Genoa, Venice, the Papal States and the Knights Hospitallers of Jerusalem, a militant order based at Malta. Their aim was to crush the Turkish fleet that was now bearing down on them before a gusty wind. Under the command of Ali Pasha, it had been marauding in the eastern Mediterranean; 352 vessels were under sail carrying 25,000 men.

The wind suddenly dropped as the two fleets approached each other in the Bay of Lepanto (now the Bay of Corinth), sails were furled and oars became the sole motive power for both fleets. At about noon the galleasses leading the Christian van opened up, pouring a hail of shot into the Turkish galleys, which had nothing to match the Venetian cannon. Suffering heavy casualties and with oars smashed, the Turks were thrown into hopeless confusion. Nonetheless, they pressed dauntlessly onwards to become locked in long and bloody combat with the galleys of the Holy Alliance. By the end of the day the Turks were in flight, completely routed, with the loss of virtually all their commanders. They lost 190 of their ships and 20,000 men were slaughtered. Ali Pasha himself was beheaded and 12,000 galley slaves released.

The galley, eminently suitable for the Mediterranean, proved to be impractical in the sterner northern waters. Those accompanying the Spanish Armada of Philip II in the 'Enterprise Against England' of 1588 were a distinct liability.

Beyond The Horizon

The very earliest mariners had an irrepressible urge to see beyond the horizon, a need to explore the unknown. This urge, whether in the name of religion, trade, colonization, personal curiosity, or just plain piracy, drove them to take untold risks and suffer fearful hardship. Putting aside a superstitious dread of sea monsters, water demons and jealous gods who, at their whim, could turn a placid sea into a raging maelstrom, the early explorers pointed their prows towards the horizon and sailed into the unknown. More often than not their discoveries came as a result of being blown off course by a storm. Such accidental sightings, when recounted on their return, inspired others to follow wittingly in their tracks.

Phoenician Traders

The Phoenicians sailing out of Tyre were motivated solely by trade, a need to establish new outlets for their glassware, bronze artifacts and dyes, in particular Tyrrean purple, the 'royal' purple used only for the robes of kings. Their ships returned laden with linen, cotton, 'wheat from Minnith', 'horns of ivory', emeralds and other precious stones, honey, oils and balm, and the raw materials of the mysterious Tarshish. There is more than a touch of envy as well as a prediction of doom behind Ezekiel's Biblical reference to Tarshish and the ships of Tyre. 'Tarshish was thy merchant by the multitude of all kinds of riches; with silver, iron, tin and lead, they traded in thy fairs.' (Ezekiel 27:12) His description of their ships is no less envious: 'Thy borders are in the midst of the seas, thy builders have perfected thy beauty. They have made all thy shipboards of fir trees of Senir; they have taken cedars from Lebanon to make masts for thee. Of the oaks of Bashan they have made thy oars: the company of

Ashurites have made thy benches of ivory, brought out of the isles of Chittem. Fine linen with broidered work from Egypt was that which thou spreadeth forth to be thy sail: blue and purple from the isles of Elishah was that which covered thee. The inhabitants of Zidon and Arvad were thy mariners. O Tyrus, that were in thee, were thy pilots. The ancients of Gebal and the wise men thereof were in thee thy caulkers.' (Ezekiel 27:4 to 9)

Although they generally hugged the coast, it nonetheless took great courage to penetrate strange seas, to land on potentially hostile shores and to venture beyond the Pillars of Hercules and face the possibility of falling off the edge of the world into the abyss. Herodotus was highly sceptical of an account he heard during his travels in Egypt that told of a Phoenician circumnavigation of Libya (the name given to the whole of Africa in classical times). Yet there is a ring of truth about the story. According to a Greek historian, Necho II (610–594 B.C., the Egyptian pharaoh who decreed the cutting of the canal linking the Nile with the Red Sea) sent an expedition of 'Phoenician men in ships', ordering them to sail back through the Pillars of Hercules until they came to the 'Northern Sea' (Mediterranean) and 'thus to Egypt'. This presupposes a knowledge that Africa was surrounded by sea except where it borders Asia, and poses the question, 'Had other explorers preceded the Phoenician expedition?' Seemingly the Phoenicians in their trading 'hippos' made their way into the Southern Sea (Indian Ocean) and crept down the east coast of Africa, sailing by day and putting ashore each night. Unfortunately there is no account of the native tribes and animals who would surely have been drawn to investigate their cooking fires. When each

Opposite: A Phoenician trading ship of the 1st/2nd century.

autumn came they put ashore and planted corn, settling there until it became ripe and could be harvested, then once again they would take to the sea. No doubt during this time they took the opportunity to careen the hulls of their ships, overhaul their sails and rigging, and make good any damage sustained on the voyage. Rounding the Cape of Good Hope, the explorers made their way up the west coast, reaching the Pillars of Hercules in the third year. If the Phoenicians did in fact undertake this voyage, then they must have sailed the best part of 14,000 miles (22,400 km), which would say a lot both for their determination and for the strength of construction of their ships.

It has even been suggested, though the evidence for this is extremely scanty, that the Phoenicians preceded the Vikings and Columbus in discovering the New World. As 2,000 years were to elapse before the introduction of the magnetic compass to guide mariners across open seas, they could only have been driven helplessly westwards by prevailing winds, probably making a landfall somewhere on the coast of Brazil.

Viking Exploration, Rapine and Plunder

The Mediterranean galley with its banks of rowers was completely unsuitable for the sterner seas of the north. An entirely different type of ship evolved there, one designed to withstand the mountainous waves, racing tides and fierce winter winds of these inhospitable waters. A superficial resemblance to early Greek ships has led to the supposition that northern ships and boats were based on Mediterranean designs that had found their way across Europe. This can hardly be the case, as rock carvings of boats have been found in Scandinavia dating back to 2000 B.C., hundreds of years before Mediterranean mariners ventured into the Atlantic. This suggests that the ships of northern Europe developed independently and that faced with similar problems of boat construction, the northern Europeans arrived at similar solutions. These early craft were most probably made from animal hides stretched across a wooden frame, stitched together and waterproofed. They were light enough to be easily carried across land on the shoulders of the crew, in much the same way as the Irish curragh or coracle is today.

As early as the 3rd century, the Irish were sending out expeditions to explore beyond their shores, sometimes with a strictly religious motive, but more often with piracy and marauding in mind. In 222 A.D. Cormac MacArt left Ireland in command of a sizeable fleet on a three-year cruise of outright piracy, ravaging the English coast to such an extent that a special force had to be raised in the West

Irish monks, seeking solitude, sailed into the unknown in flimsy vessels. From a medieval illuminated manuscript.

Country. He reached as far north as the Orkneys, and it was as a result of this voyage that the Irish priests and monks began to undertake their long voyages to set up religious settlements in the northern seas. The national character of the Irish has always produced acolytes drawn to religious enclaves built on remote islands and it is natural that some should have settled in Iceland. Their claim to have discovered North America before the Vikings, is by no means impossible. Iceland is only a short distance from Greenland, a natural stepping stone to the American mainland. In Irish legend the three sons of Ua Corra collected five companions and sailed west for 40 days and 40 nights, reaching a mythical land; from there they contrived to get back to Spain in 540 A.D.

Sadly, the early Irish priests who settled in Iceland kept no records; deliberately cutting themselves off from the world, they had no wish to encourage visitors. Much of our knowledge of these adventurous clerics who were prepared to brave heavy seas in their flimsy boats in search of solitude comes from chance references in old Norse sagas. Around the 9th century, the Viking Naddod, returning home to the Faroes from a voyage to Norway and being overtaken by a gale, ran before the wind – the usual practice of seamen of the day. His flimsy ship was tossed westwards, until on the tenth day the crew sighted an active volcano. Their miserable plight overcoming their superstitious terror of the volcano, they made a landing, where they found 'woods without end and fair pastures dripping butter'. Remaining there throughout the summer, they left at the onset of winter naming the country Snowland. They were followed by other Norsemen who brought

Early Irish wicker vessel.

31

Model of the Gokstad Viking ship in the Science Museum, London.

back evidence of Irish settlement. One of these expeditions had come upon a group of white-robed priests and acolytes singing on the shore and, without a moment's thought, they had wantonly butchered them. Eventually Iceland was colonized by hardy farmers, traders and unruly ne'er-do-wells, outlawed from their native Norway.

The era of the Vikings, originally the men of the '*viks*' or bays, began around 800 A.D. and lasted for about 500 years. Before long the name came to be associated with the Norse sea-rover, the scourge of honest folk from the Orkneys to the Black Sea. Although the Norwegian Vikings laid claim to the actual title 'Northmen' for themselves, the term in history really embraces other Scandinavian people also –

Angles, Saxons, Jutes and the Wends of the Baltic. Whatever their nationality, all became a terror to the more settled communities of northern Europe. The sea was in their blood. The title 'Sea-king' which was given to the leaders of the marauding bands was synonymous with honour and nobility. But even if the sea was 'in their blood' the Scandinavians took to the water as much from necessity as from choice. The Viking story is firmly linked with their emergence as the undisputed masters not only of the turbulent northern seas but also of the calmer waters of the Mediterranean. They lived by the sea, scouring it for loot in coastal raids and piratical sorties, trading with distant lands and voyaging into uncharted seas to settle and colonize. It has been suggested that there were more Danes at sea during the first part of the 9th century than there were on land.

All this was made possible by the skill of their shipwrights, whose contribution to ship design had a crucial bearing on the development of future northern European vessels. The ships of the Vikings, double-ended with high prows and sterns, were the culmination of several centuries of refining previous successful designs. Mainly by trial, error and practical experience, they created a ship which was stout enough to brave the wild North Atlantic seas and take them into the sub-Arctic latitudes of Iceland and Greenland. The seaworthiness of these craft was proved beyond doubt by Captain Magnus Anderson and his crew in 1893, when they built an exact replica of a Viking ship found in a burial mound at Gokstad in Norway and sailed it across the Atlantic Ocean. Putting out from her Norwegian home port on 30 April, she headed into the Atlantic and 28 days later made landfall in Newfoundland. She rode out a number of fierce gales without damage and at times reached speeds of 10 or 11 knots when under sail. A later replica, the *Hugin*, built at Frederikssund near Copenhagen in 1949, sailed with a crew of 53 'Vikings' from Esbjerg in Denmark to the coast of Kent in two weeks. This 'snekja', or snake, 71 ft (21.6 m) long with an 18-ft (5.5-m) beam, is still to be seen at Pegwell Bay near Ramsgate.

Fierce, ruthless and without pity, the Vikings would swoop out of the blue to sack and pillage the coastal towns of north-western Europe, carrying off their gold, raping and enslaving their women and

A relief of a 10th-century Viking ship and warriors at Gotland.

33

THE VIKING SHIP

The longship, the most advanced craft of her day, has become the accepted symbol of the Viking. There were no finer shipwrights in Europe than Norse shipwrights, no finer seamen than Norse seamen. Between them they snatched the mastery of the seas from other European maritime nations. To them the ship was the symbol of power, a way of life and a companion in death. A sea-king was buried in his ship – seated or lying at the stern, he was surrounded by his weapons, often with his favourite battle-axe or broadsword grasped in his dead hand, and facing the prow for the voyage to another life. Before him was piled food, treasure, tools, household goods and the ship's equipment; the horses and dogs, sacrificed for his benefit, were placed round the ship. Ship and warrior were buried under a mound of earth, or in a pit. Sometimes a mortally wounded sea-king, along with his dead comrades, would be set adrift in a blazing ship.

It is precisely this custom of burying warriors in their ships, particularly when it occurred in heavy blue clay, that has given us so much information regarding the construction of their vessels. Unlike the early people of the Mediterranean, the Norsemen have left considerable evidence of their ship lore. Not only are there the burial finds, but also there are highly informative drawings which have been incised or carved into stone, some vigorous impressions scratched on to scraps of wood and various detailed accounts in their sagas and chronicles. The best preserved examples of Viking ships have been excavated from burial mounds around the Oslo Fjord at Gokstad, Oseberg and Tune. (Many other examples have been found in other burial sites, but these are less well preserved.) Although their basic construction is the same, there is sufficient variation to indicate that numerous specialized types of ships had been developed.

The Norse system of defining the size of a ship is a complex one. Smaller vessels were classified by the number of oars, the 'tolfaeringr' (12-oared boat) being the biggest of this class. For ships which had between 12 and 26 oars, classification was made by the number of rowers on each side; the larger ships (more than 26 oars) were defined by the number of bench places (each bench place was called a 'sess'). The type of Viking ship used to plunder the coasts of northern Europe during the 8th and 9th centuries was usually a 'fimtansessa' (15-bencher), but in some cases '20-benchers' were used. The 'rum', the space or room between the benches, was also at times used to describe the size of a ship. Of the warships, the 'snekkja' or 'snake' was the one most commonly employed. Usually a '20-bencher', it had an overall length of over 70 ft (21 m), with an 18-ft (5.5-m) beam and carried up to 150 fighting men. The biggest warships of all were the dreaded 'drekar' or dragons, ships of 32 'rum' – '32-benchers.' The longship of Olaf Tryggvason, the *Ormrinn Langi*, or *Long Serpent*, a vessel of 34 'rum', has been described by Snorre the skald – 'of all the ships in Norway she was the best made and at the greatest cost', rowed at speed, she looked like 'the flutter of an eagle's wings'. Built by the shipwright Thorberg, she was, according to the saga of Olaf Tryggvason, '... 180 ft [55 m] long with a beam exceeding 38 ft [11.6 m] and with stem and stern posts rising 15 ft [4.6 m] above the water'. In Snorre's account, eight men sat at each oar and 30 'stafnbúi' stood in the prow, but a crew of 574 is hardly credible; this number was most likely inflated as the legend grew.

The Vikings gave their craft fanciful names, probably referring to the carved prows: *Visundr* (Bison), *Trani* (Crane), *Stigandi* (Strider). A chronicler of 1013 describes some of the carvings on the ships of King Sven's invasion fleet about to set out for England.

'On one side lions moulded in gold were to be seen on the ships, on the others birds on the tops of the masts indicated by their movements the winds as they blew, or dragons of various kinds poured fire from their nostrils. Here there were glittering men

Top two pictures: Close-up of the construction of a Viking ship from a model.

Above right: This model clearly shows the sweeping lines that made these ships so seaworthy.

Right: The prows were usually decorated with the carved heads of animals and birds.

of solid gold or silver nearly comparable to live ones, there bulls with necks raised high ... One might see dolphins moulded in electrum, and centaurs in the same metal...'

The Gokstad ship, built about 900, was discovered in 1880 buried in layers of blue clay which had preserved its woodwork almost intact. Unlike the Mediterranean galleys which were 'carvel-built' (the planks of the hull being set flush, edge to edge), its planks, or strakes, overlap each other in 'clinker' construction and are riveted together.

The keel, T-shaped in cross-section, is adzed from one single piece of oak, scarfed to which are the stem and stern, rising in an elegant but sharply defined curve. The 19 ribs, 3 ft (0.9 m) apart, which run the length of the keel are firmly married to the crossbeams which tie the ships together. Incidently the crossbeams also carry the pine decking, which is not nailed down but laid loose, enabling it to be taken up for bailing or stowing gear. The strakes, each skillfully scarfed, are about 1 inch (2.5 cm) thick, except for the 'main plank' which runs along the waterline and the fourteenth strake which bears 16 circular holes for the oars; these are left somewhat heavier to bear the added strain. Below the waterline the strakes are not nailed but are lashed to the ribs using pliable spruce roots. This allowed the vessel considerable 'give', reducing the stress and strain on her and the consequent danger of the ship breaking up in heavy seas. Above the waterline the strakes are nailed with wooden pegs to naturally grown knees, L-shaped pieces of wood attached to the crossbeams. They are riveted together with iron nails clenched over a washer on the inboard side of the vessel. To make them watertight, the strakes have been caulked with loosely woven wool-yarn and horse-hair, then the whole vessel is coated with tar to make doubly sure. In bad weather, or under sail, the oar-holes – each with a vertical slit to take the blade of the oar – were closed on the inside with circular wooden discs, swivelled on a nail.

When she was excavated, the Gokstad ship had 64 overlapping shields hanging from a rail just below the gunwale, 32 each side; these were painted alternately black and yellow. It appears that the crews hung their shields in this fashion when in harbour, possibly for recognition – they would certainly have been stowed inboard when at sea. The oars, made from pine, vary in length from 17 to 19 ft (5.2 to 5.8 m), to ensure that they would strike the water together, despite the curve of the ship's side. As there are no built-in benches and the holes for the oars are too low down for the ship to have been rowed from a standing position, it is assumed that the oarsmen either sat on their sea chests or had removable thwarts. When under sail the oars were stowed in T-shaped racks, 7 ft (2.1 m) above the deck. She was steered by means of a rudder with a detachable tiller, mounted on the starboard quarter. Shaped like a heavy, broad oar, it projects about 18 inches (46 cm) below the hull of the ship and can be swivelled round on an oak

block to a horizontal position. From the 11th century onwards, ships carried a richly decorated bronze weather vane, most likely placed at the prow of the vessel – several are displayed on the prows of a fleet in a Norwegian wood-carving. Longships usually carried one or more small boats, either stowed on deck or towed; these were graceful, clinker-built versions of the ship itself. Of the three found at Gokstad, one was 30 ft (9.1 m) long with three pairs of oars which were rowed from rowlocks.

Frames for roomy tents, their gables carved with grotesque animal heads to ward off the evil spirits of the night, were also found at Gokstad, along with dismantled bed frames. While in habour it was the custom to erect these tents on the deck to sleep under, but on coastal voyages, they would be pitched ashore each night. Once ashore, a fire would be lit and the cooking gear brought out. Freshly caught meat or fish might be roasted on a spit, but when it was dried or smoked, it would almost certainly be stewed in a huge bronze or iron cauldron and eaten with a spoon or a knife from a wooden bowl.

In contrast to the Gokstad ship, whose austere beauty lies in the stark functionalism of her graceful lines, the ship discovered at Oseberg in 1903 is richly carved and decorated. In general construction it is similar to the Gokstad ship, though a few feet shorter in length, but the amidships gunwale to keel measurement, scarcely 3 ft (1 m) deep, points to its being used as a ceremonial vessel, or at best, a pleasure cruiser of a chieftain designed for the sheltered waters of a fjord. It lies far too low in the water for an ocean-going vessel. At stem and stern it is lavishly carved with spiralling arabesques, sinuous interlaced animals and coiling snakes which are sometimes fearful, sometimes humorous, but always grotesque.

STATISTICS OF THE GOKSTAD SHIP

Length	76 ft 6 inches (23.3 m)
Beam	17 ft 6 inches (5.4 m)
Depth amidships	6 ft 5 inches (2.0 m)
Length-breadth ratio	4.50:1
Displacement – unloaded	9 tons (dead weight) (9 tonnes)
Loaded – crew and equipment	circa 18 tons (18 tonnes)
Draught	3 ft (0.9 m)
Crew	70
Oars – made from pine	32 – from 17 to 19 ft long (5.2 to 5.8 m)
Height of mast	approx 40 ft (12.2 m) – made of pine, up to 1 ft (0.3 m) circumference
Width of yard	approx 16 ft (4.9 m)
Number of strakes	16

burning their crops and dwellings. The old litany 'From the fury of the Northmen, good Lord deliver us', was an all-too-common prayer in those times. Dreaded beyond all others were the 'Berserks' or 'wolf-skins'. Surrounded by mystery, regarded with horror even by their own people, these half-crazed warriors were dedicated to frenzied butchery, stimulating themselves to animal fury by rhythmical baying and leaping. Sometimes clad in animal skins with the head as a mask, at other times naked, they, according to one saga,

'. . . advanced without mail-coats, and were as frenzied as dogs or wolves; they bit their shields; they were as strong as bears or boars; they struck men down, but neither fire nor steel could mark them. This was called Berserk Rage.'

The larger Viking piratical raids against Britain, which began about 789 A.D., were

An Anglo-Saxon version of a Viking Dragon ship, from a 10th-century manuscript.

never haphazard affairs. They all basically followed a similar plan. Initially a strong reconnaissance force of two or three ships would arrive to prod and probe along the coast, looking for a likely place to attack and a good position to set up a base that could be easily defended. This usually turned out to be an island at the mouth of a river, which the bigger expedition, following the reconnaissance group, transformed into a fortified camp, supply dump

and arsenal. From there, sorties thrust inland, pillaging and looting as they went. Their aims in life were plunder, women and drink, yet these cruel sea-rovers were often drawn to settle down, assimilating easily with those Britons left alive.

Their cruelty, especially towards prisoners, was as much a matter of policy as sadistic pleasure. Future victims would fly leaving their treasures behind, rather than face the possibility of being flayed alive. In extreme cases when local weapon-men had killed or maimed many of their number, the Vikings inflicted the dreadful death of the 'Blood Eagle' on them. Stripped to the waist, the victim's ribs were carefully opened up like those of an eagle and their pumping lungs drawn out; the lucky ones died at the first initial shock.

In a raid on the coast of Northumbria, Ragnor Lodbrok, one of the more violent of the sea-kings, was captured, while plundering his way inland, by Ella the king. Unwisely, Ella put Ragnor to death by having him thrown into a pit of poisonous snakes. When the news of this reached Denmark, Ragnor's sons, incensed at their father's terrible death, began to raise a fleet to exact revenge. Descending on the east coast in 867, they captured York, and, using it as a base, spread into Northumbria. They took Ella prisoner and Ragnor's sons not only subjected him to the death of the 'Blood Eagle', but added the refinement of tearing his ribs apart with red-hot irons before ripping out his lungs.

After their first raids on the English coast, the Vikings left the country alone for a time, turning their attention to Ireland, the west coast of Scotland and the Isle of Man. They returned in 835 to capture Thanet and the Isle of Sheppey. Their 'Great Army' landed in 865 to begin a systematic invasion of England. It was finally, 13 years later, forced to accept the terms of Alfred the Great who had become King of the West Saxons in 872. Although it was Alfred's predecessor, Ethelred, who first fought a naval engagement against the Norsemen in which he captured nine of their ships and scattered the rest, it was Alfred, however, who laid the foundations of a permanent navy. He saw the importance of facing an enemy at sea, scattering his fighting ships and transports before a landing could be achieved – a policy which maritime nations have followed ever since.

Not only did Alfred have an uncanny grasp of naval tactics, but he realized that sea power depended very much upon the number and quality of ships within a fleet and their strategic disposition round the coast. The Saxon Chronicle records that the king himself designed and introduced new types of ships. These ships were twice as long as their contempories with a higher freeboard, which gave archers and spearmen the advantage of hurling their missiles down upon the enemy. Fast and seaworthy, steadier at sea than others of their day, they had 60 or more oars, though the Chronicle also mentions ships of 40 oars. In action, the king ordered, Norsemen were to be regarded as pirates and no quarter given. The Chronicle in one part refers to Alfred's brother and valued adviser Saint Neot as fighting on shipboard in 851; such militant priests were by no means uncommon at the time.

Frustrated by the opposition put up by Alfred's fleet, the Norsemen turned their attention to France, sailing up her rivers to attack and lay waste the inland towns. Rouen was sacked, and burning and plundering, they continued up the Seine to

Drawings of Saxon ships from Stratt's Chronicle of England, based on Saxon illuminations.

attack Paris. Here, the fortified Isle de Cité held out and the marauders had to content themselves with looting the abbeys and sweeping upstream as far as Melun. Despite being bought off by Charles the Bald, they returned to the Seine in 885 with a powerful fleet commanded by the notorious sea-king, Hastings – sometimes called Siegfried. This invasion force of 700 warships carrying 30,000 weapon-men (the combined fleets of the Danes in England, the Jutes and the Frisians) laid seige to Paris, where once again they were bought off, this time by Charles the Fat. Finally, to put an end to their depredations, Charles the Simple, King of the Franks in 912, gave a coastal province to Rollo, the chief of the sea-kings, which he promptly named Normandy. For a century and a half the Normans were content to farm their new-found land, but always they had an eye cocked towards England on the other side of the Channel.

The ravaging hordes of Norsemen often

fought among themselves. The old sagas tell of a mighty naval engagement that took place at Bravalla off the coast of Scania *circa* 755. And the skalds in their poems tell of a sea battle in which all the sea-kings of the time took part, over one thousand vessels. The two opposing fleets made the engagement as much like a land battle as possible. Each side roped their ships closely together in line abreast and sailed head-on to meet the enemy, the crews screaming insults and battle cries as they came on. 'In front of the fleet the sea looked as it does in heavy rain in still weather. This shower came quickly on and it was arrow fall. Then shields were needed.' As the bowmen fired into the air, the 'stafnbúi' (stem dweller) – forecastle man – crouched behind his circular wooden shield which was covered in leather with an iron boss in the centre and was often a yard across. Soon hacked to pieces by battle-axe or broadsword, it was nevertheless effective against flying arrows. As the warships of the two fleets crashed together, hand-to-hand fighting broke out at the prow and forward parts, the 'stem-dwellers' slashing and stabbing at each other with broadsword, battle-axe and spear. To be a 'stafnbúi' was a mark of distinction, the sure sign of a weapon-man of repute. The men in the after parts fired a constant stream of arrows into the enemy, the spearmen hurled throwing lances; 'twisting-spears' with cord wound round their shafts so that they spun in flight. Should a 'stafnbúi' fall, one of these would race forward to take his place. Victory went to the 'stem-dwellers' who wore down the enemy in order to board and clear his ship. Among the most fierce of these were the Skoldmeyars. These women-warriors or 'Buckler Virgins' asked no quarter and gave none. Tied together as they were, the fleets had little manoeuvrability, although individual ships could cut themselves loose to pursue an enemy ship or to flee from one.

The Viking story is not only one of rapine and plunder. The Vikings were also great traders, opening up trade routes through Russia to the Black Sea, the Caspian Sea and the Arab world. Taking out furs, animal skins, bird feathers, walrus tusks and slaves, they brought back on the return voyage, gold, silver, woollen goods, spices, silks and wine. These trade goods flowed through the great marketing centres that grew up at Kaupang in Norway and Hedeby in Denmark, thriving ports whose ships sailed to all parts of the known world. Their traders, more often than not warriors themselves, were as intrepid as the marauders, often venturing into little known regions in search of trade and merchandise. Othere, a rich Norwegian chieftain and merchant who visited the court of King Alfred in the 870s, described to the king how he voyaged beyond the northernmost whaling grounds into the White Sea—a voyage of exploration 'to find out how far the land continued to the northeast and whether anyone lived to the north of that waste' and also – 'for the sake of the walrus, as they have very fine ivory in their tusks'.

Norsemen carried on a thriving slave trade, dealing mainly with the Arabs who had settled the Mediterranean coast from Spain to Asia Minor. At first, prisoners of war, criminals and the desperately poor were shipped down the Russian rivers to the Caspian and Black Sea; later, when the Church objected to Muslims owning Christians, slaves were taken from among the heathen Slavs of Russia and the Baltic, a practice to which there could be no objection. They saw nothing wrong in trading in human flesh – after all, the gods had ordained that there should be 'greater and lesser offspring'. In Nordic myth, the god Rig came to earth and, in much the same way as Zeus, consorted with human women. Firstly, he consorted with Edda (great-grandmother) who bore a swarthy son, Thrall, from whom were descended the race of slaves. Then he entertained Amma (grandmother) whose ruddy-complexioned son, Karl, was the first of the yeomen. Finally he visited Moðir (mother); her son, Jarl (earl), was born with fair hair, red cheeks and piercing eyes and from him descended the earls and kings.

The traffic was two-way. Arabs often came north to trade on the spot. One merchant from Cordova in Spain who visited Hedeby in the 950s, left an account of this 'very large town beyond the furthest end of the ocean'. He hardly sounds impressed with the Danes, their customs, or their town.

'Its inhabitants are worshippers of Sirius, except for a few who are Christians and have a church there. . . . The town is poor in goods and treasure. The main food of the inhabitants is fish. When a child is born, they often throw it into the sea to save expense. Among them, women have the right to claim divorce, and the woman arranges her own divorce whenever she wishes . . . Never have I heard such hideous singing as that of the people of this town: it is a growl that comes from the throat, like the baying of dogs, only even more like a wild beast than that.'

Beyond Iceland

The great northern voyages of the Vikings began in 984, with Eirik the Red. According to the Greenlanders saga, 'Thorvald and his son Eirik left Jaeren (in Norway) for Iceland because of a killing', and settled in the northwest of the island. Having married Thjodhild, a woman of noble birth, Eirik moved south to Breidafjord. Without doubt he was an outstanding leader and a mighty warrior, but Eirik the Red was also a man of ungovernable temper. Once, being refused the repayment of a debt, he slew the debtor. Unfortunately for him his victim was of a powerful family and the Thones court of Iceland outlawed Eirik. Thus, he fitted out his ship, persuaded his karls and a number of discontented Icelanders to join him and pointed his prow west. A Norse trader had once told him of a fabled land to the west, a land of mountains, that had been glimpsed through a haze.

Though without compass, Eirik's navigation was anything but haphazard. There were the landmarks to be observed such as mountain peaks, the reflection of icefields beyond the horizon, the flight of land birds, the angle of wind across the face. Sometimes ravens were released from shipboard cages. Should they circle high above the vessel, the sea-king knew there was no land close by, but if, on the other hand, the birds flew off, he set course after them, confident that there was land in the near vicinity. Early voyagers remembered signs and passed them on to others; a later chronicle recording the route from Norway to Greenland is a typical example.

'From Hernar in Norway set sail due west for Hvarf in Greenland. You are to sail to the north of Shetland in such a way that you can just sight it in clear weather: but to the south of the Faroes, in such a way that the sea seems to be half way up the mountain slopes; and steer

A Viking ship unloading furs on the River Foss.

south of Iceland, in such a way that you can sight birds and whales from there.'

These observations were all very well in clear weather, but sailing through murk and fog, or on long ocean crossings far from land, called for different navigational techniques. In these conditions the Vikings resorted to latitude sailing, steering a course by the Pole Star at night and by the sun during the day. Having established that a certain point on the Norwegian coast was on the same latitude as a position in Iceland, they endeavoured to hold a steady course, using the direction of the wind and

A romantic view of a Viking Sea King – in reality they were ruthless, bloodthirsty and rapacious.

waves as indicators. To steer by the sun was not easy; only twice during the year, at the Spring Equinox in March and the Autumnal Equinox in September, does the sun bear due east as it rises and due west as it sets. The Vikings were aware of this and calculated sets of tables that made allowances for its seasonal variation.

Each day at noon they established their position. If the height of the sun had remained constant, they were keeping the correct latitude; on the other hand, should the sun appear higher in the sky, they knew they had wandered too far south, if lower, too far north of their course. Providing they were able to get back on the chosen latitude, no mean feat in heaving seas, it was simply a matter of sailing due east or west, to arrive eventually at their destination. To steer course the helmsman used a bearing-dial which was a notched wooden disc, divided into eight points of the compass, established by reference to the sun or Pole Star.

On the voyage from Iceland, sailing west as directed by the trader, Eirik and his crew were at no time able to land, pitch tent and light cooking fires. Most of the time they were forced to live on their plentiful but monotonous supply of dried or smoked meat and fish, stale bread and rancid curds washed down with flat ale, mead or water. Only on calm days did they dare to light a cooking fire in a box packed with sand.

Eventually the look-out sighted land, a mountainous country of snow and ice, as unpromising a place to colonize as one could imagine. Undeterred, Eirik the Red spent three years systematically exploring this seemingly inhospitable land, naming it Greenland. Cynically he remarked to his crew, 'Men will be the more easily persuaded to come here if I give it a fair name'. In fact, on returning to Iceland he did indeed persuade 25 shiploads of men, women and children, about 400, to accompany him to Greenland to found a colony. Packed to the gunwales with people, horses, sheep, cattle and goats, as well as planting corn and crude farming implements, the fleet set out, only to run into heavy weather. Out of the 25 ships that originally left Iceland, only 14 reached southwest Greenland, the rest were either lost or turned back. Yet enough survived to found a colony. Building huts of turf and stone, they lived by rearing cattle and sheep, fishing and hunting. As the settlement grew, they exported furs, hides, walrus tusks and live falcons to Norway.

Throughout the Norse sagas, particularly in the 'Flatey Book', there is mention of a trader, Biarni Heriulfsson, who, in 985, was blown off course on his way to Greenland – as so many Norsemen were – and sighted a land which he called Helluland. Although these sagas were folk legend, handed down from generation to generation and no doubt embellished with each telling, there is nevertheless enough geographical, botanical and zoological evidence contained in them to identify Helluland as Baffin Island. On finally reaching Greenland, Biarni's tale of this strange land to the west – he had not allowed his crew to land – fired the imagination of 'Leif the Lucky', son of Eirik the Red.

One account states that Leif Eiriksson was returning from Norway with a commission from Olaf Tryggvason, the Norwegian king, to proclaim Christianity in Greenland. He was blown off course to the southwest and made landfall on Helluland. Another account suggests that Leif deliberately set out to the southwest, retracing Biarni's course in the opposite direction. A caption on a map of 1440, a surprisingly accurate map of Greenland which shows a huge island to the southwest marked 'Island of Vinland', ascribes the distinction of discovering America, 500 years before Christopher Columbus, to Leif and Biarni 'in company'. 'By God's will, after a long voyage from the island of Greenland to the

The Viking ship showing:
1. The vessel when taken to Christiania.
2. As she must have looked sailing before the wind.
3. The rudder, oars, a shield and one of the tilt-heads.

43

south towards the most distant remaining parts of the western ocean sea, sailing southwards amidst the ice, the companions Biarni and Leif Eiriksson discovered a new land, extremely fertile and even having vines, which island they named Vinland.'

In the Greenlander saga, Leif Eiriksson, after coming upon the land – Helluland (Baffin Island) – discovered by Biarni Heriulfsson, worked his way south to the forested Markland (Labrador) and then into far warmer regions where grapes grew wild, a country he named Vinland or Wine Land (Newfoundland). For the past 200 years scholars have debated the exact location of this fabled country. Various theories have put Vinland anywhere from Florida in the south to Hudson Bay in the north, but the consensus of opinion has favoured the areas where grapes grow wild – Chesapeake Bay, Long Island and the coast of New England. Wherever the Vinland of the sagas is situated, there can be little doubt that Vikings raised settlements in North America. Six house sites, a smithy, a steam-bath house and a number of unmistakably Norse artifacts, carbon-dated *circa* 1000 A.D., have been excavated at L'Anse au Meadows, on the north tip of Newfoundland.

There is a poem attributed to Thorhall the Hunter, who accompanied a later expedition in search of Vinland, which suggests that even then there was some doubt as to its whereabouts. The Vikings are somewhere on the coast of North America and are arguing whether to sail to the north or south.

THORHALL'S POEM

Famous leaders told me I would have
The best of drink when I came hither,
Therefore I cannot blame the land.
But see, you helmeted Champions,
How instead of drinking wine
I must raise this pail (of water)
Which I had to stoop to fill at the spring.

Let us go to that quarter
Discovered by our countrymen
We will explore well
Beyond the keel place and the sweeping sands,
Travelling on the sea
While these great Warrior Chiefs
Who think so highly of this land
Remain behind and gorge upon
Whale meat on this marvellous strand.

Voyages of discovery continued – some, like Madog's, lost in legend, others well authenticated. Prince Madog, sailing from Wales in 1164, is said to have landed in Newfoundland. Returning home, he fitted out an expedition of ten ships, with the intention of sailing west to reinforce the 120 of his people he had left behind to guard a fortified settlement. After encountering ferocious storms, the would-be colonists eventually made contact with those that remained from the first expedition and although no further reinforcements came from Wales, they hung on, and, so it is said, intermarried with the natives of the country. This gave rise to numerous stories of the existence of Welsh Indians, theories supported by such distinguished investigators as Humboldt.

There is more substance to the saga of Earl Rognvald of the Orkneys, who led a pilgrimage to Palestine in 1150. Setting out late in the year, with a fleet of 15 ships, he ran into storm after storm as his ships skirted the coasts of England, France and Spain. By the time they entered the western Mediterranean, six of his fleet had already had enough and made for Marseilles. The remainder of the pilgrims, sailing on towards the Holy Land, saw nothing inconsistent in taking a Moorish ship off Sardinia, seizing her valuable cargo of merchandise and trading the slaves aboard themselves. After wintering in Constantinople, Earl Rognvald returned home overland.

Other explorers turned northwards. King Alfred records that Othere, a Norseman from Helgeland (near modern Trondheim), rounded the North Cape into the Barents Sea and brought back stories of the midnight sun – a terrifying spectacle for a superstitious Viking. There is far less evidence to support the vague claim that a Carmelite monk, Nicholas of Lynn, made an Arctic voyage in 1360. Without a doubt the monk existed, but whether he sailed into the Arctic in an attempt to reach the North Pole is very much open to question. But there can be no question that Basque seamen, in their quest for whales, scoured the seas well to the west of Iceland, and were most likely working the Grand Banks by the middle of the 14th century.

The 14th century marks the end of the era of early exploration in which seamen, sailing into the unknown, were driven by chance winds to discover new lands. After a period of inactivity, the golden age of exploration opened; an age when mariners sailed forth with a definite purpose in mind, though on many occasions their discoveries were certainly far from what they expected.

Left: Norman ships on the Bayeux Tapestry.

Below: Model of a double-ended ship of the early 14th century at the Science Museum, London.

Escosia

Irlanda

ingalaterra

flade

franca

itali

a

bordes

As Ilhas terceiras

seçilia

tunis

As canarias

Mõ

te as claros

Africa

Ilhas do cabo verde

mina

Reino de benins

46

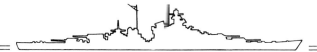

Naval Power Grows

Henry the Navigator

When he brought back news of the lands he had discovered across the Atlantic, Christopher Columbus changed the balance of world power and set in motion the struggle for control of the seas that was to follow. Already Portuguese navigators had probed the coast of West Africa in search of a route to the Spice Islands and Cathay (China). The existence of such exotic places had been known in Europe since early times and Marco Polo's account of the rich and powerful Eastern potentates he had met on his travels encouraged the establishment of an overland route to Cathay. This route, however, was long, expensive and dangerous, and the Muslim Turks who controlled it did not welcome Christian interlopers. It was a need to find

Opposite: 'The Discoveries of Fernão Gomez (1470–75)'. An early map of Lazaro Luis, 1563.

Below: The Santa Maria *of Columbus, from a drawing by the author.*

7

47

a sea route to the East coupled with a desire to make contact with the legendary Christian monarch, Prester John, that prompted Prince Henry the Navigator to found a college of seamanship. Isaac Newton wrote of Henry, '. . . one man by faith and persistence, drove a nation to look for its prosperity overseas and launched it on a career of discovery and conquest'.

The ideal vessel for this already lay to hand – the caravel. The early caravels, evolved from local fishing vessels, were small, sturdy craft which were able to stand up to the continual buffeting of long voyages across immense wastes of un-

charted oceans. Low in the water, with a draught of no more than 6 or 7 ft (1.8 to 2.1 m), they carried three lateen sails: one at the mainmast; a smaller one at the mizzenmast; and furthest aft, a smaller one from the 'bonaventure' mizzen. The most remarkable feature of the caravel was its ability to beat windwards, and it was this asset more than anything else that enabled the Portuguese pilots to make their voyages of discovery. For years they had groped their way down the northwest coast to Africa, never daring to round Cabo Bojador for fear of being unable to return against the northerly winds, and because of

A navigator on Columbus's first voyage.

LAPIS POLARIS, MAGNES.

Lapis reclusit iste Flauic abditum   Poli suum hunc amorem, at ipse nauita.

A 16th-century scholar at work on a navigational treatise.

a superstitious dread that the fabled boiling hot seas at the Equator would melt the coat of tar on the underside of their ships. With laudable confidence in the caravel, Gil Eannes rounded the cape in 1434 and proved that it was possible to tack safely back to Portugal against the prevailing winds. He was closely followed by other seamen, who, sailing past Cabo Blanco in 1441, reached Guinea to open up a lucrative trade in slaves and gold dust. Finally, Bartholomew Diaz, despite a near mutiny, returned from his southern voyage in 1488, to tell of a high promontory that he believed to be the tip of Africa. The name he gave to it, Cabo Tormentose (Stormy Cape) did not meet with the approval of the king, who re-christened it Cabo da Boa Esperance (Cape of Good Hope) – the way to the East was open.

However, the 'caravela latina' had its drawbacks. She was difficult to handle in a rough sea and needed a large crew to dip the spar round the mast at every change of tack. This led to the 'caravela redonda', a far more seaworthy vessel that needed a far smaller crew to handle the square sails

rigged to the fore and mainmasts and the lateen-rigged bonaventure mizzen. It was in such a 'caravela redonda', also carrying a spritsail at the prow, that Columbus made his voyage to the New World.

The Voyage West to Reach Cathay

On 3 August 1492 his tiny fleet weighed anchor, sailing from Palos, Spain into the 'Ocean Sea'; the Admiral's flagship was the *Santa Maria* of 100 tons (102 tonnes) and it carried a crew of 52. With him were the *Pinta*, another 'caravela redonda' of 50 tons (51 tonnes) with a crew of 18, commanded by Martin Pinzon and the 40-ton (41-tonne) *Niña*, also with a crew of 18, and commanded by Vincente Yanez Pinzon. The *Niña*, a 'caravela latina' was later re-rigged when its lateen sails were found to be unsuitable to take full advantage of the northeast trade winds. Fiercely committed to the theory that the world was round, Columbus had persuaded Ferdinand and Isabella of Spain to finance an expedition to sail west, first to Cinpangu (Japan) then onwards to open up trade with the Khan of Cathay, to whom he carried a letter of introduction. At that time the size of the world was not known, but the theory of philosophers, astronomers and cosmologists, made it larger in circumference than Columbus could afford to admit. By somewhat doubtful means he convinced his royal patrons that it was smaller than was generally believed and that the Indies lay a relatively short distance west of Europe.

As few had wanted to join this expedition into the unknown, the task of manning the ships was eased by extending a royal pardon to any condemned felons prepared to ship on the voyage. Thus, laden down with trade goods he hoped to exchange for spices and gold, Columbus set course for the Canaries, and although he fully intended to revictual there, his ships were nonetheless well-stocked with maritime victuals of the day. As well as an abundance of salt fish and bacon, there were wine, water, olive oil and vinegar, hard ship's biscuit and flour. The fleet made the Canaries after an uneventful voyage, and, revictualling, quit San Sebastian on 6 September, leaving the isle of Hierro to starboard as they sailed from the known world.

Caught in the easterlies they were swept westwards, but by the 19 September, Columbus, beginning himself to have doubts, resorted to falsifying the log to allay the grumblings and misgivings of his crews. The method of the day which was used to judge a ship's speed, and consequently the distance covered, was to drop a stick over the bow and then walk aft alongside it until it came to the taffrail. Any estimate would

Ferdinand Magellan, the first man to sail around the world.

50

and could prove inaccurate. In the event, it has since been established that because of a tendency to overestimate distances, Columbus's falsified log is actually more accurate than the private one he kept for himself. Grasping at any and every indication of nearby land, he wrote on 20 September: 'There came to the flagship two pelicans and later another, which was a sign of nearness of land. By hand they took in a bird that was a river bird, not of the sea, though its feet were like a gull's. There came to the ship at dawn two or three land-birds singing and later before daybreak they departed.'

The murmuring grew as they entered the seaweed-infested Sargasso Sea; fearfully the seamen recalled the legends of monsters who haunted the depths with the express purpose of dragging down unwary ships, and what more likely place than this desolate bog of weed? Morale was at its lowest ebb, murmuring escalated into near mutiny and demands to return home; some of the more desperate hatched a plot to throw Columbus overboard. It took all the Admiral's prescience to avert the 'accident' and all his powers of persuasion and bold confidence in success to cajole the mariners

to continue the voyage.

By the 10 October 'the crew could endure no more'. The bitterly expressed assertion of Martin Pinzon that they had overshot Cinpangu caused Columbus to change course to the southwest, in the hope of reaching the mainland of Cathay. The second day on this new course brought unmistakable signs of populated land, and the 'Admiral had it for certain that they were next to land' – according to Las Casa – and he added a bolt of silk to the prize offered by the King and Queen to the first person to sight land. During the last few weeks of the voyage the cry 'Tierra, tierra!' (Land, land!) had been raised time and time again, only to prove false. The look-outs were more than eager to win the annual pension of 30 crowns guaranteed by their Catholic Majesties to the first man to sight the promised land. Land birds were seen in the distance, three branches floated past, the excitement of the crew reached fever pitch. That night the Salve Regina was sung with greater fervour, the watch kept with more vigilance. Although the Admiral himself reported seeing a light during the night, it was not until 2 a.m. on 12 October, that the now familiar cry 'Tierra,

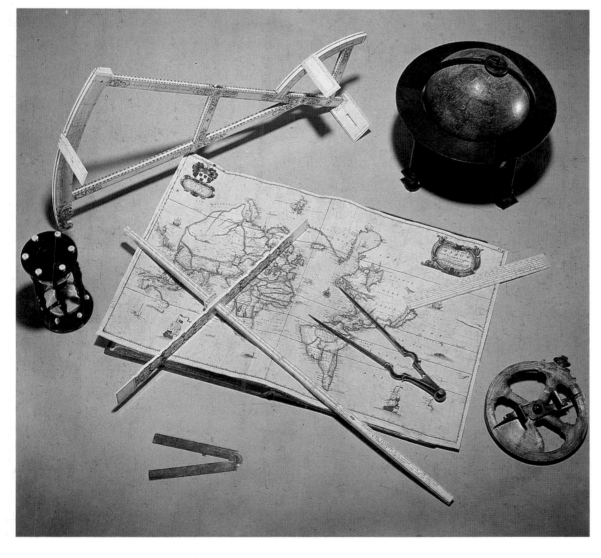

Sandglass, globe dividers, astrolabe, cross-staff, Gunter's scale and selector.

tierra!' rang out – but this was no false alarm. The mast-head look-out aboard the *Pinta*, Rodrigo de Triana, had earned the sovereigns' pension – the signal gun crashed out – there in the tropical moonlight, dead ahead, lay land – hymns of thanksgiving to God broke out from the three little ships.

The next morning Columbus, holding aloft the Royal Standard, was rowed ashore by a well-armed party. Watched by wide-eyed natives who had flocked to the beach from the woods, he fell to his knees, kissed the ground and gave thanks to God. He next took possession of the island in the name of Ferdinand and Isabella, calling it San Salvador, 'in remembrance of the Divine Majesty'. With some horror he later wrote of the people whom he took to be natives of an island at the southern tip of India. 'The people of this island and all other islands which I have found and of which I have information, all go naked, men and women, as their mothers bore them, although some of the women cover a single place with the leaf of a plant or with a net of cotton which they make for the purpose.'

For some time Columbus cruised the Caribbean, still believing that Cinpangu lay only a short distance ahead, taking possession of Cuba, Hispaniola and other islands in the name of Spain. It was off Hispaniola, present-day Haiti, that the *Santa Maria* came to grief and had to be abandoned. The Admiral returned home in the *Niña*. Before returning from the New World, Columbus built a fort on Hispaniola, leaving 44 of his expedition to man it while he returned to Spain for supplies. After a stormy passage the *Niña* finally limped into the Tagus on 3 March 1493, and anchored off the Portuguese capital. King John II, furious at the successful outcome of a voyage he had himself refused to sponsor – one, moreover, that would bring greater gains to his Castilian rivals – held Columbus in custody. Later, seeing nothing to gain, he reluctantly released him. 'Don Cristobál Colón, Admiral of the Ocean Sea, Viceroy and Governor of the Islands he had discovered in the Indies', presented himself, his gold samples and captured 'Indians' before an admiring Castilian court at Barcelona, sometime in April.

By the autumn of 1493 he was at sea again heading west, this time with a much larger squadron. As one expedition followed another, more and more land came under the control of Spain. The gold, silver, precious stones and other merchandise which flowed, as a result, into her coffers made Spain the most powerful maritime nation in Europe. Other European maritime countries, in particular England, turned an envious eye on her success. This resentment was increased as a result of a Bull granted by Pope Alexander VI. He decreed that any land discovered west of a line drawn 100 leagues from the Azores should belong to Spain, any land to the east of that to Portugal. Later, when Portugal protested, this line was moved to 370 leagues from the Azores, enabling Portugal to retain possession of Brazil, discovered by Pedro Cabral in 1500, as it was found to be east of the line. The full effects of this partition were seen in Ferdinand Magellan's circumnavigation of the globe, made between 1519 and 1522. A Portuguese sailing under the banner of Spain, he sought and found a way round the newly discovered land mass (America) into the Great South Sea, sighted by Vasco Nunez de Balboa six years before from the Isthmus of Panama. By sailing westwards to reach the Spice Islands, which Spain greedily coveted, Magellan believed he would be able to annex them without offending the Pope. Magellan was killed in a native quarrel in the Philippines in 1521 and only Juan Sebastian del Cana, commanding the *Vittoria*, made it back to Spain with 31 men, all that remained of the original expedition. But her log revealed the true size of the world and the vastness of the Great South Sea with its enormous trade potential.

Although all the maritime nations of Europe readily accepted the concept of possession by right of prior discovery, only the Catholic countries conceded to Alexander VII's Papal Bull. Even then, France felt herself strong enough to put her national interest in the scramble for trade before her allegiance to the Pope. The emerging Protestant countries of the north, led by England, needed to show no such allegiance; they were governed only by political expediency and the military – not religious – power of their Catholic rivals. For the next 300 years England was to seek a northern route into the Great South Sea. John Cabot and his son Sebastian ventured northwards, discovering Labrador and Newfoundland which they solemnly annexed on behalf of the king. But these were not treasure houses to compare with the Spanish possessions in the New World. Martin Frobisher and John Davis vainly searched for the legendary 'Northwest

Passage' to Cathay, thwarted by ice in the Polar Sea, north of Canada. Attempts by Sir Hugh Willoughby, Richard Chancellor and Stephen Burrough to reach Cathay by sailing northeastwards around the top of Europe and Asia, met with similar failures. The only access to the wealth of the New World and the East Indies seemed to be by sailing east or west. Either way meant falling foul of the powerful Spanish and Portuguese Empires, to say nothing of the Pope and the Holy Roman Emperor Only a country with a powerful fleet of superior ships could hope to compete – the race for sea power was on.

In their search for a bigger ship to bring back the wealth of their new-found possessions, Spain and Portugal abandoned the caravel. Lively, tough and easy to handle, the caravel was ideal for seeking out these possessions, but too small for carrying back the rich cargoes. Instead they turned to the carrack, adopting her as both a trading vessel and a fighting ship. By the middle of the 16th century carracks of up to 1,200 tons (1,220 tonnes), some even bigger, were being launched, with higher and higher 'castles' fore and aft. The Venetian carrack in its early days was a two-masted, carvel-built vessel carrying a single large square sail on the mainmast and either a smaller square sail or lateen sail on her mizzen. Towards the end of the 15th century it is reported that ships of 1,500 tons (1,524 tonnes) burthen were being built at Genoa, three or four-masted with topsails added above mainsails and multiple decks. Although stately, they were bluff-bowed with a rounded stern and square counter – impressive but cumbersome. One built at Nice in 1530 for the Knights of Malta, was over 1,700 tons (1,730 tonnes) burthen, the mightiest ship of her time, and could carry a crew of 300. Four-masted with six decks, two of them under water, she was protected against the 'worm', (*terredo navalis*, the shipwright's great enemy) by a thick sheafing of lead which made her sluggish through the water.

As the 16th century progressed, the carrack was modified into the galleon or 'Great Ship'. She was still high out of the water with lofty castles fore and aft, but her hull was slender and more graceful, giving her better sailing qualities. The forecastle no longer overhung the bow, but was moved back behind a beak head, which among other things housed the crew's heads or toilets. Even with a length-to-beam ratio of 3:1, she still held the wind and strained her hull when she rolled, hardly suitable for long ocean voyages. The steering oar fixed over the starboard quarter, which had long since been replaced in favour of a rudder on the centre line, was now controlled by means of a whipstaff, a vertical extension of the tiller.

Gunnery at Sea

Naval tactics remained very much the same – in essence, a land battle at sea. At the first opportunity ships came alongside to grapple the enemy, prior to boarding and taking the battle to his decks. The lofty fore and aft castles made ideal vantage

points for bowmen, and for others to hurl missiles and Greek fire grenades into the waist of enemy ships. But the use of heavy ordnance in more manoeuvrable ships was soon to alter the whole pattern of war at sea. The first mention of the use of cannon in ships was at La Rochelle in 1342 (though handguns were being carried afloat 20 years earlier) and by the beginning of the 15th century it was common practice to arm ships with guns. Even so the 750-ton (772-tonne) *Holigost* of Henry V, built in 1414, carried only six pieces and she was the most heavily armed ship in the English fleet. The value of cannon as 'man-killers' was fully appreciated towards the end of the century. The *Regent* of 1489 carried no less than 285 serpentines, many of them mounted on the rails of the

forecastle and quarterdeck to sweep the waist of the ship should she be boarded.

From the serpentine, whose shot weighed only a few pounds, cannon began to grow in size. Gradually they established themselves as naval weapons, eventually becoming 'ship-smashing' pieces that could hurl heavy cannon balls up to 2,500 paces. And the seamen became the naval gunners. Prior to this it was the heavily armed sea-soldiers who did the fighting – the sailors were merely there to work ship. Now, as the ship truly became a 'warship', the role of the sailor changed: he became a fighting man as well as a mariner. The land battle at sea was beginning to give way to an entirely new concept of naval warfare. This called not only for different strategy and tactics, but for bigger and sturdier ships to house the increasingly heavier ordnance. It also meant that the ships had to be designed to fight, the old interchangeability, merchantman turning into warship in time of war, became a thing of the past – the great master shipwrights emerged.

Cannon continued to grow in size, power and accuracy, and the latter part of the 16th century saw a large variety of guns ranging in weight from 70-lb (32-kg) shot to 1⅛-lb (0.5-kg) shot, 'ship-smashers' and 'man-killers' respectively. By the time of the Armada engagement of 1588, there were over 20 different types of cannon.

Apart from the main types of armament, there were further variations – for example, the Narborough (Nuremberg) culverin fired 20-lb (9-kg) shot and the falcon fired 2½-lb (1.1-kg) shot. Some threw balls of stone, others balls of iron.

Naval gunnery was rudimentary for a number of reasons. Not least of all was the fact that individual cannon varied fractionally in calibre and individual shot in weight and diameter. The best, the most sought-after gunmakers in Europe were to be found in the Weald of Kent and Sussex in the south of England. In fact, despite government intervention and legislation, many of the guns mounted in the Spanish Armada came from there. For all their variety in size, weight and detail, the cannon fell into two basic categories – 'breech-loading' and 'muzzle-loading'. The 'breech-loader', built up of wrought-iron staves welded together and strengthened with iron hoops, had a detachable powder chamber. These, lying close to the deck on a stock carriage, were fired through apertures in the bulwarks of the upper deck and the castles. They could be trained to right and left by means of a training lever applied to the rear of the carriage. The cannon ball, usually of stone, was inserted into the breech end of the barrel; then the separate breech piece – into which a measure of gunpowder had been ladled – was slipped into grooves on the carriage and hammered home with a wooden wedge to hold it secure.

The 'cast' gun, on the other hand, had no detachable breech and had to be loaded from the muzzle. The powder charge, usually in a cloth bag, was slid down the barrel and wadding rammed home to hold it firm and keep the powder dry. The shot was next rolled down the gun's throat and held secure against the roll of the ship by ramming further wadding on top. The Spanish and Portuguese tended to fire on the upward-roll of the ship, aiming to demast the enemy; the English fired on the downward-roll to pepper the hull and send deadly splinters of wood flying among the enemy gunners. The muzzle-loader, cast in

Overleaf: Henry VIII's 'Great Harry' of 1546 from the Anthony Anthony Rolls at Magdalene College, Cambridge.

Below: The Ark Royal, designed and built by Sir Walter Raleigh, was bought from him by the Navy. Its main armament was of 24 brass and cast-iron muzzle loading culverins mounted 12 along each broadside.

ŋ Thys the ffyrſt Rolle declaryng th[e]
Naem. wth theyr Tunnage and No[mber]
for Warre. ffor the Armyng and [...]

The Harry Tunnage · x̄ı ·
Grace A Dieu

Gonnes of Brasse.

Cannons	iiij
D Cannons	ij
Culueryns	iiij
D Culueryns	ij
Sakers	iiij
Cannon peeirs	iij
ffawcons	ij

Gonnes of yron.

porte peeirs	iiij
Slyngs	iiij
D Slyngs	ij
ffowlers	viij
Bassys	lx
Topp peeirs	ij
hayle shotte peeirs	vl
handgonnes complete	c

Gonnepowder

Serpentyn powder in Barrell	j laſt
Corne powder in Barrells	vj

Shotte of yron

for Cannons	c
for D Cannons	lx
for Culueryns	cc
for D Culueryns	lx
for Sakers	cc
for ffawcons	c
for Slyngs	c
for D Slyngs	c
Crosse barre shotte	c
Dyce of yron for	iij
hayle shotte	

...mbre of the kyngs Maiesties owne Shyppes Wᵗʰ eu[er]e Shyppe and Shyppes
...e of men. As Alsſ the ordenaunce Artillary Munycions and Habillment
...nce of eu[er]y of the sayd Shyppes Agaynst theyr enemyes vppon the See.

What ys to Saye

Men

Souldiours ccclx[...]
marynas ccc.l
Gonners c

Bowes Bowestrynys Arrowes Morryshe pyke Byllys Dartts for toppes   **Munycions**   **Habillment**

Iren & leade		Bowes Bowestrynys Arrowes Morryshe pyke Byllys Dartts for toppes		Munycions		Habillment
Cannon perer	lxx	Bowes of ewgh	vc	pyke hamers	xx	Ropes of hempe for
porte peces	ccc	Bowestrynys	xgred	Ledyps of yron	vi	wolnyng & breechyng
fowlers	c	Lyuere Arrowes	byel	Crowes of yron	vi	Naylles of sundery sor
Toppe peces	xl	m shaffs		Comaunders	vijf	Barrys of hylder
haffes	vijj	Morres pykes	cc	Tampions	v.ij	Shyvyns wᵗ ponlies
te of leade		Byllys	cc	Canuas for		Lyme poss
handgonnes	vijj	Dartts for toppes	c	Cartowches	xi m̃yo	Spare Wheles
te of leade	vijj	m donssen		paper Ryall		Spare truckell
				for cartowches	j quer	Spare sptrys
				Sponnes for	vj	Ships skynnys
				cartowches		Tymber for ſorloſk

one piece in bronze or iron and mounted on truck carriages by means of trunnions, could not only be traversed from right to left, but could also be elevated through 20 degrees using a quoin. Although more expensive to produce, the cast cannon was stronger, more accurate and quicker to fire. Eventually it totally superceded the breech-loader, which on numerous occasions had the nasty tendency to explode on itself.

The actual firing was the same for both types of cannon. The gunner 'pricked' the touch-hole clear, primed it with a shake of powder from a horn and applied a glowing linstock to the touch-hole. As the cannon roared off, its leaping recoil was checked by block and tackle running from the ship's side to the gun carriage.

Meanwhile a revolution in shipbuilding, gunnery and naval tactics was taking place in England that was to have a significant effect on naval warfare for centuries to come. In the past as merchantmen doubled as fighting ships and soldiers fought land battles at sea, the cog or 'round ship' with a low length-to-beam ratio had been adopted rather than the Venetian carrack. Admirable though it was as a cargo ship with its deep belly, this slow, wallowing craft was found totally unsuitable as a warship, especially with the advent of more efficient naval gunnery. As early as the time of Henry V it was realized that warships had to be designed solely for fighting; a number were built and many of them were large. The 'great' ship *Jesus* of 1,000 tons (1,016 tonnes), built for the war with France, the *Holigost* (760 tons or 772 tonnes) and the *Trinity Royal* (540 tons or 549 tonnes) were far cries from the 200 tonners (203 tonnes) of the early part of the 14th century. While the Spanish and Portuguese stuck to the carrack, the English, French and Dutch extended the cog, adding two more masts to the existing one, making her carvel-built instead of clinker-built and giving her more racy lines.

BUILDING AN ELIZABETHAN GALLEON

'For galions or ships for the wars made for the most advantage of sail. Length of keel three times the beam, depth of hold two-fifths beam.'

When the shipbuilding programme of 1577 was put under way, most of the ships were built in the Royal dockyards at Chatham on the River Medway and at Deptford and Woolwich on the Thames. These sleek, graceful, yet-so-seaworthy ships were built with only a handful of tools, but wielded by skilled craftsmen under the direction of a master shipwright, they became instruments of great precision. Various types of axes were used, to fell and trim trees, 'blockout' the keel and shape 'treenails' (wooden nails that pinned the ship together). Adzes, chiefly employed for shaping curves and smoothing planks, were expertly swung with the accuracy of a plane. A collection of hammers, each for a particular use with its own individual name, drove wedges to split or 'rive' logs, hammered home 'treenails' and tapped in oakum. Together with a number of specialist saws and augers to drill holes, these were the only tools required to create an elegant 500-ton (508-tonne) galleon.

Before Sir John Hawkyns became Treasurer of the Navy Board and put master shipwrights on a regular set salary and a pension of a shilling a day for life, the shipwright was paid £5.19s.5d per ton to build a ship. So the *Elizabeth Bonaventure* of 448 tons (455 tonnes) burden (unloaded weight) would have cost £2,675 to build. From this sum he had to pay for timber, masts and spars, ironwork, and wages and lodgings for the workmen, but he was spared the cost of ordnance, sails and fittings. His shipwrights received 10d. to 1s. a day and their assistants, 3d. a day, but lodging was provided or, in lieu of that, 1s. a week lodging money. Accounts show that Mistress Leighton of Deptford charges 4d. a week for all-in board and lodging; Bayley's wife in Limehouse only 1½d. a week, but her house was verminous. Caulkers, who drove the oakum into the ship's seams to make them watertight, were also paid as skilled craftsmen, 6d a day; their 'oakum boyes', who picked the old rope into strands and rolled them into strips for them, just 2d. a day. 'Bartholomew Moptide the elder, at 6d. the day by 7 days, 4s. 9d,' reads one account.

Often the master shipwright went down into one of the Royal forests in the winter – the best time for cutting – with his sawyers to select and cut his own wood, which would be drawn on ox-carts to the river, then floated by barge to the dockyard. Other times he would buy wood already cut into: 'thick stuff', planks of 4 inches (10 cm) or more, up to 12 inches (30 cm) wide; 'plank', 1½ to 4 inches (4–10 cm) thick; and boards, 1½ inches (4 cm) thick. Mature oaks and elms were selected for straight timber, which after seasoning, was cut into planking in a saw pit by the 'top-sawyer' and the 'pitman'. Although it was the usual practice to scour the forest for naturally curved branches, 'compass' timber for ribs, knees and other curved parts of ships, many shipwrights, rather than leave it to chance, deliberately bent branches during their growth. 'Compass oaks' were so named because their curving branches and surface roots pointed to all direction of the compass. Planks themselves were shaped by attaching a heavy weight to each end and suspending them over a fire pit while apprentices kept the topside soaking wet.

While the sawyers and 'scavelmen' (semi-skilled craftsmen who worked closly with the shipwrights and maintained the dockyard) cut and dragged the timber to the slipway, the master shipwright padded about bare-footed in the 'mould loft', drawing a full-scale plot of his draft in chalk on the smooth boards. From this would be cut wooden templates to act as a guide to the shipwrights and joiners.

From 5 o'clock in the morning the dockyard became a hive of clamorous activity; sheer-legs and cranes were erected around the slipway and an incline built so that timbers could be dragged up as the ship's frame rose. The thud of adzes mingled with the shriek of saws, the clang of blacksmith's hammers from the temporary forges and the creak of ropes and pulleys – men had to shout to be heard above the din. Once the keel had been laid, made up of huge blocks of straight elm 'scarfed' and bolted together, the ship quickly began to grow. (Scarfs were long, tapering joints which held two blocks of timber together; adzed to a perfect fit they were bolted together and 3-inch/8-cm hard wood pins driven in the length of the joint.) Ribs or 'futtocks' rose from the keel, clad, carvel fashion, in 4-inch (10-cm) planking to

The Elizabethan Fleet

The whole role of a national navy was in the melting pot. No longer was it just a question of safeguarding home waters against invasion or putting down piracy, for the real issue had become the protection of the trade routes against privateers who were operating with the covert sanction of their governments. To safeguard the rich cargoes flowing out of their newly discovered lands, Portugal and Spain required large navies to ward off both privateers and downright pirates. England, even while attempting to colonize the coastal strip of the American continent between the French possessions in Canada and the Spanish sphere of influence to the south, was unofficially encouraging her freebooters to take their toll of Spanish treasure. The English merchants, dissatisfied 'with the short voyages commonly then made to the known coasts of Europe', cried out against the 'Papal Bulls of Partition'. It was, however, a religious conflict as much as anything; English privateers, little better than semi-official pirates, were treated when caught as Lutheran heretics and handed over to the Holy Inquisition for questioning by rack and strappado. At best they could expect upwards of 200 lashes and endless years chained to the rowing bench of a galley, at worst the fire, led out to an *auto-da-fe* wearing the yellow garb of a penitent. The bitterness that grew on both sides was finally to erupt into a full-scale confrontation, but the years between were to be taken up with minor skirmishes, diplomatic squabbles and private vendettas.

Meanwhile, the increasing size, weight and power of naval cannon made it impossible to fire a broadside from the upper deck without endangering the stability of the ship. To combat this, the heavier guns were mounted on the lower decks and the hull of the ships pierced with gun ports. Vertically hinged lids could be lowered to the 'breadth' of the ship – elm below the waterline, oak above. From the 'breadth' to the gunwale the planking was 2-inch (5-cm) oak. Then the orlop, the lowest deck, was laid, followed by the main deck, upperdeck, quarterdeck and forecastle. Gun ports were cut into the hull, the lowest being 4 ft (1.2 m) above the waterline.

Once the hull had been caulked, the ship would be launched and secured by cables to quayside bollards and the masts seated in the keelson. Top masts and yards would then be rigged and the sails cut and made up.

Once ordnance was aboard and mounted in position, the ship was ready to be painted and decorated with gold leaf. The cost of this varied; the *Revenge* had £121.13s.8d. spent on her for decoration; the *White Bear* as much as £379.10s. But the latter had 'an image of Jupiter sitting upon an eagle with cloudes, before the heade of the shippe XI^{li}' and 'the greate pece of Neptune and the Nymphes about him for the uprighte of the sterne VI^{li}Xs'. Banners, streamers and flags were taken aboard and the crew 'pressed'. (In Elizabethan times this meant paying the crew an advance in pay, the notorious 'press gangs' came later.)

Once the ship was victualled, she was ready for trials and service at sea. Carrying a crew of 250, the *Elizabeth Bonaventure* would indent the following stores for a month.

	£	s	d
Fresh beef 5,252 lb (2,384 kg) at 18s. the cwt	42	4	0
Baye salt for the fresh beef, 25 bu at 8d the bushel		16	0
Bisket, at 11s. the cwt 7,000 lb (3,178 kg)	38	10	0
Canvas bags for same – 140 bags	6	8	0
Bacon at 3d. the lb – 1,000 lb (454 kg)	12	10	0
Peas, at 24s a quarter – 16 quarters	19	4	0
Casks for them, at 10s. the ton – 5 tons	2	10	0
Stockfish, at 4d. the piece – 1,250 pieces	20	16	4
Butter, at 4d. the pound – 312 lb (142 kg)	5	4	0
Cheese, at 2d. the pound – 624 lb (283 kg)	5	4	0
Beer, with casks, at 45s. per ton – 28 tons	63	0	0
Necessaries, at 4d. each man, per mensum	4	3	2
	£220	9	10

Statistics for Her Majesty's Ship *Elizabeth Bonaventure*

Commander during the Armada Engagement – Earl of Cumberland (a well-known privateer of noble birth)

Keel – 80 ft (24 m)
Beam – 35 ft (11 m)
Depth of hold – 16 ft (5 m)
Burden (unloaded weight) 448 wine tons
Loaded weight – 560 wine tons
Forerake – 28 ft (9 m)
After rake – 4 ft 10 inches (1.5 m)
Foremast – Mainmast – Mizzen mast – Bonaventure Mizzen mast
Fore and Mainmast – square sails – Course, Topsail, Top-gallant
Weight of masts and yards – 14 tons 14 cwt (14.9 tonnes)
Mizzen and Bonaventure – Lateen sails
Weight of rigging and tackle – 12,300 lb (5,580 kg)
Number of anchors – 6
Weight of anchors – 9,600 lb (4,350 kg)
Weight of ordnance – 40 tons (41 tonnes)

'Ship Smashers'
Demi-cannon – 4 (32 pounders)
Cannon periers – 2 (24 pounders)
Culverins – 6 (18 pounders)
Demi-culverins – 8 (9 pounders)
Sakers – 6 (6 pounders)
Minions – 2 (4 pounders)

'Man-killers'	Crew
Port pieces – 4	Mariners 150
Fowlers – 6	Gunners – 24
Bases – 12	Soldiers – 76
Falcons – 2	

protect the gun ports in heavy seas and raised when the ships went into action and the guns run out. These proved to be dangerous time and time again, especially when the lowest gun ports were cut only inches above the waterline. As late as 1628, the 1,400-ton (1,422-tonne) Swedish warship *Vasa* had hardly begun to sail across Stockholm harbour on her maiden voyage before being hit by a freak squall. As she heeled over, water rushed through her open gun ports and despite frantic efforts she plunged to the bottom.

The need to create the 'lower gundeck' close to the centre line of the ship, inevitably led to a pronounced 'tumble-home', which became a marked feature of wooden warships. From the deck, the hull bellied out sharply to its widest point at the waterline which helped steady the ship in the water, particularly during the firing of broadsides. The practice of designing ships by eye and experience was rapidly giving way to the master shipwright's precise 'draft', a drawing of a ship's lines which acted as a blueprint for the dockyard craftsmen. In the past a ship was built on the banks of a river estuary, or at best on a slipway surrounded by a mud embankment thrown up around it to act as a dry dock; either way it would be necessary to wait for the next spring tide to float it off. As ships grew in size, timber dry docks were introduced with flood-gates which allowed ships to be launched at normal high tides.

Throughout Europe shipbuilding and the raising of fleets ceased to be a haphazard affair; Navy Boards and Royal dockyards sprang up everywhere, with officials responsible for carrying through properly constructed naval programmes. Henry VIII, left behind in the race for colonial possessions, had, by 1512, realized the need for a strong navy and the administrative machinery to control it. Lord Edward Howard was made Lord High Admiral with Robert Brygandine, Clerk of Ships; but perhaps more important was the appointment of a royal master shipwright in the person of William Bond. In 1514 he built the *Henry Grâce à Dieu* – known as the 'Great Harry' – which was claimed to be the biggest and most advanced warship of her day (though most likely Spain, Portugal and possibly France were building equally large, if not larger, ships). A towering four-masted vessel carrying topsails and topgallants on fore, main and mizzen masts, she was more a floating fortress than a ship. She had little or no 'tumble-home' and her lofty, stacked decks

fore and aft made her unstable. She was totally rebuilt between 1536 and 1539 and although she still remained a liability as a fighting ship, her list of armament was impressive. She had two rows of gun ports housing 21 muzzle-loading bronze cannon, too heavy to be mounted high in the castles. She also mounted 122 medium-sized cannon, primitive breech-loaders, and 30 'man-killers', murderers, swivels and falconets. The danger of top-heavy ships with gun ports cut close to the waterline was underlined when, in 1544, the *Mary Rose* went down in Portsmouth harbour. Standing on *Southsea Castle*, Henry VIII saw the *Mary Rose*, one of his finest ships, sail out to face a French squadron. Her gun ports, just 16 inches (41 cm) above the waterline, were open and her guns run out; as she heeled in a tight turn, the sea poured into her lower gundeck and she sank like a stone.

Queen Mary, the daughter of Henry VIII, inheriting a paper fleet of rotting ships, introduced an extensive naval programme, encouraged strangely enough as it turned out, by her husband, Philip II of Spain. During her reign Spain was an uneasy ally, but on her death and the accession of Elizabeth I, a convinced Protestant, the scene changed dramatically. Philip's religious zeal, fanned by the Pope, inclined him to an 'Enterprise Against England', a situation exacerbated by the inroads being made into his treasury by English privateers. Martin Frobisher, John Hawkyns, John Oxenham, Fenton, Cavendish and hosts of others preyed upon his treasure fleets; but the worst of them all was Francis Drake. Known to the Spaniards as '*El Draco*' (The Dragon), he became the scourge of the viceroys and governors of the New World, not only plundering their treasure ships, but sacking their townships as well. A half-hearted attempt to land Spanish troops to encourage and support insurrection in Ireland in 1579 not only caused Philip to lose 800 infantrymen, but roused great bitterness in England against Spain and the Catholic League – the two countries were on an inevitable collision course towards war.

When she came to the throne of England, Elizabeth I, with grudging reluctance, carried on her sister's shipbuilding programme, but a quarrelsome and often corrupt Navy Board slowed down its progress – until Hawkyns was appointed Treasurer of the Queen's Navy Board. He quickly pushed through a programme to build 18 new ships, but ships with a difference, ships

WHSMITH

WHSMITH

Record Department

WHSMITH

WHSMITH

WHSMITH

WHSMITH

WHSMITH

WHSMITH

WHSMITH

WHSMITH

WHSMITH

Record Department

Type of gun	Range in paces	Weight of shot		Weight of gun		Length of gun		Diameter of shot	
		lb	kg	lb	kg	ft	m	inches	cm
Eldest double cannon	1,700	70	32	8,000	3,600	12	3.7	8	20.3
Cannon	1,700 to 2,000	50	23	7,500	3,400	11–12	3.4–3.7	7½	19.1
Demi-cannon	1,700 to 2,000	32	14	6,000	2,700	11–12	3.4–3.7	6½	16.5
Cannon-periers	1,600	24	11	5,000	2,300	10–11	3.0–3.4	5¾	14.6
Culverins	2,500	18	8	4,300	1,950	12–13	3.7–4.0	5	127
Demi-culverins	2,500	9	4	2,464	1,119	10	3.0	4½	11.4
Sakers	1,700	5½	2.5	1,400	540	8–9	2.4–2.7	3½	8.9
Minions	1,700	3¾	1.7	1,000	450	8	2.4	3	7.6
Falconet	–	1⅛	0.5	400	180	–	–	2	5.1

GUNS CARRIED BY THE TWO FLEETS – from 4-pounders upwards

Gun-carrying ships – Spanish – 124 with an average of 9 per ship.

English – 172 with an average of 11.5 per ship

Type of gun	Range in paces	Weight of shot		Number of guns	
		lb	kg	Spanish	English
Cannon }	1,700–2,000	50	23	} 163	55
Demi-cannon }		32	14		
Cannon-periers	1,600	24	11	362	43
Culverins	2,500	18	8	165 }	153 }
Demi-culverins	2,500	9	4	137 } 635	344 } 1,875
Sakers	1,700	5½	2.5	144 }	662 }
Minions	1,700	4	2	189 }	715 }
			Total:	1,124	1,972

Total weight of shot fired .... 19,369 lb (8,785 kg)   14,677 lb (6,657 kg)

Average weight per ship .... 156 lb (71 kg)   85 lb (39 kg)

Average weight per gun .... 17 lb (8 kg)   7½ lb (3.4 kg)

that would change the face of naval warfare. The Portuguese and Spaniards with the help of Italian shipwrights had produced the galleon. English 'sea-cogs' thought the galleon to be impractical for long ocean voyages. They advocated fast 'galions', low-slung ships with a small crew of experienced mariners and gunners, ships that could stay at sea for longer periods without the crew becoming sick.

The two great master shipwrights of the day, Matthew Baker and Peter Pett, going along with the ideas of the 'sea-dogs', had altered the draughts of their vessels to produce the 'race-ship', a sleek ocean greyhound, with forecastle and quarterdeck trimmed low. Close to the water like a galleass, her keel three times as long as her beam, she had a 32-ft (10-m) forerake and beak head to shatter the heavy seas, preventing them breaking on board. The 'deep-sea' captains, led by Sir John Hawkyns, were determined to change the existing concept of naval warfare, despite the opposition of the Navy Board, which comprised mainly 'Narrow Seas' commanders who were reluctant to part with their lofty, impressive 'fights' – 'Wicked fools,' Hawkyns called them. The 'sea-dogs' no longer meant to come alongside, grapple and sweep the deck with their man-killing pieces and hailshot, but intended to lay off and pound the enemy with long-range 'ship-smashing' culverins firing 18-lb (8.2-kg) iron shot. The culverin, 12 ft (3.7 m) long, accurate, with a range of 2,500 paces, be-

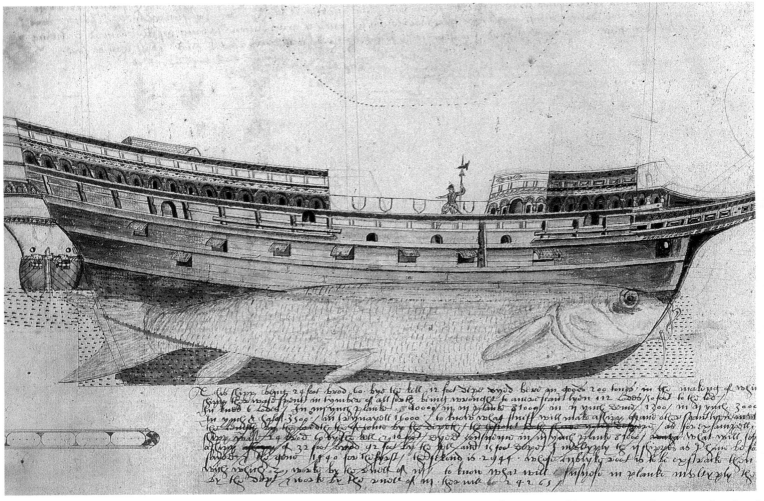

came the main armament of the Elizabethan fleet. As the result of this co-operation between the men who designed and built the ships and the seamen who fought in them, warships like the *Revenge* came into being. This forerunner of the new type of fighting ship, built in 1577, was still, according to Sir Francis Drake, the best fighting ship 11 years later, when he chose her for his flagship for the Armada engagement.

Drake's Circumnavigation of the Globe

Rumour had been rife in Plymouth in 1577 when Drake's fleet of five small ships set sail on a bleak December. Even Vice-Admiral John Wynter and the gentlemen adventurers had no idea where they were going – as far as they were concerned they had joined an expedition to explore 'Terra Australis', that legendary continent in the Antarctic. Most of the seamen thought that the fleet was bound for Alexandria to take on a cargo of currants, but the wiseacres aboard knew better. As the armament came aboard their suspicions were confirmed: 18 demi-culverins designated for the flagship alone; an immense amount of cannon shot; barrel upon barrel of gunpowder, bows, arquebuses, calivers, pikes and part-armour. In no way could this be a peaceful

trading expedition to pick up a load of Egyptian currants.

The old hands who had sailed with Drake before, noting the amount of victuals going aboard – casks of salt beef and pork, ship's biscuit, flour, hogsheads of ale, peas, beans and lentils, dried fish and fresh cheeses, wine, water and vinegar – guessed they were heading for the Main and the Spanish treasure 'Flota'. On paper the Elizabethan sailor lived well – certainly few labourers ashore enjoyed such a high standard of living – but he was at the mercy of corrupt merchants, dishonest Admiralty victualling officers and, in far too many cases, the cupidity of his own captain and ship's purser. Often even as it came aboard the butter was rancid and the bacon acrid, the beer short and flat – brewed without hops it would soon sour anyway, the meat and fish far from fresh and the ship's biscuit weevil-ridden.

At sea, mariners of the period were allowed 8¼d. for a day's victuals on a 'Flesh' day (when they were served meat) and 4¾d. on a 'Fish' day – in harbour this was less. 'Flesh' days were Tuesday, Thursday, Saturday and Sunday; the remainder were 'Fish' days. Each man was victualled for a month of 28 days and this extract from a 'Pipe' account of the time shows how the rations were broken down.

Goldar sculp.

S.ʳ Francis Drake.

63

THE PROPORTION OF VICTUALLING FOR THE SEAS.

Note 28 days to 1 month: whereof –

Fish days 12
Flesh days 16
Fish days .... 24 meals.
Flesh days .... 32 meals.

The fare of fish days for every man per diem.
Biscuit 1 lb [0.5 kg] .... 1d.
Beer (1) gallon [4.5 litres] . 1¾d.
In fish, 1 qr. of stockfish or the 8th part of a ling .... 1d.
In butter, half 1 qr. of a pound [57 g] .... ½d.
In cheese, 1 qr. of a pound [113 g] .... ½d.

The fare of flesh days
Biscuit .... 1d.
Beer 1 gallon [4.5 litres] ... 1¾d.
Beef 2 lb [1 kg] .... 5½d.

To this was added 1 pint of 'pease', salt, vinegar and, at odd times, usually when putting in to the Canaries, wine. The rations for Spanish and Portuguese seamen were much the same and according to Gregorio de Sotomeyer who sailed with the Armada, they suffered the same injustices – '. . . King Philip did command that the fleet should be victualled for 6 months, but Luis Hezar and Francisco Duarte of Cadiz did victual them but for 4 months, and with that which was nought and rotten'.

Daily rations
Sunday, Tuesday, Thursday
⅓ of an 'azumbre' (an azumbre was nearly half a gallon) of wine.
1½ lb [680 g] biscuit or 2 lb [900 g] fresh bread.
6 oz [170 g] bacon
2 oz [57 g] of rice
Monday
to the wine and biscuit were added, 6 oz [170 g] cheese and 3 oz [85 g] beans.
Wednesday
to the wine and biscuit were added, 6 oz [170 g] of tunny, squid or cod or five sardines, 6 oz [170 g] cheese, 3 oz (85 g) beans, oil and vinegar (¼) pint [142 ml]
Friday, Saturday
to the wine and biscuit were added, 6 oz [170 g] of fish, 3 oz [85 g] beans or chick peas, with oil and vinegar.

When the Armada finally sailed from Lisbon, rotten food was being thrown overboard long before they even reached Corunna, where they had to revictual.

Only Drake knew where the fleet was heading. His flagship was the *Pelican*, length 100 ft (30 m), displacing 100 tons (102 tonnes). Others in the fleet were the *Elizabeth* of 80 tons (81 tonnes), the *Swan* of 50 tons (51 tonnes), the *Marigold* of 30 tons (30 tonnes) and a 15-ton (15-tonne) bark, the *Christopher*. Against the advice of Lord Burghley, the Chancellor of England, who hesitated to upset the Spanish king, members of the Queen's Council, including the Queen herself (albeit clandestinely), had financed Drake to make his way into the Great South Sea in search of new lands and, as they privately hoped, plunder. Drake and his fleet set course southwest by south into the Torrid Zone, the Doldrums, the Devil's Sea, where day followed monotonous day as the fleet

limped along making use of whatever faint breezes came its way. The meat became rotten, worms grew fat in the ship's biscuit and the living conditions became foul.

At sea 16th-century ships were hot-beds of disease and infection brought about by lack of proper sanitation, cramped sleeping conditions on hard decks ('hammacoes' – hammocks – were not introduced until later in the century), wet and condensation. The fact that mariners wore their only suit of clothes day and night throughout a voyage did not help. Typhus (gaol fever), consumption and skin complaints were prevalent, as was the 'flux' or dysentery, brought on by rotten food and sour wine and beer. But the most dreaded disease on a long voyage was scurvy. A few observant commanders of the period had an inkling that it occurred as a result of dietary deficiencies and fed their 'people' fresh vegetables, lemons and lime juice whenever possible. Yet centuries were to

pass before it was determined that scurvy was caused by a lack of Vitamin C. The scurvy sufferer first became listless; then his skin broke into angry boils, his gums began to swell and bleed and his teeth fell out. Within days arms and legs became dreadfully swollen, ugly black bruises appeared and breathing was almost impossible. This was followed by coma and death.

The men, huddled together, slept either on the hard planking of the gundecks or, as they sailed into the tropics, the upper deck. The Navy Board had long since stopped the practice of bringing straw aboard to soften the hard decks for the risk of fire was far too great. They ordered that '. . . no Captain suffer any beds of straw within the ship, for it is perilous for fire work; and the said Captain to cause 2 hogsheads to be cut assunder in the midst and chained to the side; the soldiers and mariners to piss in them that they may always be full of Urin, to quench fire with, 2 or 3 pieces of sail

An Elizabethan galleon in a heavy sea, from a drawing by the author.

65

Caca Fogo.

Caca Plato.

ready to wet in the piss, and always cast in on the fire work as need shall require'. The stench below must have been indescribable. Added to this factor was the mingled smell of tallow, burning oil, unwashed bodies, sour ale and, in rough weather, with the gun ports shut tight, the smell of vomit. All was suffered for 6s. 8d. a month in pay, although the ship's officers received rather more – the Master (who handled the sailing of the ship) £2.10s.; the Master Gunner, 10s.; the Purser, 11s. 8d. plus his pickings; and oddly enough, the trumpeter was rated at a princely 15s. a month. But their wages were nothing compared with their share of any loot taken.

When Thomas Doughty, a gentleman adventurer and a spy for Lord Burghley, incited a mutiny in an attempt to get the fleet to turn for home, Drake gave him short shrift. Tried before a jury of 40 men, he was convicted and sentenced. Two days later he was led out to the block on an island in St. Julian's Bay – after taking communion and sharing dinner with Drake – and beheaded. Although swift and sharp, punishment aboard ship was governed by the Laws of Oleron, believed to have been instituted by Queen Eleanor of Aquitaine, wife of King Henry II. They covered everything from blasphemy to gambling and the issue of sailors' victuals. A seaman caught stealing was tarred and feathered, then forced to run the gauntlet of the whole crew, finally being dismissed from the ship. A murderer was lashed to the body of his victim and thrown overboard. For blaspheming, offenders had 'a maudlin-spike, viz. an iron pinn, clapt into their mouths until they are very bloody; an excellent cure for swearers'. Drawing a knife on a shipmate could result in the loss of the right hand.

After experiencing dreadful storms, Drake made his way into the Great South Sea and marauded up the west coast of South America. The fleet chaplain, Francis Fletcher, wrote of the storm in his journal, 'The day being come the sight of Sun & land was taken from us so that there followed as it were a palpable darkness by the space of 56 days without sight of sun, moon or stars. . .' Later in the voyage when the parson upset Drake, the Admiral had a placard hung round his neck, carrying a pun on his name – FRANCES fLETCHER YE FALSEST KNAVE THAT LIVETH.'

His ship, now named the *Golden Hind*, was full of plunder obtained mainly from the Spanish treasure galleon, *Nũestra Senora de la Concepcion*. Drake turned eastwards for home and arrived at Plymouth Sound on 26 September 1580. His haul represented the best part of £500,000 which when translated into modern values probably amounted to nearly £25,000,000 or $35,000,000. This should have been the last straw for Philip II, but still he hesitated. If he should depose Elizabeth, then she would be succeeded by the half-French Mary Queen of Scots, and he had no wish to see a French influence on the affairs of England. With the execution of the Scottish queen in 1587, the final obstacle was removed and the die was cast – the 'Enterprise Against England' got underway.

The Enterprise Against England

Aided by 1,000,000 ducats from the Pope and with the assistance of other Catholic maritime powers, the Spanish king began to assemble a powerful fleet. This fleet was to sail up the Channel to link up with the army of the Duke of Parma in the Netherlands for the combined invasion of Lutheran England. By the beginning of 1588 a vast fleet of ships crammed with soldiers – and called the Most Happy Armada – lay in Lisbon harbour ready to sail against England, but the crews were far from happy. Typhus, brought on by filthy conditions, lack of food and verminous clothing, raged throughout the fleet; they were on the point of mutiny. The Armada had been due to sail the previous year, but a daring raid by Sir Francis Drake on the supply ships assembled at Cadiz had put back the invasion date – Philip II wrote in this journal, 'The loss was not very great, but the daring of the attempt was very great indeed'. Another far more serious setback occurred in January 1588; the Captain General of the Armada, the ageing Marquis of Santa Cruz, the greatest admiral in Spain, died of fever and was replaced by Don Alonso Perez de Guzman el Bueno, the seventh Duke of Medina Sidonia. A landsman given to violent seasickness, he protested his unfitness for the task, but the king peremptorily ordered him to Lisbon. Arriving there he found the Armada in a dreadful state. Of the original 22,000 soldiers with the fleet, over 4,000 were either sick, dead, or had deserted ship.

The Duke, no sailor, ignorant of ships and with no knowledge of naval warfare, nonetheless threw himself into the job of Captain General with a will and by early summer the fleet was in good order, ready to sail. After a false start from Lisbon, the

Opposite: Drake in the Pelican *takes the Spanish treasure ship* Cacafuego.

67

Above: Fire ships attack the
Armada at anchor in the
Calais Roads.

Below: The Armada is
harassed in the Channel.

Armada finally set out from Corunna,
bound for the English Channel: 130 ships,
carrying 8,000 seamen, 2,000 rowers,
19,000 soldiers, 1,500 volunteers and non-
combatants including 180 friars (to the
horror of the seamen who thought a priest
aboard unlucky). In tight crescent formation, they were off the Lizard on 19 July
1588, beating towards Plymouth and

hoping to take the English fleet by surprise.
However, Tom Flemyng of the bark *Golden
Hind* spotted the Armada off the Scilly Isles
and raced to Plymouth to warn the Lord
High Admiral, Lord Howard of Effingham,
who lost no time in putting to sea.

Tacking westwards along the coast
throughout the night, the English fleet
were to windward of the Armada the

following morning and the chase up the Channel began. The low-slung English galleons buzzed around the Armada like a swarm of angry wasps, completely outsailing the 'stiff elephants' of Spain, pouring in long-range broadsides from their 18 pounders and then scurrying away. Only occasionally did they allow themselves to get within range of the heavier Spanish guns. However, the gunnery was of no high standard, the wooden hulls too stout for the shots. In any event, only two Spanish ships were sunk during the action, and one of those, the *San Salvador*, was blown up by a disgruntled German mercenary, a gunner who had been flogged by Captain Priego. By the 27 July the Duke of Medina Sidonia had reached Calais to join up with the Duke of Parma, his fleet virtually intact. During the night the English sent in seven fireships; the first one was dragged clear into the shallows, but the other six got through to scatter the Spanish fleet. As dawn broke on 29 July, the ships of the Armada were strung along the French coast and were being driven into the North Sea by a brisk southwesterly wind. A broken man, Medina Sidonia decided to sail for Spain around the north coast of Scotland. Less than half the Armada that had sailed so proudly from Corunna returned to Spain – 63 were lost. Other than the two sunk during the battle, three were abandoned to the enemy, five ran ashore and 35 disappeared without trace; the remainder were wrecked off the rocky coasts of Scotland and Ireland, where their crews were invariably butchered. Luckily for the defeated Spanish Captain General and his commanders, King Philip II took a philosophical view of the disastrous end to the Enterprise Against England – 'I sent my ships to fight against the English, not the wind and waves'. But really the defeat of the Armada demonstrated for the first time the futility of sending soldiers to fight sailors at sea.

The Spanish Armada in a storm, detail from a painting by Henrik Cornelius Vroom (1566–1640).

Wooden Walls and Frigates

As the naval power of Spain declined, the naval power of England grew, until her navy became the finest fighting force at sea. Yet by the mid-17th century her maritime supremacy was being seriously challenged by one of the smaller countries of Europe. Having finally thrown off the Spanish yoke, the United Provinces of Holland set out to become one of the great sea trading powers of the world – in the Narrow Seas as cargo carriers, and in the East and West Indies as merchant adventurers. Her long coastline and intricate waterways flowing into wide estuaries, made it inevitable that Holland would become a strong maritime nation. Of her population of two and a half million, no less than one-fifth were involved in either fishing or her growing mercantile marine.

At first, along with the English navigators, the Dutch looked for a Northeast Passage to the Orient, but this was abandoned when Jan Huygen van Linschoten rounded the Cape of Good Hope in 1595 and turned into the Indian Ocean. Within two years he returned having established the foundation of an empire in the East Indies, which the Dutch jealously guarded against foreign competition, particularly against English aggression. Towards the end of her reign, Queen Elizabeth had granted a charter to the British East Indies Company. This group of merchant adventurers had the privateering Duke of Cumberland among their backers and were prepared to fight the Dutch and Portuguese for a share of the wealth of the East. An endless series of more or less private skirmishes broke out between the armed merchantmen of Holland and England, but the real reason that set the two countries on a collision course towards war was occurring in the Narrow Seas.

Cromwell's Commonwealth when it came to power made an effort to suppress the corruption that had been rife throughout the time of the early Stuarts – the *Bonaventure*, for instance, was being cared for and maintained at the Navy Board's expense, seven years after she had been broken up, and someone had received £1,700 on account for her successor that was never built. Cromwell also turned a jealous eye on the Dutch Mercantile Marine which had achieved a virtual monopoly as the cargo carriers of northern Europe. Nine out of ten English trade cargoes were carried in Dutch ships. To put an end to this situation the Navigation Act was introduced in 1651 which banned all foreign ships carrying cargo to English ports unless the cargo had originated in their own country. This was really, to all intents and purposes, a declaration of war. The following May fighting broke out between a Dutch squadron of 40 ships under Marten Tromp and 21 English ships under the English 'General at Sea' Robert Blake. The battle raged from six in the evening until dark and although the English took one of the Dutch warships, ten of their own were badly mauled, including the flagship, *James*, which took more than 70 cannon shot. War was formally declared by the Commonwealth on 17 July. Cromwell, realizing the importance of sea power, not only increased the navy, but kept it fully occupied, though not always successfully. It was the policy of the Commonwealth to give naval commands to soldiers, indeed they were officially termed 'generals at sea'. The story that during his first naval engagement Robert Blake, who had formerly been a colonel in the Parliamentary army, ordered the fleet to 'wheel to the right', although unconfirmed, could well be true.

There was a marked difference between the ships of the two navies. The Dutch built their smaller ships for speed and manoeuvrability, with the additional virtue that their shallow draught enabled them to sail into shoal water. The English, on the other hand, went for massive, cumbersome ships, 'so clogged with timber that there was no room for stores'. The English built their ships to last 70 years, the Dutch for seven. The result was that many of the latter were sunk by gunfire (a rare happening before this conflict). However, on the other hand, the Dutch ships had little difficulty outsailing the English ships, showing them a clean pair of heels. It was during this period that warships began to be rated by the number of guns they carried. First-rates mounted 90 to 100 cannon, second-rates from 80 to 90, third-rates from 60 to 80, fourth-rates 40 to 60, fifth-rates 28 to 40; below that they were sixth-rates. Despite the attraction of fast, light, manoeuvrable ships that could deliver a broadside and sail swiftly out of harm's way, it was borne home to European navies that

for sheer 'ship-smashing', warships had to be big and powerfully armed. Minor adjustments were made to hull and rigging but, by and large, the only major change was a continual increase in size and armament, a situation that was to continue until the introduction of steam and iron-cladding. In fact, there was little radical change in ship design from the time of the Elizabethan galleon.

In the first half of the century, ships were richly carved and gilded – the English *Sovereign of the Seas*, launched in 1637, was a typical example of an ornately decorated first-rater. The £66,000 needed to build her was raised by 'Ship Money' tax, a determining factor in the Civil War that brought about the fall and execution of Charles I. A three-master displacing 1,700 tons (1,730 tonnes), she was a powerful warship mounting 102 guns on her three decks. Later, in 1652, she was cut down to a two-decker by the master shipwright Peter Pett (the Pett family had produced master shipwrights since the time of Henry VIII) and re-christened *Royal Sovereign* at

Engraving of a Dutch warship of the 17th century.

the Restoration. With the advent of Cardinal Richelieu, 'Father of the French Navy', France began to accumulate a fleet, building some herself, buying others from the Dutch. At the time of the cardinal's death they had 63 ponderous 'wooden-walls', even more ornately decorated than the English ships, but the costly gilding and carving was protected during battle by matting. Sensibly, the Dutch built their ships solely for fighting, with little or no adornment – they could see no reason for costly decoration which could be obliterated at the first broadside.

Once war was officially declared, the English naval commanders, Blake, Monck and Sir George Ayscore (a professional naval officer), concentrated on attacking the rich merchant convoys and herring fishing fleet. The Dutch admirals, Marten Tromp, Michel de Ruyter, Jan Evertsen and De Witt, seamen to a man, inflicted early defeats on the Commonwealth fleet, and had the better of a number of other fiercely fought engagements. So successful were the Dutch that it gave rise to the popular legend that Tromp hoisted a broom to his masthead after his defeat of an English fleet of Dungeness in 1652, in order to indicate that he had swept the English from the seas. Doubtless Tromp did fly a broom when he returned to port, but a broom at the masthead was the age-old sign of a ship up for sale, and the Dutch admiral had captured a number of prizes during his cruise.

The following year when Blake defeated a Dutch fleet in a running fight down the Channel that lasted three days, he is said to have hoisted a whip to show he had whipped the Dutch off the seas, but a whip had been commonly worn by warships well before Blake's time. The final decisive battle of the first Dutch war was fought off the North Foreland on 11 June 1653, when Monck with 110 ships encountered Tromp with 90. Both fleets had their problems; the English had difficulty crewing their ships, for although the rates of pay for seamen were far higher than in the Royalist navy, there was just as much delay in getting it, so the result to the sailors was very much the same. Press gangs were put hard to work replacing the large numbers deserting to the Dutch, ostensibly to support the Royalist cause, but really as a mark

Sovereign of the Seas, *the pride of the navy of Charles I.*

of discontent over pay and conditions. On the other hand, many of the Dutch captains were not fully committed to the action and Tromp was, at one point, forced to fire on his own ships in an unsuccessful effort to stop them retiring from the battle. The Dutch lost ten ships, and 1,350 men (including six captains) were captured. But the English admiral was denied an overwhelming victory by the brilliant seamanship of the enemy who navigated their smaller ships among the sandbanks of the Scheldt, where their heavier opponents with a greater draught dare not follow.

Peace between the two countries was declared in April 1654 after a final skirmish off Schenveningen, during which Marten Tromp was killed by musket fire from the enemy tops.

The uneasy peace lasted only ten years. The Dutch had never ceased to harry the English ships in eastern waters, and when Charles II on his restoration, ambitious for a fleet capable of subduing any other European navy, introduced an even more stringent Navigation Bill, hostilities broke out once more between the two countries. France, with her growing fleet, came into

The English ship Resolution *in a gale, from a painting by Willem Van de Velde, (1633–1707).*

The Dutch in the Thames.

the war on the side of the Dutch in 1666. A number of inconclusive engagements followed – indeed both sides claimed victory – but by and large the Dutch usually had the better of things; certainly the English lost more men and ships. The British had more success on the American frontier, however, when they captured New Amsterdam which they renamed New York. But they suffered a humiliating reverse at the hands of Michiel Adrianszoon de Ruyter, the Dutch admiral-in-chief.

Peace negotiations at Breda broke down when Charles II demanded impossible terms from the United Provinces, terms that the English fleet was in no condition to enforce. He and the Lord High Admiral, his brother James, Duke of York – later King James II – had allowed the fleet to deteriorate, and had bitterly disappointed the seamen by failing to honour an early promise of better pay and conditions. Many English sailors, finding themselves living in the same old squalor, went over to the Dutch and among them were several experienced river pilots who were used to picking their way through the shoals and

shallows of the River Medway, the entrance to the Royal naval base and dockyard at Chatham. In an operation carefully planned down to the finest detail, de Ruyter put to sea with 51 ships-of-the-line – three frigates, 14 fireships and a number of smaller vessels – with the intention of sailing up the Thames and Medway, to destroy shipping, dockyard installations and naval stores and to blow up arsenals. It had been conceived as a combined operation in which the landing party was put under the command of a Parliamentary soldier, Colonel Dolman. The Dutch knew from the deserters exactly where each English ship lay, and the Medway pilots aboard the leading vessels guided the fleet safely through the treacherous entrance to the river. The 20 June 1667 saw terrified Londoners in a panic as the Dutch sailed serenely up the Thames. 'Trading ceased, banks suspended payments, people left their work and gathered in the streets; many of the inhabitants fled, taking their valuables with them.'

With a mass of helpless ships lying ahead, the wind changed as Admiral van

Ghent, leading the fleet, reached Gravesend, and he was forced to turn up river to attack Chatham. Despite a boom chain and four fireships with a handful of craft behind them, the Dutch broke through and mauled the anchored men-of-war, many of which were unmanned, others were without guns. In all, they burnt six warships before they withdrew, taking along with them the *Royal Charles*, the pride of the English fleet. A chastened Charles II offered more reasonable terms and the war was concluded by the signing of the Peace of Breda in 1667. But it did not last long. Five years later England was again fighting the Dutch, but this time with the French as allies.

The Growing French Navy

Once the French seriously began to build a navy, they set about it in a characteristically scientific manner. The French ships sent across the Channel to supplement the navy of Charles II so impressed the king that he ordered a number of ships to be laid down along the lines of the *Superbe*. By constructing ships which were in advance of their time in dimension and line, the French, soon to be followed by the Spanish, gained a reputation for building faster and more satisfactory sailers than any other country in Europe – a reputation that lasted for generations.

The weight of shot fired by 17th-century warships was very much the same as during the Spanish Armada engagement, ranging from 3 lb (1.4 kg) to 42 lb (19 kg), but by the end of the century, the individual names, cannon, semi-cannon, culverin and so on, had been dropped in favour of a designation of shot-weight only: '42-pounders', '18-pounders' and so on. Although the oaken hulls of ships were extremely strong, heavy shot fired at 'half pistol shot' (about 100 yards), the range at which naval battles were usually fought, could cause considerable damage if it splintered its way through a gun port into the

A highly decorated French warship of 1657, an engraving after Boisseau.

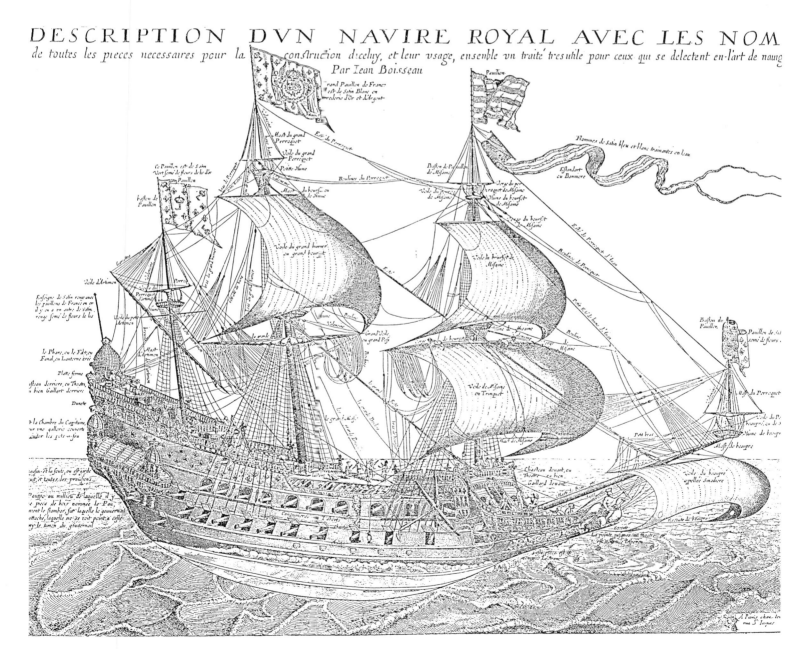

75

congested gundeck. However, first-raters had little to fear in the way of crippling damage from a broadside engagement. The smooth-bore cannon, firing solid iron shot, was reaching the height of its destructive power, but the hulls of ships-of-the-line had become more massively timbered to counteract this. (Only the first three rates were classed as ships-of-the-line; fourth-raters were termed 'cruisers'; and fifth- and sixth-raters were called 'frigates' and never fought in the line.)

Naval warfare had by now developed from the individual mêlée of the Dutch wars into the broadside battle in which ships fought line-ahead firing into each others' hulls. They were forced into this strategy as their guns were unable to train fore and aft; they could only effectively fire at right-angles to the centre line at an enemy directly on the beam. When France took up the cause of the deposed James II towards the end of the 17th century and England and France found themselves at war, their ships had arrived at a warfare pattern that was to persist with only detail alterations until sail was superceded by steam. The same statement can, in general, be applied to the naval tactics of the day. Later, in the 1750s, by 'breaking the line' of an enemy squadron, a naval commander could pour a deadly broadside through the stern lights of an enemy, his heavier shot scything through the flimsy transverse partitions from one end of the ship to the other. *Victory*'s first broadside at Trafalgar, fired at point-blank range through the stern lights of *Bucentaure*, tore through the gundecks, dismounting 20 cannon and killing or wounding nearly 400

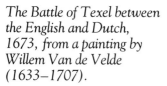

The Battle of Texel between the English and Dutch, 1673, from a painting by Willem Van de Velde (1633–1707).

men, half of the ship's crew.

One innovation to the art of naval warfare was the 'bomb ketch' which first made its appearance in 1682. The French had long been aware of the value of the mortar which fired a 200-lb (91-kg) bomb with a high trajectory, and sought to use it at sea for systematic land bombardment (it was never used against other ships). This called for a specially designed vessel, built to absorb the enormous shock of firing such a large missile (the nearest in weight and destructive power was the 42-lb/9-kg shot) from such a short-barrelled piece of ordnance. Iron 'knees' replaced the ones traditionally made from oak; heavy 'beam bridges' strengthened the deck; and the foremast was removed to make room for the mortar and to allow it to fire dead ahead. The ship itself was trained on the target in much the same way as a submarine fires a torpedo. Two anchors were run out, and by means of springs the 'bomb' could achieve a high degree of accuracy.

When James II came to the throne of England, he alienated both Parliament and the public by his obstinate religious bigotry, and in 1688 the crown was offered to William, Prince of Orange, the husband of James's daughter Mary. As William III, the new king conceived a 'Grand Alliance', whereby Louis XIV, who supported the cause of ex-king James, found France arrayed against the rest of Europe. His navy was no match for the combined Anglo-Dutch fleets, although a brilliant delaying action was fought by the French admiral De Tourville off Barfleur in 1692.

In 1704 the capture of Gibraltar by Admiral Sir George Rooke gave Britain a

commanding naval base that led to her control of the Mediterranean. The French navy met with further reverses during the Seven Years War (1756-1762), in which Canada and a number of West Indian islands were lost and the British gained a firmer foothold in India. France's Spanish allies fared little better as one by one her former possessions were wrested away from her, with her fleet unable to do little more than fight a series of defensive actions. But from 1778 onwards, the French saw an opportunity for revenge by siding with the newly emerging United States of America.

Although there had been little change in the hull shape of warships, particularly the first-raters, there were nevertheless new ideas in the offing. The *Architectura Navalis Mercatoria*, written by the Swede Frederick Hendrik af Chapman in 1768, followed in 1775 by his *Tractat om Skepps Buggereit (Treatise on Shipbuilding)* were to have a profound effect on ship design of the future. Chapman, the grandson of a Yorkshire shipwright who had settled in Gothenberg, made a careful study of the hydrodynamics of hull shapes in relationship to their speed through the water. Experimenting with models in tanks – he was the first naval architect to test models under such conditions, controlling their speed through the water by an ingenious

The lower gundeck of the Swedish ship Wasa *after the completed excavation.*

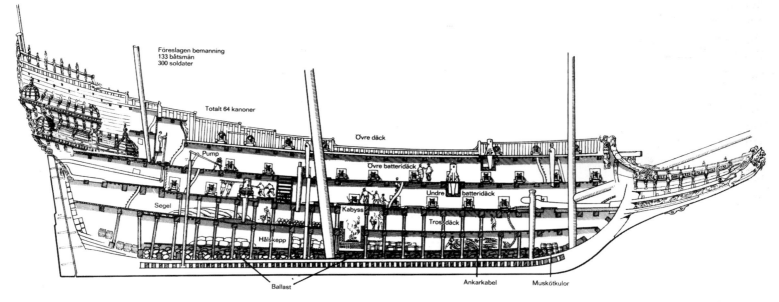

Föreslagen bemanning
133 båtsmän
300 soldater

Totalt 64 kanoner

Övre däck

Pump

Övre batteridäck

Segel

Undre batteridäck

Kabyss

Trossdäck

Hålskepp

Ballast

Ankarkabel

Muskötkulor

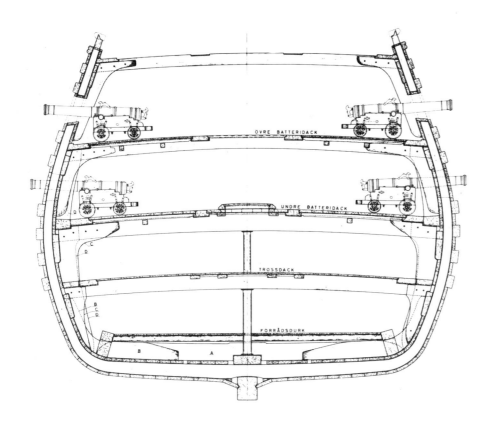

ÖVRE BATTERIDACK

UNDRE BATTERIDACK

TROSSDACK

FORRÅDSDURK

Top: A cut-away of the Wasa.

Above: A cross-section of Wasa's main gundecks.

system of dropping weights – he came to the conclusion that a ship's speed could be increased by giving her a finer entry into the water and a cleaner sweep aft. This lesson was put to good use by the builders of the American frigates that were to enjoy such remarkable success.

The American Frigate

Following the Treaty of Paris signed in 1763 which brought an end to the Seven Years War, the French, realizing the inadequacy of their navy, threw themselves into a crash shipbuilding programme. In a short time they built a strong and powerful fleet; but their efforts were not solely directed at

shipbuilding for they also re-established their Naval Academy and set up gunnery and medical schools. By 1771 the ambitious programme which called for 80 ships-of-the-line and 44 frigates was three parts complete; 64 ships-of-the-line were in commission and 50 frigates – six more than the target set. Together with their Spanish allies, they were able to put to sea 90 ships-of-the-line when, in 1778, they sided with the Americans in the War of Independence. On the other hand, no such dynamic shipbuilding programme had been undertaken in Britain. There, incompetent naval administration, low service morale, corruption and political intrigue had allowed the fleet to deteriorate to such a level that, in 1778, the Royal Navy could muster only 72 ships-of-the-line for service.

At the outbreak of the American Revolution in 1776, the emerging country had no recognized fleet, though George Washington had chartered a number of fishing boats and merchantmen that were armed and fitted out as cruisers. Seeing the need for a fleet, the revolutionary Congress had authorized the building of 13 warships, which became the nucleus of the new Continental Navy, though the navy was not officially established until an Act of Congress was signed in 1794. Relying on the support of French sea power, the Americans made no attempt to build ships-of-the-line, but concentrated on designing fast, hard-hitting frigates.

Frigates, 'the eyes of the fleet' according to Lord Nelson, were small, swiftly moving, highly manoeuvrable vessels employed out of the line of battle for reconnaissance, convoy duty and as 'repeating ships' (free from the smoke of an engagement, they would repeat an admiral's orders, running up signal flags to be seen by the rest of the fleet). The original frigate or 'fregata' of the Mediterranean was a small-oared tender that served a big galley; later it became lightly armed to enable it to take part in skirmishes. In the second half of the 16th century, the English frigate, believed to have been introduced by Francis Drake, was a miniature galleon used for despatch work. The *Constant Warwick*, built in 1646 for the privateering Earl of Warwick and later bought for the navy, is generally considered to be the first English naval frigate, mainly because of her longer keel-to-beam ratio and lower freeboard. It was not until the mid-18th century that the true frigate began to appear: fast, small ships mounting a relatively heavy armament on a single gundeck. The value of the frigate was soon realized and most navies began a rapid building programme. Britain, for example, had 35 frigates afloat in 1760; by 1770 this figure had risen to 100; by the end of the century to 159. Gun for gun, the British and Dutch favoured a lighter craft than the French, Spanish and American navies. Both the British *Brilliant* and French

A view of Gibraltar in 1705.

Aurore, launched in 1757 and 1758 respectively, were 36-gun frigates, but their dimensions varied considerably.

Brilliant

Keel	106 ft 2½ inches (32.4 m)
Beam	35 ft 6 inches (10.8 m)
Depth	12 ft 4 inches (3.8 m)
Weight	718 tons (729 tonnes)

Aurore

Keel	118 ft 9 inches (32.2 m)
Beam	38 ft 6 inches (11.7 m)
Depth	15 ft 2 inches (4.6 m)
Weight	946 tons (961 tonnes)

A first-rate 18th-century ship-of-the-line, at anchor and a cut-away section.

All frigates had two things in common: they were three-masted with square sails and had a length-to-beam ratio of nearly 4:1, as opposed to the 3:1 ratio of a ship-of-the-line. These finer lines gave them the edge in speed over the bigger ships and they were able to sail closer to the wind. The early frigates carried 28–30 guns, 9-pounders, on the upper deck, but by the 1790s the standard frigate mounted 36 18-pounders.

The frigate was the ideal ship for the rising United States Navy. Fast and manoeuvrable, they were the best possible type of ship for escorting convoys, for

SHIP.

A FIRST RATE SHIP of WAR with Rigging &c. at Anchor.

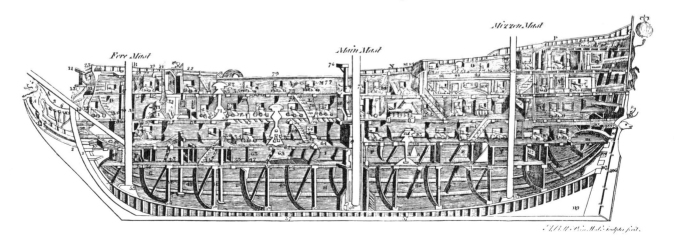

The Section of a First Rate Ship of War, Shewing its various Timbers and Apartments.

Fore Mast   *Main Mast*   *Mizzen Mast*

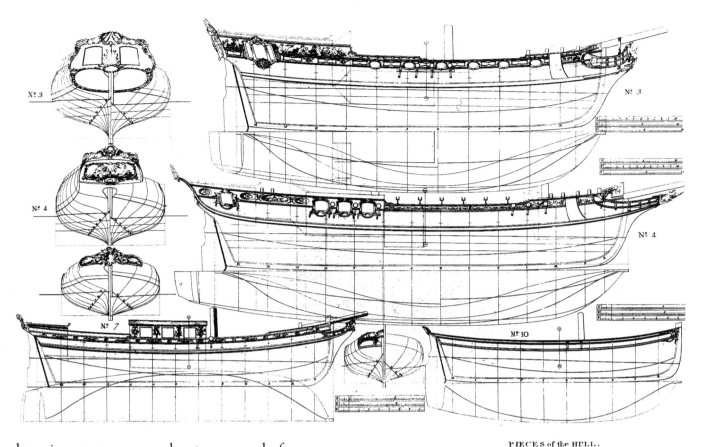

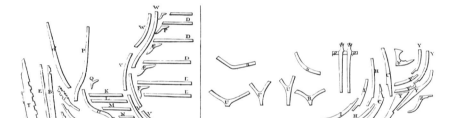

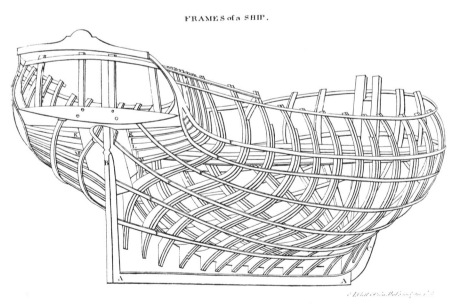

FRAMES of a SHIP.

harrying enemy merchantmen and for making lightning coastal raids, as John Paul Jones proved so effectively. From the beginning, American shipbuilders and naval architects were faced with the age-old problem of speed versus stability. Hogging (becoming curved upward in the middle) through strain generally developed if the ship had too sharp a prow and taper; bluff ends made the vessel slow through the water. The compromise reached by the Americans, incorporating as many good features as possible, produced an effective fighting ship when manned by experienced crews. Of the first 13 built, eight were of 32 guns; the other five carried 28 guns, the main armament on a single flush gundeck, with chase guns on the forecastle and quarterdeck. Later the forecastle and quarterdeck were connected by gangways running down each side, giving the impression of a continuous upper deck. The Americans then introduced the 'double-back' frigate, in which the number of guns was raised from 32 to 44.

One of the first of the original 13 frigates, the 32-gun *Hancock*, was considered at the time to be the fastest frigate in the world. Launched at Newberryport, Massachusetts, in 1776, she had been built by Jonathan Greenleaf and Stephen and Ralph Cross, who were among the best American shipbuilders. Her first success, in June 1777, occurred when, in company with the 24-gun *Boston*, she captured the British 28-gun frigate *Fox*. Ten days later, in spite of her potential speed, she fell to the 44-gun *Rainbow*, after a chase lasting 36 hours. Repaired in the British naval dockyard at Plymouth, England, she was taken into the British fleet and renamed *Iris*, but not before careful drafts of her lines had been made for future reference in frigate building. When with the British

Top and above: Proportions of 18th-century craft.

fleet, she captured a number of enemy vessels, including the *Trumbull*, another of the original 13 frigates. She was herself captured by the French in 1781, who used her as a powder hulk at Toulon until she was finally destroyed by the British when they took the port in 1793. By now the American shipbuilders were gaining a reputation for the design of their frigates and one of them, William Hackett, became the best-known ship designer of his day.

'. . . in human affairs the sources of success are ever to be found in the fountains of quick resolve and swift stroke: and it seems to be a law inflexible and inexorable that he who will not risk cannot win.' These words of John Paul Jones, the first hero of the young American Navy, sum up the attitude of their frigate commanders. Many individual actions were fought by these hard-hitting ships during the War of Independence and the War of 1812, in which the American ships and seamen had remarkable success. Early on, Lord Nelson realized the growing threat when he wrote, 'There is in the handling of those transatlantic ships, a nucleus of trouble for the Navy of Great Britain'. The sentiment was echoed by Napoleon who said that England had been given 'a maritime rival that will sooner or later humble her pride'.

One such single action was fought to the death off Flamborough Head on the northeast coast of England on 23 February 1779. Paul Jones had arrived in Nantes from the United States of America in December 1777, commanding the 18-gun *Ranger*. By April he was at sea again harrying British shipping in the Irish Sea and raiding towns along the West Coast. Heading north, he set the port of Whitehaven ablaze and captured the *Drake*, the first British warship to be taken in the war. The French, impressed by his success, gave him the *Duc de Durras* – which he promptly re-named *Bonhomme Richard* – and put him in command of a raiding squadron consisting of the 32-gun frigate *Alliance*, two armed merchantmen, the *Pallas* and *Vengeance*, and the 18-gun cutter *Cerf*. Taking a few prizes in the Irish Sea, he rounded the north of Scotland into the North Sea with the intention of attacking the Firth of Forth. When this venture proved unsuccessful, due in the main to the laxity of his second-in-command Landais, captain of the *Alliance*, the squadron headed south, until on 23 February 1779 they sighted a convoy of 41 merchantmen escorted by the 44-gun *Serapis* (under Captain Richard Pearson) and the 20-gun *Countess of Scarborough*.

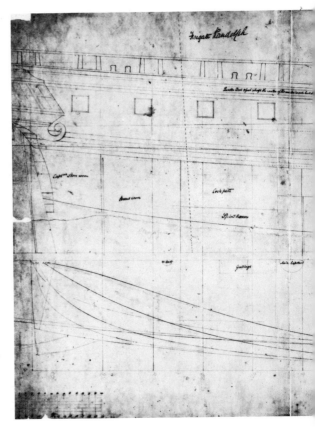

Jones, following his maxim, without hesitation ran up the signal to attack, but they had been spotted by the British and Captain Pearson sailed his two warships between the Americans and the Baltic convoy. In the dusk light, the *Serapis* and *Bonhomme Richard* sailed side by side on a parallel course, close enough inshore to be clearly seen by a crowd gathered on the Flamborough cliffs. Paul Jones closed the *Serapis* to within musket range, with the crews of both ships hurling insults and challenges to each other – in the case of the *Bonhomme Richard*, in the many different tongues of her multi-national crew.

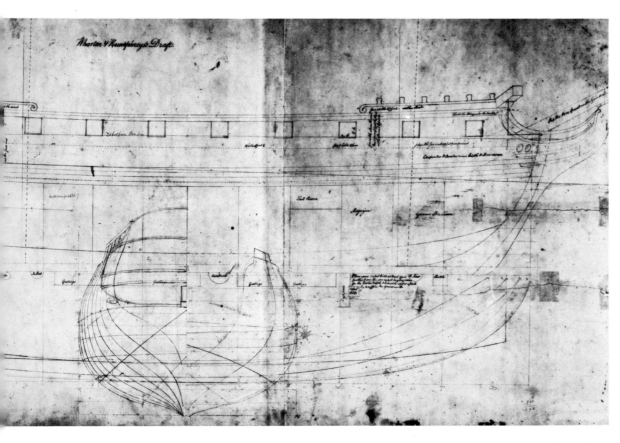

The *Bonhomme Richard*, mounting six 18-pounders on her lower gundeck, 28 12-pounders on her upper deck and eight 9-pounders fore and aft, opened up with a broadside at 1920 hours. Before the smoke had time to clear, a broadside crashed into the American ship. To Jones's horror there was a fearful crash from below and smoke and flame belched from the lower gundeck. The explosions, however, were not the result of a British shot; rather two of his own 18-pounders had burst on firing.

The cramped gundeck, now completely out of action, was a bloody shambles; bodies lay everywhere, flung among the shattered and dismounted 18-pounders. The 'loblollies' (surgeons mates) were carrying the screaming wounded through the dense powder smoke, across decks slippery with blood, to the surgeon's cockpit. Jones urged on his upper-deck gunners at their 12-pounders, but they had little chance against their more heavily armed adversary, manned by a better disciplined crew; before long they were silenced and the deck strewn with dead gunners. With only three

of her 9-pounders still firing and taking water through a number of shot holes, the *Bonhomme Richard* was in a sorry plight. The crew called on Jones to strike. From the *Serapis* Pearson called on him to surrender. But the American commander had no intention of giving in. Raising his speaking-trumpet he shouted across to the Englishman, 'I haven't begun to fight yet!'

Jones's only hope, however, was to board and enter the enemy. His first attempt to do so failed, but as the two ships crashed together for the second time, he himself, oblivious to the withering volleys of musket fire crackling along the enemy's side, flung himself into the after rigging, lashing it to the bowsprit of the *Serapis*. The two ships swung together, bows to stern. The American crew surged aboard the English frigate, and furiously slashing and hacking with their cutlasses, relentlessly drove the enemy aft. Frantically the gunners of the *Serapis* fired point-blank into the *Bonhomme Richard*, shattering her hull but causing no casualties among her crew as they were all ranged along the upper deck. A lucky grenade, thrown down a hatchway by one of the American attackers, found the powder room. The explosion that immediately followed caused frightful havoc on the gundeck, men and cannon were hurled in every direction. With acrid, yellow smoke billowing round them, the British seamen on the upper deck still fought on, holding the boarders at bay.

By now the *Bonhomme Richard* was in a

LIFE ABOARD AN EIGHTEENTH CENTURY MAN-OF-WAR

In times of peace the Royal Navy allowed its personnel to run down. At the beginning of the Napoleonic War – known as the Great War – there were scarcely 16,000 seamen available to man the ships. But in a short space of time this figure had risen to 100,000. Less than one-fifth of these were volunteers. Rather, these 'sailors' were usually men whose life ashore was a grim struggle to survive, orphans and waifs, and gaol-birds who had seized the opportunity to serve King and Country in exchange for a free pardon and bounty. (Not that they necessarily got the best of the deal; Dr. Samuel Johnson, after visiting a man-of-war, remarked to Boswell that 'serving in a ship was like being in prison with a chance of drowning'.) Furthermore, the notorious press-gangs who roamed the streets of ports provided another means of obtaining manpower – no waterfront tavern was safe. Suddenly the door of a public house would crash open and sailors and marines would stream into the bar to 'take' any able-bodied men present. Anyone foolhardy enough to resist stood the chance of being laid flat with a heavy wooden marline pin. Certain categories were exempt by law – apprentices, fishermen, pilots and the like – and they were not allowed to 'take' boys under 18 years or men over 55 years, but the Lieutenant in charge often turned a blind eye if his ship's crew was much below strength.

The largest single source of recruitment, and certainly the best from ship's captain's point of view, came from homeward-bound merchantmen, fishing fleets and coastal trading vessels. At the beginning of the war, the merchant marine numbered around 80,000 and soon 50,000 of these had been 'pressed' into 'service'. During the peace between 1801 and 1812, American ships 'lost' no less than 6,000 men to the Royal Navy – though many of these had deserted from the Royal Navy in the first place. To relieve a captain of the task of 'pressing' his own men, an 'Impress Service' was set up. Armed with 'warrants', these men operated in likely ports, sending their 'catch' of 'landsmen' – an expression introduced into the Navy to rate these unfortunates – to 'guard' ships there to await a draft to individual men-of-war.

One such 'landsman', calling himself 'Jack Nasty-Face', wrote of the appalling conditions he found aboard a guard ship. After a cursory medical examination, he was pronounced seaworthy and battened down with 200 others in the hold with 'rats running over us in numbers'. Guarded by marines with loaded muskets and fixed bayonets, 'as though we had been culprits of the first or capital convicts', he writes of their introduction to Navy life. 'In this place we spent the day and following night huddled together for there was not room to sit or stand separate, for indeed we were in a pitiable plight, for numbers of them were sea-sick, some retching, others were smoking, whilst many were so overcome by the stench that they fainted for want of air . . . scarcely any of us were free from filth and vermin.'

Once aboard ship, conditions were hardly better. The men, slinging their hammocks from the ship's crossbeams on a gundeck cramped with cannon, had to crouch low to pass under them, sometimes receiving a flow of naval invective having jostled a dog-tired off-watch hand. A seaman's hammock was his most important possession. He slept in it, used it stacked in weather-deck netting as a protection against flying grape-shot (small balls in a cluster used to make a scattering charge for cannon) and musket balls, and finally, should he die aboard ship, as his coffin (the Boatswain would then sew him into it with tarred thread, putting the final stitch through his nostrils to make sure he was dead). As each man had just between 16 and 18 inches (31 and 46 cm) of space in which to sling his hammock, their close proximity to each other did nothing to improve health and hygiene; diseases ran through a ship like wildfire.

Disease killed vastly more men than did enemy shot. As a direct result of continual damp, undernourishment, overcrowding, verminous filth and the noisome vapours rising from stagnant bilges, of the 185,000 men enlisted at the beginning of the Seven Years War, 130,000 had perished from illness by the Peace of 1763 – that is more than 70 per cent! A good captain would take what precautions he could. Ships were fumigated by burning a mixture of gunpowder and vinegar in iron pans placed around the lower decks, the acrid fumes rolling through the ship setting the seamen coughing and their eyes streaming. At other times the gun ports were slammed shut and tobacco or flowers of sulphur were burned on the gundecks, or a red-hot iron bar (a 'loggerhead') was plunged into a bucket of tar. In spite of these precautions, seamen went down with rheumatism, lumbago, consumption, bronchitis, ague (malaria), dysentery, smallpox and, on long voyages, scurvy. These latter two were held at bay by Jenner's new method of inoculation and the issue of lime juice. But it was fever that the sailors feared the most, fever that could sweep through a ship with lightning speed leaving a trail of dead in its wake. Typhus or 'gaol fever' – often brought aboard by 'pressed' men straight from prison – and 'Black Vomit' (yellow fever), which killed within 24 hours, were by far the worst. As the gun ports on the lower decks were open only in the calmest of seas, the men who messed there lived in almost permanent gloom, relieved only by flickering candles in battle 'lanthorns', lanterns, or a 'pusser's glim', a crude wick floating in an iron saucer of reeking oil.

Surgery at sea was swift and hideously painful, but the surgeons were either incredibly skillful, or the seamen incredibly tough, as the majority of them lived to fight again. At 'beat to quarters', the surgeon and his assistants, 'loblollies', would form a platform of seamen's chests to

parlous condition, sinking rapidly with very few of her crew available to man the pumps. Jones, ever resourceful, convinced the prisoners that he had taken from previous successful battles that their only hope of survival lay in manning the pumps – this they did with a will. At this point the *Alliance* broke away from the engagement between the *Pallas* and the *Countess of Scarborough* and raked the now-defenceless *Serapis* down the port side. For most of the action, Landais, the French commander of the *Alliance*, had circled the *Countess of Scarborough*, firing indiscriminately, but totally ineffectually at British and American alike. When, at 2230 hours. *Serapis*'s mainmast came crashing down, Pearson struck his colours. The *Bonhomme Richard* was beyond hope of saving and a jubilant Paul Jones transferred his crew and prisoners to the British ship which he triumphantly sailed back to France. Although he had achieved a splendid victory, for some reason he was afforded no recognition in the United States of America at the time, neither did he ever receive another U.S. command.

Without doubt the most famous frigate in the history of the American Navy was the *Constitution*, launched in 1797, one of the 'six original frigates' called for by the 1794 Act of Congress. With an overall length of 204 ft (62 m), a beam of 43 ft 6 inches (13.2 m) and a depth of hold of 14 ft 3 inches (4.3 m), she displaced 2,200 tons (2,240 tonnes) and mounted 44 guns. During the War of 1812 she fought a

act as an operating table in the 'cockpit' on the orlop deck. Another set of chests would be used to lay out the surgical instruments – catlins (double-edged amputating knives), saws, needles and tourniquets. A kid (a half-barrel), filled with hot water, was used for dipping instruments to warm them; another was used to take the amputated limbs. Sponges, used to save money because lint could only be used once, became a source of infection after a time, and the slightest wound could lead to an amputation. After being given a heavy tot of rum – there were no anaesthetics – the wounded man would bite on a leather gag as the surgeon went swiftly to work. After amputation the stump was sealed with hot pitch.

Point-blank actions accounted, by and large, for less casualties than those fought at a distance. Close to, the shot entered the hull leaving a clean hole with few splinters, but a near-spent ball produced a jagged hole, sending out a shower of lethal splinters which did more damage than the shot.

The food issue was much the same as in Elizabethan times! Tuesday and Saturday were 'beef' days with an issue of 2 lb (0.9 kg) of salted beef; Sunday and Thursday were 'pork' days; on Monday, Wednesday and Friday (Banyan days), the men were given dried fish, oatmeal or pease, butter and cheese. (Banyans were Hindu merchants who, as often as not, ate no meat.) But unscrupulous naval victuallers were given to supplying meat that was far from fresh, beer that had already gone flat and ship's biscuit riddled with weevil and worm – raw recruits were usually advised by old hands to eat them in the dark, so they would be unaware of the nature of the soft parts. The pound of ship's biscuit and gallon of 'small beer' (weak ale) issued each day was often in short measure, owing to the cupidity of the purser and, in some instances, the captain.

On Banyan days during long voyages, the hands were given 'Portable Soup', the 18th-century equivalent of dehydrated 'instant' packet soup.

This was about as popular as the 'Krout' that Captain Cook insisted his crews ate to prevent scurvy – salted cabbage with juniper berries. An Admiralty instruction for serving 'Portable Soup' reads:

Directions for serving Portable Soup to the Well men on board the *Endeavour* Bark on Banyan Days (Viz).

On the Days it is served with Pease. 1 Qt of Water to Each Oz Pease with 10 Oz of the Soup When pease are boiled soft, the Soup is to be dissolved in them, and in a quarter of an hour it will be fit for use, after the Soup is put in it should be kept stirring all the time it is on the fire to prevent its burning the copper.

On the Days it is served with Oatmeal. 1 Qt of Water to 2 oz Oatmeal, with 1 Oz of the Soup The Oatmeal and Water to be boiled about 20 minutes, then put in the Soup, and when it is well dissolved which will be in about a quarter of an hour, it will be fit for use.

NB: One Ounce of the Soup is thought sufficient for a man a day.

The food was made more palatable by an issue of two gills (½ pint or 284 cc) of rum, proof strength; a gill was given at midday and another with the evening meal. Brandy was sometimes given in lieu. Admiral Vernon, believing 'neaters' too fiery, insisted that the rum issued in his squadron should be watered down, three parts of water to one part rum, this led to it being nicknamed 'grog' after the Admiral's custom of wearing a grogham coat.

It was the dreadful quality and state of the food – if a barrel of meat should be found to be half-rotten on opening it was still issued – in conjunction with the unhygienic conditions and meagre pay (when he got it) that had not been increased for 150 years, that triggered off the mutinies at Spithead and the Nore. At one end of the scale, a Vice-Admiral, such as Nelson, received £74.10s. a month, plus table money of £1 per day and other 'perks'; a Landsman, at the other end of the scale, received only £1.2s.6d. per month; an Ordinary Seaman, £1.5s.6d.; an Able Seaman, £1.13s.6d.; and a boy, just £4 per *annum*. The Warrant Officers did considerably better; Carpenter, Gunner, Boatswain and Purser got £4 per month and the Chaplain, although paid a nominal salary of 19s. a month, received a 'groat' (4d.) for every head of the ship's company and, in the case of a first-rater, this was quite substantial.

Discipline aboard ship was strict, and punishment, at the discretion of the captain, harsh. Much could be borne if the punishment was just and deserved, but 'flogging' captains would inflict 'lashes' for the least possible offence. A man deserting ship could expect a 'Flogging round the Fleet'. Stripped to the waist and lashed to a grating, he would be rowed from ship to ship in the anchored fleet, receiving 25 lashes at each from the 'cat o'nine tails', delivered by a bosun's mate, so his fellow shipmates could see the sentence carried out. Sometimes this could amount to as many as 300 lashes. With him in the boat was the Master-at-Arms, a warrant officer responsible to the captain for discipline aboard ship, and the surgeon, or one of his mates, would be standing by to revive the prisoner with vinegar and salts should he faint – in some instances he could well die from the ordeal. Minor offences would bring a dozen or two dozen lashes, meted out at the gangway, on the stroke of seven bells in the forenoon watch (11.30 a.m.), after 'Hands to witness punishment had been piped'.

Yet in spite of these unthinkable conditions, the seamen of both sides at Trafalgar (it was much the same, if not worse in the French and Spanish navies) fought bravely, working their guns to the death.

number of successful single-ship actions. The one in which she captured the British 38-gun frigate *Guerriere* earned her the nickname 'Old Ironsides'. Later in the year she took the *Java* and in 1815 scored victories over the *Cyane* and *Levant*.

The Fight Between the *Shannon* and the *Chesapeake*

Many believe that the greatest individual dual was fought between the British frigate *Shannon* and the American *Chesapeake*, 15 miles (24 km) off Boston on 1 June 1813. They were evenly matched (both carried 50 guns) and the battle was conducted with all the formality of a medieval tournament. Captain Broke of the *Shannon* issued a challenge, and Captain Lawrence took it up and sailed out of Boston to meet him in the *Chesapeake*. After a fast and furious gun battle (the action took less than 15 minutes and during that short interval both captains were seriously wounded), the *Shannon* was victorious – but not before the dying Lawrence uttered the phrase that was to be taken up by the American Navy down the years, 'Don't give up the ship'.

Boarding the American frigate Chesapeake *in 1813.*

The Siege of Yorktown

Meanwhile, while the frigates were fighting individual actions, the great ships-of-the-line (most first-raters were well over 2,000 tons/2,032 tonnes) were slogging it out in pitched battles, fought at point-blank range. Of all the battles and skirmishes fought between the British and French ships-of-the-line in the Caribbean and along the Atlantic seaboard of North America, it was the Battle of Chesapeake Bay in 1781 that had the most far-reaching effects. The battle itself was no major engagement and no outstanding victory was gained by either side, but it was, nonetheless, to alter the whole course of history. The British general Cornwallis in his advance through Carolina and Virginia was making for Hampton Roads in the expectation of receiving the badly needed supplies which were essential to his being able to continue his campaign. Wrongly believing a French fleet under Admiral de Grasse to be further north, Rear-Admiral Sir Samuel Hood took his squadron up the coast to blockade the Hudson River. Five days later the French Admiral arrived off the Virginian Capes and anchored without opposition in Cape Henry, put troops

The Battle of Virginia Capes, 1781.

ashore and blockaded the Rivers York and James. Invested by land and sea, Cornwallis had little choice but to retire with his army to Yorktown.

When Hood was joined by his commander, Admiral Graves, it was decided that the combined squadrons should make for Chesapeake Bay to offer assistance to Cornwallis. As he sailed his fleet of 20 ships-of-the-line southwards before a stern wind, Graves had no idea that de Grasse was already there; he believed him to be cruising somewhere off Cuba. The French were no less taken by surprise when their guard frigates raced into the anchorage firing their warning guns to announce the number of enemy ships approaching – ten – 15 – 20. The order was given to slip anchor, and one by one the massive French ships (the *Ville de Paris*, the flagship, was the biggest ship in the world) made open water. Had Graves followed Hood's advice and picked off the enemy piecemeal as they left harbour, the whole course of history might well have been changed. Instead he allowed the French fleet to come out and form up line-abreast. It was 1600 hours before action was joined and the British had been sighted at 1000 hours. The French had the better of an inconclusive engagement, suffering 220 casualties to the 336 of the British, but many more British ships than French ones had been severely damaged.

For five days the two fleets lay within sight of each other; then came a shift of wind. De Grasse, knowing that reinforcements were on the way, returned to anchorage, confident that the British would need to go north to repair their fleet before

they attacked again – which indeed they did. Washington and Rochambeau, the French commmander, tightened their hold on Yorktown and Cornwallis was forced to capitulate – victory in the War of Independence was in sight. Washington himself was in no doubt as to the value of the Chesapeake Bay engagement and the value of naval power when he wrote, '. . . a decisive naval superiority is to be considered as a fundamental principle and the basis upon which every hope of success must ultimately depend.'

War with Revolutionary France

When revolution broke out in France in 1789, the command of the navy suffered at the hands of the more extreme elements of the newly established Convention. The majority of the regular naval officers who were not guillotined or hanged in the streets either quit the service or fled the country. They were replaced either by raw recruits with only bravery and revolutionary zeal to commend them or, at best, by very junior officers lacking experience. Nevertheless, a fleet under Villaret de Joyeuse – 'General Villaret' as he was called – acquitted itself well at the Battle of the 'Glorious First of June', against the fleet of the battle-seasoned Lord Howe. Villaret, who had rocketed to command by the elimination of the regular senior officers, was closely supervised aboard his flagship, the 120-gun *Montagne*, by Jean Bon St. André, a People's Commissary, an 18th-century political commissar. Of the 36 ships under his command, only one was captained by an officer who had commanded a ship-of-the-line before the Revolution. Although Villaret was defeated, losing six of his ships to the enemy, he in a sense, succeeded: the vital grain convoy from the United States of America that he had been sent to protect reached Brest without loss.

British frigates off Dover, by Thomas Whitcombe (1752–1824).

Wooden Walls and Iron Men

The British fleet in which Horatio, Lord Nelson was to gain such unqualified success during the Napoleonic Wars was not without its problems. Mutiny broke out in the Royal Navy. Originally occurring aboard a single ship, the *Culloden* at Spithead, it

spread to the fleet there which refused to weigh anchor. From Spithead the mutiny spread to the ships at the Nore and even to some of the squadrons at sea. In isolated cases the ship's company murdered its officers and took the ship over to the enemy, but these occasions were rare. When, in 1800, the crew of the frigate *Danae* took her into Brest, they were astonished when the French clapped them into irons and showed their officers every consideration. The mutineers had a definite grievance: it was not a revolt against authority – they, indeed, continually maintained that they were loyal subjects of the King – but it was a revolt against intolerable conditions and delay in pay.

At a point in its history when morale was

ADMIRAL LORD NELSON, K.B. and the VICTORY of the NILE

at its lowest ebb, the Royal Navy found itself faced with the combined fleets of France, Holland and Spain – the latter pair had formed an alliance with the French Republic. Not that Napoleon had much faith in the Spanish Navy, being more than forthright in his criticism. 'The Dons make fine ships – they cannot, however, make men. Their fleet has nothing but bad crews and officers who are still worse.' In spite of the unrest among the 'lower deck',

the British gradually gained control of the seas, mainly through the series of brilliant victories, often unorthodox, won by Vice-Admiral Lord Nelson. Following his successes at the Battle of the Nile and at Copenhagen, Nelson was appointed Commander-in-Chief of the Mediterranean and hoisted his flag on HMS *Victory* in May 1803. After a frustrating 18 months spent trying to entice the French fleet out of Toulon by means of a loose blockade,

Nelson was mortified that when the French did come out, they easily gave him the slip. The French Admiral Villeneuve took his ships through the Straits of Gibraltar into the Atlantic in the direction of the West Indies, belatedly pursued by Nelson. When Nelson failed to make contact with the French, the British admiral clapped on all sail and raced back, actually passing the French without seeing them as they returned to Europe. Following an inconclusive battle fought against Admiral Calder's squadron, 120 miles (190 km) off Cape Finesterre, Villeneuve sailed for Cadiz.

He had hardly arrived there when Napoleon ordered him into the Channel to give support to an invasion of England – 'Leave at once, you have only to sail up the Channel to ensure our becoming masters of England.' However, strong northeast winds

closely packed crescent formation. His command comprised 18 French ships-of-the-line and 15 Spanish vessels under Admiral Gravina. The British admiral, splitting his fleet of 27 ships-of-the-line into two squadrons, sailed line-ahead to attack the enemy at right-angles and break his line. Ignoring normal custom, both Nelson and Vice-Admiral Collingwood, commanding the lee-squadron, put themselves at the head of their battle line; Villeneuve's flagship, *Bucentaure* was twelfth in the Franco-Spanish line.

Drums rolled aboard the *Victory*, beating 'clear for action'. Within ten minutes she was ready to fight. Decks had been sluiced down and sanded to prevent men slipping as surfaces became bloody during the action. The ship was cleared from prow to stern, stripped of everything unnecessary to

prevented Villeneuve reaching the Channel and he once again returned to Cadiz to the fury of the Emperor, who wrote, 'What a navy! What an admiral!' The invasion plans were scrapped and the French fleet at Cadiz ordered into the Mediterranean. Narrowly deciding against a courtmartial, Napoleon sent a replacement for Villeneuve, but the French admiral had already reluctantly put to sea.

'At daylight saw the enemy's combined fleet from East to E.S.E. Bore away, made the signal for order of battle, the enemy with their heads to the southwards.' Nelson's last entry in his diary was made on the morning of Monday 21 October 1805, 21 miles (34 km) off Cape Trafalgar. On sighting the British, Villeneuve 'wore' his fleet round to head back to Cadiz, taking up a

the coming engagement: baggage and furniture were stowed in the hold; stern windows were removed and stern chaser guns run out. Nets were rigged on the upper decks to catch falling blocks and spars; hammocks were stacked to guard against wooden splinters, grape-shot and musket balls. Ships boats were swung outboard to be towed aft; they would be required after the action and it would also lessen the liability of deadly flying splinters.

Soaking wet 'fearnought' screens of canvas had been rigged below decks to reduce the risk of fire. On the gundecks, the ports were opened and the cannon run out. Each gun on the three gundecks had beside it a rope bag with a dozen shot, a kid of water for cooling the gun, rammers, reamers and borers. To hand were half-

Sailors relaxing aboard HMS Hector, drawn by Thomas Rowlandson (1756–1827).

pikes and cutlasses for boarding and close work. 'Powder monkeys' (Thomas Twitchet, the youngest aboard the *Victory*, was 12 years old) stood by with flannel cartridge bags – each charged with 3½ lb (1.6 kg) of gunpowder – ready to dash to and from the hanging-magazine four decks below, to keep the guns fed throughout the action.

Again the drums rolled as the marine drummers 'Beat to quarters'. William Willmet, *Victory*'s Boatswain, was already stationed beside the port-side carronade mounted at the prow, gripping the firing lanyard, bracing himself against the heaving swell as the ship wallowed towards the enemy making a bare 3 knots. On the quarterdeck, Nelson, wearing all his stars and decorations despite the pleas of his captain, Thomas Masterman Hardy, turned to his Signal Lieutenant. 'I'll now

amuse the fleet with a signal. Mr. Pascoe, send, "England expects that every man will do his duty".' The signal flags, run up the halyards in Popham's telegraphic code, were closely followed by 'Engage the enemy more closely'.

To Willmet, unprotected on the open prow, the looming Franco-Spanish first-rates looked enormous. The Admiral was making for Villeneuve's *Bucentaure* to pass him astern. The French ran up their colours and the Spanish mounted large wooden crosses at their mast-heads. At 800 yards (730 m), flame flickered down the port sides of the nearest ships – the first ball had dropped short. The second drenched a gun's crew on the lower gundeck as it threw up a column of water alongside. The third tore through the main topsail. At 600 yards (550 m), the mizzen top-mast was shot away and the

The British ships-of-the-line of Earl St. Vincent, Admiral of the Blue, 1797.

steering wheel smashed while a double-headed shot sliced through some marines. Alongside the Admiral, his secretary, Mr. Scott, was all but cut in half by a cannon ball. 'This is too warm work, Hardy, to last long.' Nelson's words raised a nervous laugh. Not for the first time Willmet knew fear as the *Victory* closed with the Frenchman as if to ram. Less than a stone's throw away, their marines were firing muskets from the fighting tops – and still the order to fire did not come. They were brushing the stern of the French flagship, *Victory*'s main yardarm caught in the enemy's after rigging, he could have reached out and touched the limply-hanging Tricolour.

At the command 'Fire', the Boatswain jerked the lanyard of his carronade, the 'smasher'; a 68-lb (31-kg) ball and a keg of 500 bullets tore their way through the stern windows of the *Bucentaure* – it was just 1259 hours. One by one the *Victory*'s broadside of 52 guns, some double-shotted, the remainder treble-shotted, poured in a

withering fire at point-blank range as the ship swept past. Through the flame and smoke the Boatswain could hear the screams of the French gunners as the first deadly broadside ploughed through the gundecks, dismounting 20 cannon and killing or wounding nearly 400 men – half the ship's company.

However, it was while engaging the *Redoutable* that Nelson fell. A French marine who was perched in her fighting top, 15 yards (14 m) above, sent a ball through the Admiral's left epaulette which drove through the lung to lodge in his spine. Gently he was carried below to the surgeon's cockpit, where he died three hours later, but not before Hardy was able to report a complete victory: 19 of the enemy had struck their colours. So fierce was the gunnery on both sides, that at the end of the battle the *Victory* was almost a complete wreck, with 57 men killed and 103 wounded. Things were even worse aboard the *Redoutable*. With 490 of his 'people' dead and 81 wounded out of a crew of 600, the diminutive Captain Lucas – he was only 4 ft 10 inches (1.5 m) tall – was forced to strike his colours, his crew still shouting '*Vive l'Empereur*'. A French writer was to say, 'Despite appearances it was not the flames of Moscow that dissipated Napoleon's fortune, it had already been drowned in the waters of Trafalgar.'

With the invention of the steam engine, the days of sails and 'wooden-walls' became numbered, but it was not until the mid-19th century that the full effect of this revolution was to be felt.

Vice-Admiral Nelson explains his plans of attack to his officers before the Battle of Trafalgar.

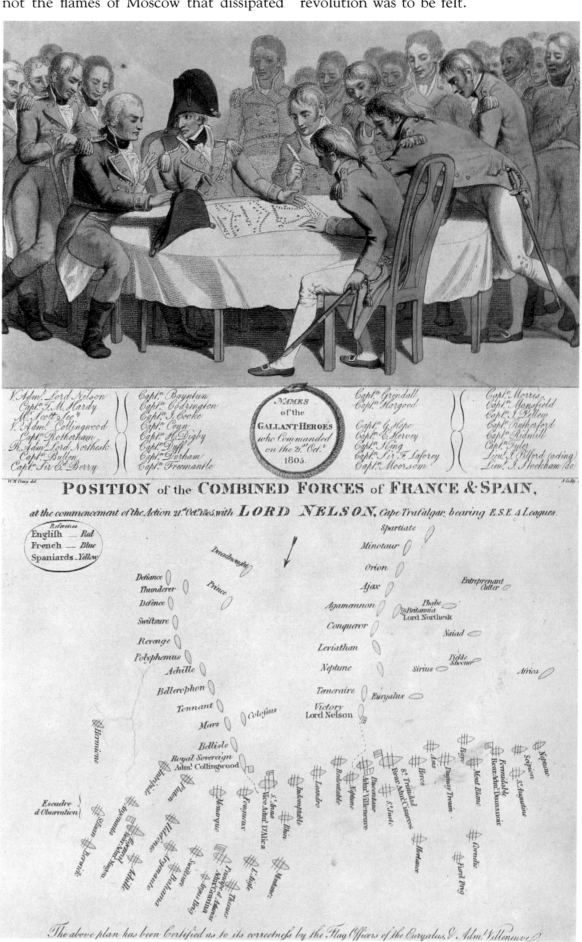

Opposite:
HMS Victory in dry dock at Portsmouth.

Steam Versus Sail

'The largest ships, with only one guiding them, will be carried with greater velocity than if they were full of sailors.' These words of Roger Bacon, a 13th-century philosopher, epitomizes the 'scientific dreamer's' prophetic outlook towards ocean transport. Long before this was written, however, mariners and shipbuilders with enquiring minds had been searching for mechanical means of propelling ships through the water, means that would free them from the vagaries of 'wind power'. The direction of the wind always placed a limitation on the course the ship was able to steer and, when tacking to take advantage of an oblique wind, she might sail three, or even four, times as far as on a direct course. Without a breath of wind to fill her sails, which was a common enough occurrence in tropical waters, she was completely helpless. Over the years sailing ships had been improved by adding to tradition and experience, but mechanical propulsion called for new, revolutionary thinking and experiment.

In pre-Christian times, some of the legions of Claudius Claudex were carried to Sicily in ships propelled by paddle wheels turned by oxen, and a bas-relief of 527 A.D. shows that Roman naval architects were by then experimenting with a warship carrying three pairs of paddle wheels. In the 7th century A.D. the Chinese, too, were using paddle-driven warships, the power being supplied by slaves walking a treadmill, but they, like the Romans, concluded that rowers with oars or sails were more efficient. Fanciful ideas were sketched out by Leonardo da Vinci and in the early 17th century a scheme for a 'jet-propulsion' system employing a large bellows was patented by Toogood and Hayes in England. Although the innovators clung to the paddle wheel, the more thoughtful of them realized that something more efficient than manpower was needed to drive it. The introduction of steam power successfully solved the problem, and eventually, after many trials and difficulties, put an end to 'wind power' as a commercial proposition.

Early Steam Power

Although engineers had been experimenting with steam as a source of power since the end of the 16th century, it was not until Thomas Newcomen built the first practical steam engine some 150 years later, that an efficient propulsion unit was developed. At the time this 'atmospheric' engine was used only to pump excess water from mines, but later inventors were quick to see the viability of using it as a means of propulsion. James Watt produced a vastly superior power unit in 1765, based on Newcomen's original idea which was a rotory-action engine which allowed steam power to be utilized in a number of different ways. Improving on Newcomen's principle, Watt made the cylinder double-acting by adding a condenser which allowed steam to be admitted both above and below the cylinder. This produced a reasonable supply of power, and with the invention of the centrifugal governor, power at a constant speed. It was the development of this engine that powered the first steamships.

Technically speaking, the first steamboat was the *Pyroscaphe*, a long clinker-built vessel invented by the French Marquis Claude de Jouffroy d'Abbans in 1783– unfortunately the French Revolution put an end to his experiments. The *Pyroscaphe* managed to move against the Saône River current for 15 minutes, but her boilers were unable to sustain the effort. The race to build steamships was entered early by the Americans and by the last decade of the century a boat service had been introduced on the Delaware River. The *Experiment* made a total of 11 trips, covering 2,000 miles (3,200 km), but was never a practical proposition. Nonetheless, this confident advertisement appeared in a Philadelphia newspaper on 14 July 1790. 'The STEAM-BOAT is now ready to take passengers and is intended to set off from Arch Street Ferry in Philadelphia, every Monday, Wednesday and Friday for Burlington, Bristol, Bordertown and Trenton, to return on Tuesday, Thursday and Saturdays.'

To all intents and purposes the first viable steamboat was the *Charlotte Dundas*, built on the River Clyde by William Symington, first in a long line of Clydeside shipbuilders. Commissioned by Lord Dundas and named after his daughter, she was built to replace horses which hitherto had towed barges up and down the Forth and Clyde canals. A stern-wheeler with a single tall funnel, she made her first trip in 1802, pulling two 70-ton (71-tonne) canal boats against a 19 mph (30 km/h) head wind. More like a conventional ship than her predecessors, she was a wooden vessel with a 58-ft (17.7-m) keel, a beam of 18 ft (5.5 m) and an 8-ft (2.4-m) draught. Her paddle was driven by a single-cylinder steam engine which developed 12 horsepower, giving the boat a speed of 3 knots. The *Charlotte Dundas* was short-lived – her wash was damaging the canal banks – but she had established the fact that steamships were a viable proposition.

Robert Fulton, an American living in France – he was later to work on the concept of a submarine – latched on to the potential of the steamship. After a disastrous first attempt in which his boat broke her back and sank in the Seine, he returned to the United States of America to open up an extremely successful steamboat service. Having shipped an engine from Boulton and Watt (James Watt had gone into business with Matthew Boulton, a Birmingham engineer), as there were no engineers in the U.S. at that time with sufficient experience to construct a steam engine, he then built the 133-ft (40.5-m) *Clermont* which displaced 100 tons (102 tonnes). From the very first she was a spectacular success and on her maiden voyage she covered 240 miles (384 km) at an average speed of 3.9 knots, at times reaching a top speed of 4.7 knots. There was such a demand for her service on the Hudson River that Fulton was persuaded to build another river boat, the *Phoenix*, to cope with the passenger demand. His *North River*, which came later, was described by

The Clermont *sailed regularly from New York to Albany.*

one observer as, '. . . looking precisely like a backswood sawmill mounted on a scow and set on fire'.

As steamships grew in size and power they ventured out to sea, and by 1816 a steamship passenger service operated across the English Channel between Brighton and Le Havre. A prize of 20,000 rupees was offered for the establishment of a permanent passenger and cargo service between England and Calcutta before the end of 1826, with the proviso that the voyage took no longer than 70 days. Although the *Enterprise*, a ship of 470 tons (480 tonnes), failed to meet the target when she took 103 days, half the prize was accorded to her owners. Her best average speed for a day during the 11,450-mile (18,320-km) passage was 8 knots by steam alone, 8.79 knots under sail alone and 9.36 knots under both steam and sail. Basically the *Enterprise* was a sailing ship supplemented by steam, as was the American *Savannah* that had crossed the Atlantic to Liverpool in 21 days the previous year, using her engines for only eight hours of the passage.

'Wood Can Swim, Iron Cannot'

Up till now, hulls had been made of wood; no one had seriously considered Archi-

medes's principle of buoyancy – 'Wood can swim, iron can't', sums up the general attitude of the mariners of the period. Despite considerable opposition, the *Aaron Manby*, 106 ft (32.3 m) long, 17 ft 3 inches (5.3 m) in the beam, with a draught of 7 ft 3 inches (2.2 m), was built with an iron hull, and crossed the Channel at an average speed of between 8 and 9 knots on a passenger run between London and Paris. After a few regular passenger runs, she ended her life as a pleasure boat on the Seine, but not before she had established categorically that iron could 'swim'.

One of the problems facing marine engineers was how to carry sufficient coal to make an Atlantic crossing under steam alone. By the 1830s the actual steam engine itself was more than capable of facing up to an ocean crossing – rigged with sail just in case – but the ships were too small to carry enough coal to stoke the boilers and still make passenger-carrying a viable proposition. It had been known from early times that a ship on the crest of a wave tended to 'hog' upwards, and in the trough of a wave 'sag' fore and aft, and by experience it had been found that wooden ships over 300 ft (91 m) long were unable to stand up to these stresses. This, entirely a problem of ship design, was effectively solved by Isambard Brunel and Scott

Opposite top: The first
ocean-going screw
steamship, the SS Great
Britain, designed by I.K.
Brunel.

Opposite bottom: The
contrast between HMS
Rattler and HMS Electro,
1845.

Russell who began building bigger ships of iron – the forerunners of the giant Atlantic liners of the 20th century.

At a meeting of the directors of the Great Western Railway Company in 1837, it was suggested by one of them that the proposed railway extension to Bristol would make the line too long. Their company engineer, Isambard Kingdom Brunel, retorted that in his opinion, the line was far too short and should be extended to New York by means of a passenger steamer to be called the *Great Western*. The board were taken with the idea and Brunel was given the go ahead to build it, a ship of 1,340 tons (1,361 tonnes), developing 750 horsepower. On her maiden voyage in 1838, she crossed the Atlantic in 15 days 5 hours; her average speed was 8.8 knots and, more to the point, she still had 200 tons (203 tonnes) of coal left in her bunkers. The Transatlantic crossing by steamship was now a practical proposition.

The *Great Britain*, designed and built by Brunel in 1843, was a true Atlantic liner. An iron-hulled ship displacing 3,620 tons (3,678 tonnes), 322 ft (98.1 m) in overall length with a 50-ft (15.2-m) beam, she was screw-driven by a single propeller, 16 ft (4.9 m) in diameter. Her 1,500-horsepower engines gave the ship a speed of 11 knots and she could carry up to 360 passengers across the Atlantic in 14 days 21 hours.

She also carried 1,700 square yards (1,420 sq m) of canvas on six masts. The cramped accommodation offered in the early liners was not to everyone's liking – certainly not to Charles Dickens, who described his cabin aboard the *Brittania* as, '. . . an utterly impractical, thoroughly hopeless, and profoundly preposterous box'. Brunel and other more advanced marine engineers were already advocating screw-driven ships, but the more conservative naval circles each side of the Atlantic were reluctant to relinquish the paddle wheel. The matter was resolved by a test carried out in 1845 between a trial vessel, HMS *Rattler*, which was screw-driven, and the paddle sloop, *Electo*. Both ships had engines of 200 horsepower. In the speed trials over a distance of 100 miles (160 km), the *Rattler* proved to be faster, but for the final trial the ships were secured stern to stern with a towing hawser and their engines taken to full revolutions: this finally clinched the matter – *Rattler* towed the *Electo* astern at 2.8 knots.

The *Great Eastern*

Yet when Brunel came to design the *Great Eastern*, at that time the world's biggest ship, he used paddle wheels set amidships and one enormous propeller, the largest ever seen. Launched sideways in 1858, she

Below: Brunel's Great
Western.

Above: The stern view of the Great Eastern on the stocks.

Below: Longitudinal section of the Great Eastern, first called the Leviathan.

was completed in the autumn of 1859, but she proved to be a magnificent failure. A ship before her time, her gigantic iron hull too vast for her underpowered engines, she proved to be too costly to run with too-high coal consumption. Intended to be five times as large as any existing ship, her construction raised problem after problem; the building costs soared and the shipbuilders – Scott Russell, among others – went bankrupt. Under the continuous worry, Brunel's health broke down and he died of a heart attack before the *Great Eastern* went into commission.

Initially named *Leviathan,* she was built for the Far Eastern service, but instead made 11 transatlantic crossings with only a fraction of the passengers needed to make her voyages commercially profitable. She was designed to carry 800 first-class passengers, 2,000 second-class, 1,200 third-class, and a crew of 400. On her disastrous maiden voyage she embarked only 36 passengers, and she rolled so badly that prospective passengers were deterred from sailing in her. After lying idle until 1865, she was pressed into service as a cable-ship, 'an elephant spinning a cobweb', but laid only four cables in the Atlantic and one from Aden to Bombay. For the next 12 years she rusted in harbour until she was turned into an amusement ship offering a music hall and sideshows, before she was finally broken up.

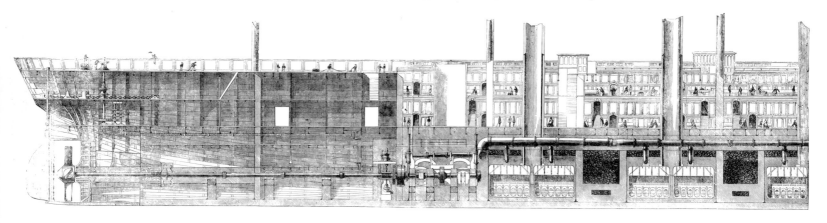

Great Eastern	
previous name *Leviathan*	
Launched	January 1858
Completed	September 1859
Displacement	27700 tons
	(28100 tonnes)
Length	680 ft (207 m)
Beam	83 ft (25.3 m)
Depth	58 ft (17.7 m)
Draught	30 ft (9 m)
Speed	14 knots –
	average speed
	11 knots
Boilers	10
Engines – for paddle	3,410 hp
for screw	4,890 hp
Cargo capacity	6,000 tons
	(6100 tonnes)
Crew	400
Passengers	4,000

Although the *Great Eastern* failed for Brunel, she led the way for the vast ocean liners that followed, whose designers gained much from his vision and learned even more from his mistakes. The 'Little Giant' had proved that iron was the material for building big ships and his introduction of an underwater shape based on the principle of hydrodynamics inspired others to follow his lead.

The Blue Riband of the Atlantic

Passenger lines began to compete fiercely with each other for the rapidly increasing passenger trade and the Blue Riband became a coveted prize, awarded for the fastest crossing to and from Europe and the United States. Companies contended for the Blue Riband not only to ensure full passenger lists, booked well ahead, but also as a matter of national pride. Everyone

Above: The Great Eastern *at sea.*

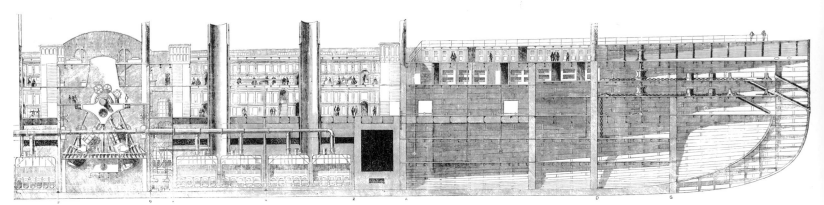

Right: Queen Elizabeth II, *the* Q.E. II.

Below: The French liner Normandie.

Opposite top: The Lusitania.

Opposite bottom left: The Mauritania *from a souvenir book.*

Opposite bottom right: A poster advertises the French liner Normandie *during the 1930s.*

A longitudinal section of an early steamship.

wanted to travel on a Blue Riband ship and when, in 1897, the 16,000-ton (16,300-tonne) *Kaiser Wilhelm der Grosse* won it, the North German Lloyd Line, her owners, had by the following year captured 28 per cent of the passengers travelling to New York. The turn of the century saw liners with treble the horsepower reaching speeds of over 23 knots, and crossings became a race against the clock with only fractions of a day separating the performances. Dickens would have had no cause to criticize their interiors; they began to resemble floating hotels with spacious lounges and dining saloons, ballrooms and bars, with food to rival the best restaurants ashore. The first-class dining saloon of the *Mauritania*, launched in 1906 and probably the most successful ship ever, was massive with carved mahogany pillars and surrounding gallery. The *Mauritania* and her sister ship, the *Lusitania*, were the first passenger liners to be powered by steam turbine engines; on her maiden voyage, the *Mauritania* crossed the Atlantic at an average speed of 27.4 knots. Easily outstripping the *Kaiser Wilhelm der Grosse*'s performance (an average speed of 22.35 knots), she gained the

Blue Riband which she held for the next 22 years.

The growing expansion in world trade and an urgent, almost explosive passenger demand from tourists, businessmen and, not least of all, immigrants to the New World, called not only for more, but for bigger ships. Bigger ships, in turn, required more powerful engines to reach competitive speeds. The lesson of the *Great Eastern* had been well learned, and from the middle of the 19th century rapid strides had been made in the development of the steam engine and its boilers. In the 1850s a newly designed boiler was introduced which raised the steam pressure sufficiently to be able to drive a compound steam engine. This invention meant that the steam was used twice in a single cycle of the engine, firstly in a high-pressure cylinder, then again in another cylinder at a lower pressure. The steam was re-used by drawing it off to a condenser and the resulting water fed back into the boiler. Not only did this increase power quite dramatically, but there was as much as a 30 per cent saving on coal. Once the Cunard Line introduced this type of engine in the *Parthia* and

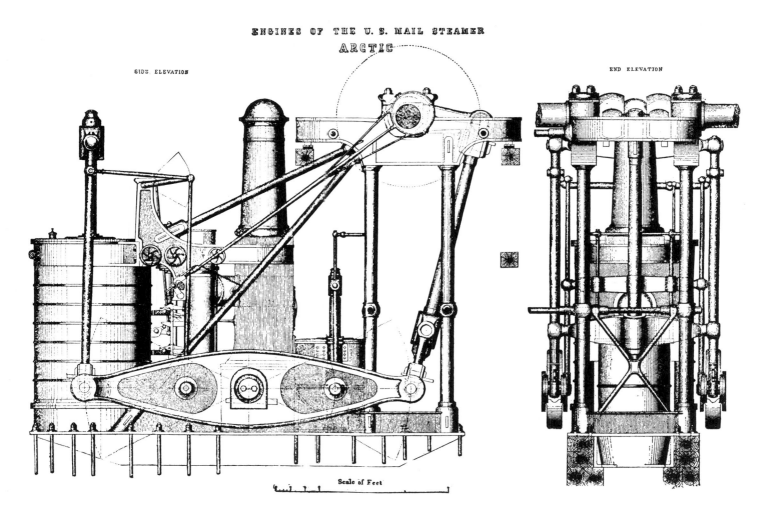

SIDE ELEVATION

END ELEVATION

Scale of Feet

Batavia, built for the transatlantic run, the other companies, in order to stay in the race, quickly followed suit.

Parsons's Steam Turbine

Further development was made with the introduction of a forced-draught boiler which, by raising the steam pressure to between 120 and 160 lb per square inch (8.4 and 11.3 kg per sq cm), enabled a triple-expansion engine to be produced. German marine engineers went one better. In 1897 they fitted *Kaiser Wilhelm der Grosse* with two quadruple-expansion engines, the biggest marine reciprocating engines ever built. Even as they were being installed, these mammoths, which stood 40 ft (12.2 m) high and generated 40,000 horsepower, were already being made obsolete by the new steam turbine engine.

The steam turbine engine, invented by Charles Parsons at the turn of the century, revolutionized marine propulsion. To gain the maximum amount of publicity he fitted a 44-ton (45-tonne) yacht, which he named *Turbinia*, with three of his engines, each driving a shaft on which three propellers were fitted, and demonstrated her at the Fleet Review of 1897 to celebrate Queen Victoria's Diamond Jubilee. To the horror of the Navy he steamed up and down the lines of anchored battleships on

the route to be taken by the Royal yacht. Frantic orders were issued, but the fast fleet picket boats sent to warn him off were totally outstripped by the *Turbinia* which had achieved a speed of 34.5 knots, unheard of in those days. Not only were Admiralty officials impressed, but so too were the representatives of foreign powers and merchant shipping lines. By 1900 iron

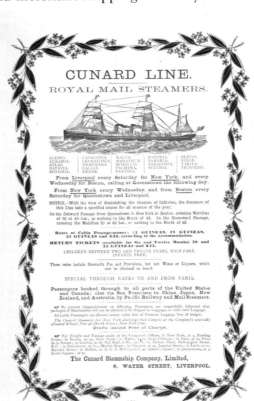

Above: A side-lever condensing engine.

Left: A sailing schedule for the Cunard Line in 1883.

Right: Parson's revolutionary Turbinia *steaming at an unheard-of rate of 35 knots.*

Below: The damage sustained by the Titanic.

THE BUCKLED PLATES

BILGE KEEL

DOUBLE BOTTOM

ICE PENETRATING THE DOUBLE BOTTOM

FIRST CLASS STATE ROOMS

POST MAIL ROOM

The above Section is taken between the Foremast and the First Funnel.

G.F.MORRELL

piston-driven ships were as obsolete as the wooden, wind-powered sailing ships they themselves had superseded.

Parsons's turbine engine worked on a principle invented by Branca, an Italian, in 1628. Until then, the piston engines had worked to and fro, but the turbine engine revolved. Compressed steam was directed through a nozzle onto fixed blades set at an angle in a drum. These deflected the steam to a set of moving blades which spun a shaft. Spinning at 3,000 revolutions a minute, this shaft, in turn, spun gear wheels which turned the propeller to drive the ship. Smaller and more compact than existing marine engines, the turbine engine used less fuel yet had a far, far higher power-to-weight ratio. Then the Siemens-Martin process ensured the production of light tough steel and this material replaced the heavy iron that had formerly been used to construct marine hulls.

The Sinking of the *Titanic*

One of the early big liners to be fitted with a steam turbine was the ill-fated *Titanic*. Launched in 1911 and the world's biggest ship – 825 ft (251.5 m) long, displacing 52,250 tons (53,086 tonnes) and powered by two four-cylinder triple-expansion engines as well as her turbine – she could cruise at 22 knots. With three passenger decks above the upper deck, she had seven decks in all; those below the upper deck were divided by a transverse watertight bulkhead every 60 ft (18 m) of her length.

The *Titanic* left Southampton on her maiden voyage to New York on 10 April

1912. Late at night on her fourth day out, she was steaming in the vicinity of the Grand Banks off the Newfoundland coast. Two seamen, Lee and Fleet, perched high in the ship's crows-nest, were just coming to the end of their two-hour shift as lookouts. The night was pitch-black and bitterly cold, but windless, with a flat calm sea. The captain had laid course beyond the normal area of field ice, but well within an area of the chart indicating, 'icebergs have been seen within this line in April, May and June'. The visibility was good. True, radio messages had been received from other ships reporting sightings of icebergs, but the captain was not too concerned and saw no reason to cut down the ship's speed of 22 knots. Normal safety precautions were in operation and the crows-nest lookouts could spot a berg at over 2,500 yards (2,300 m), plenty of time for the officer-of-the-watch to take avoiding action. The ship was ablaze with light from stem to stern, but quiet, as most of the passengers had turned in, confident that they would arrive in New York in less than 48 hours.

A startled Fleet suddenly saw a black shape looming dead ahead of the *Titanic*, less than 500 yards (460 m) away. Frantically shouting 'Iceberg right ahead' into the bridge telephone, he rang the alarm bells. On the ship's bridge the officer-in-the-watch instinctively ordered 'Hard-a-port', rang 'Full speed astern' on the engine room telegraph and pressed the automatic control for shutting the watertight doors. Below, in the engine room, the 50,000-horsepower engines were flung to full astern, but the ship had too much way on and the wildly churning propellers hardly effected her 22 knots, but her head was swinging to port. Staring down from the starboard wing of the bridge, the officer-of-the-watch heaved a sigh of relief as the dark mass appeared to slip past the starboard bow; then came the grinding sound of tearing metal. The ship lurched as the submerged part of the berg tore a 300-ft (91-m) gash in her side and water rushed in, flooding her forward compartments and then numbers four, five and six boiler rooms; engineers and stokers scrambled up the engine-room ladders through clouds of scalding steam.

Tragically, the iceberg, far from being shining white, had been dark blue, the notorious long-submerged 'black ice' of a berg that had turned over. Nor were there any warning breakers along her sides in that glassy sea. By now the *Titanic* was doomed and was slowly going down verti-cally, bow first — the captain ordered 'Abandon ship'. In the radio room, the radio officer was rapidly tapping out the distress signal, 'C.Q.D.', followed by the ship's call sign, 'M.G.Y.' Then the final tragedy occurred. Passengers, unable to believe that the 'unsinkable' *Titanic* was going down, were milling about the upper deck, reluctant to go to their boat stations. Calmly the ship's officers coaxed them into the lifeboats that were being swung outboard. Only then was the full horror of the situation realized — there were nowhere near enough lifeboats aboard. The Board of Trade in those days assessed the number of lifeboats required to tonnage, and no one had thought to increase the maximum number — 16 lifeboats and four collapsible rafts — when ships began to exceed 10,000 tons (10,160 tonnes). Of the 2,201 people aboard, 1,490 of them were doomed to perish in the icy sea unless help arrived — none did. Women and children were bundled into the boats first, then the crew to man them and lastly some men. The final list of those saved was 353 women and children, 146 men and 212 crew.

Lowering the lifeboats from the doomed liner.

As a result of the enquiry into this disaster that so shocked the world, a directive from the British Board of Trade stipulated that, in future, there must be lifeboat space for all passengers and crew.

The Clippers

In a desperate attempt to compete with the growing competition from steamships (although for the first 40 odd years of the century the introduction of steam made little impression), sailing ships underwent a dramatic change in hull design and rigging plans. Up until the 1830s, as long as the ponderous 'East Indiamen' got their valuable cargoes back to Europe, speed was of relatively little importance. But the American shipbuilders began to change all that. They started developing fast trading clippers and mail-carrying packets that could outsail all other craft afloat. This was to be the 'Golden Age' of sail and it was to continue for most of the century, in spite of the mounting encroachment of steam. This saw the beginning of speed in sea transport with captains clapping on full sail throughout the night rather than following the former custom of furling them at sunset.

It became a race to be first – first with the season's tea crop from China, first to the

goldfields of America and Australia. People were willing to pay well for fast cargo and passage. In 1866 there was a famous race between the China clippers *Ariel* and *Taiping* to bring home the first tea crop to Britain. Leaving Foochow at the same time, after 99 days and 16,093 miles (25,749 km), they were scudding up the Channel, virtually neck and neck. The *Taiping* eventually arrived *20 minutes* ahead of the *Ariel*.

With sweeping rake to bow and stern, the clippers were sleek, ocean-going ships with a vast spread of canvas – the U.S. *Challenger* of 1851 carried nearly 100,000 square feet (9,300 sq m) of sail. Donald McKay of Boston, the greatest of the American clipper builders, also built the largest. The *Great Republic*, destined for the New York – San Francisco trade, was a four-masted craft, 325 ft (99 m) long with a 53-ft (16.2-m) beam and displacing 4,165 tons (4,232 tonnes). Some of the clippers in their heyday reached speeds of 19–21 knots, given a favourable wind. For nearly 40 years, the fully fledged clippers more than held their own with their steam-driven rivals, but as the latters' engines grew more powerful, they were relegated to menial coastal trading, sometimes hauling coal for their grimy competitors.

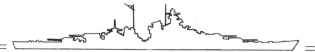

The Coming of The Ironclads

Development of Naval Gunnery

During the naval battles of the Napoleonic wars, both sides had relied on smooth-bore, cast cannon firing solid shot. At any distance, even the heaviest 42-lb (19-kg) shot had little effect on the 18-inch (45.7-cm) thick timbers of ships-of-the-line and to have any real effect, men-of-war had to slog it out with crashing broadsides delivered at point-blank range. Its defeat by the British left the French Navy an almost spent force, with a three-to-one disadvantage in ships. No naval programme, however ambitious, would enable it to overtake or even equal the strength of the Royal Navy. To come to terms with its old rival across the Channel, the French Navy needed a new innovation, a revolutionary ship or weapon that would give it the edge in a sea fight. A French artillery officer, General Henri Paixhans, believed he had the answer.

The exploding shell was nothing new – Nelson had used it to great effect at Copenhagen for land bombardment from bomb-ships at close range. In 1821 Paixhans experimented with firing a shell, a fused delayed-action projectile, from a 'long' gun with a greater range and a lower trajectory than the short-barrelled mortar. To him this was the naval weapon France had been seeking, the weapon that could well make the wooden ships of other nations obsolete. Nothing was feared by naval commanders so much as fire at sea, and Paixhans's hollow iron sphere, filled with gunpowder and then bursting inside a wooden ship, could create havoc. In his book, *Nouvelle Force Maritime et Artillerie*, he advocated the use of the shell gun as a ship-to-ship naval weapon, an idea seized upon by the French Ministry of Marine.

By 1824 his new weapon was sufficiently advanced to give it its first serious test, against an old 80-gun ship, the *Pacifacteur*, which quickly sank. Subsequent tests against other target hulks, which more often than not were set ablaze by the explosion of the shells, convinced the Ministry of Marine of the shell's value. By 1837 the shell-gun (or '*canon-obusier*') had been adopted throughout the French Navy. However, French naval supremacy was soon neutralized as other navies, seeing the enormous potential of the shell-gun, began to design their own. The year 1840 saw most heavy warships carrying a mixed battery of shell-guns and conventional cannon firing solid shot – navies were reluctant to dispense with a weapon that was more accurate and had a longer range, even if the shell had a more devastating effect – but there were additional considerations that were working to secure the shell-gun's acceptance as the standard naval weapon.

The full destructive power of the shell-gun was first demonstrated in 1838. However, an enthusiastic report by an American naval officer, Admiral Farragut, was virtually ignored by his government, and the European powers also paid little attention to the weapon. The 'Pastry War' (so called by the Americans because among other property looted was a pastry cook's shop), which was more a skirmish than a war, occurred when Mexican army mutineers plundered the property of French nationals, and the government refused reparations. Three 60-gun French frigates bombarded fort St. Jean d'Ulloa off La Vera Cruz with shell-guns, and within two hours had put it out of action. Fifteen years were to pass before the navies of the world became aware of the devastation that could be caused by shell fire and began to take the

Opposite: The first-rates of Nelson's day fought their battles at point-blank range.

precautions that would eventually spiral into the use of heavy armour plate and 15-inch (38-cm) armour-piercing shells.

At the Battle of Sinope (a port on the Black Sea) which became known as the 'Massacre' of Sinope, a Russian naval squadron of wooden-hulled ships, armed with 68-pounder French shell-guns, totally annihilated a Turkish fleet. Firing commenced at 10.00 hours and when the Russian Admiral Nakhinov withdrew at 16.00 hours, the shore batteries had been silenced and there was not a single Turkish ship afloat in the harbour. The lesson drawn from this action – the vast superior-ity of shells over cannon shot – was not lost on the navies of Europe and North America; soon they were taking a very hard look at their own ships' weaponry.

The Navies Turn to Steam

Naval Powers had shown great reluctance to turn to steam. When they finally did, the coal-fired steam engine was treated as an auxiliary to sail – as opposed to the outlook of the world's mercantile marines, who regarded sail as an auxiliary to steam.

As early as 1814 the Royal Navy had attempted to put a steam engine into a small sloop without success. The same year

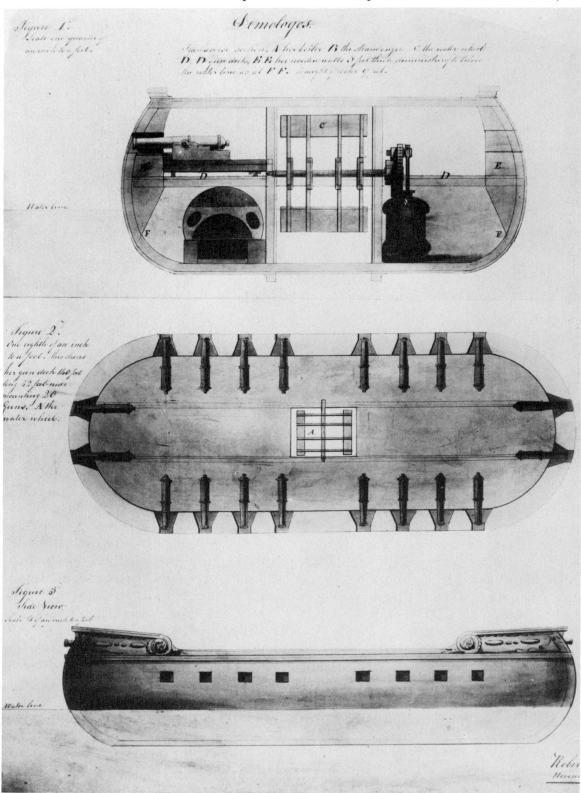

Right: Sections of Robert Fulton's Demologos *with her central paddle wheel.*

LAUNCH OF H. M. S. ROYAL ALBERT, SCREW STEAMER, 131 GUNS, AT WOOLWICH, MAY 13, 1854.

No. 1.

HER MAJESTY IS HERE REPRESENTED IN THE ACT OF CHRISTENING THE NOBLE VESSEL, AT THE MOMENT EXCLAIMING "GOD BLESS THE ROYAL ALBERT."

the *Demologos*, designed by Robert Fulton for the American Navy, was launched. This curious ship had two wooden hulls – one containing the engine and the other the boiler – with a central paddle wheel in between, and carried 30 guns arranged to fire red-hot shot. She never saw action and eventually blew up in a dockyard.

The paddle wheel itself was one reason why navies were none too keen to go over to steam. Apart from the fact that the paddle wheel was set centrally in the ship and thus broke up the line of guns for broadsides, it was also highly vulnerable – one heavy shot could shatter its relatively flimsy spokes, leaving the vessel helpless to move. In 1822 Brunel persuaded the British Admiralty to build two steamships: the 238-ton (242-tonne) *Comet* followed by the *Monkey*. Their only duty was to tow sailing men-of-war out of harbour against an adverse wind. (During the Crimean War, steamships stood by to tow the massive wooden ships in and out of action.)

Once the screw propeller was introduced, and proved in the 1845 'trial'

between the *Rattler* and *Electo*, the Royal Navy fitted its warships with steam engines, though they still retained full rigging. By 1854 the entire British fleet at the Crimea were steam-driven; at the same time, the French, who had the only comparable European fleet, were relying entirely on sail. But it was the French who first consciously applied the lesson learned at Sinope. As wooden ships were obviously vulnerable to explosive shells, the answer would seem to be to build ships of iron – already ships with iron hulls had proved their worth as merchant vessels. But gunnery tests made at Portsmouth in 1840 convinced the Royal Navy that wood offered better protection than iron. At close range, a cannon shot easily penetrated the ¾-inch (1.9-cm) thick plate of the iron-hulled steamer *Ruby*, but 8-inch (20.3-cm) oak plank withstood the shot. Moreover, the cast iron of the day was likely to crack or shatter under gunfire, spraying deadly splinters of metal. Ten years later, when the quality of wrought iron had improved, means were again sought to clad warships with metal.

The launching of the British ship-of-the-line Royal Albert *in 1854.*

The Coming of the Battleship

In 1854 the French Navy became the first to lay down five floating batteries; unwieldly, cumbersome craft, making only 4 knots, they nevertheless proved their worth the following year. About 174 ft (53.0 m) long, with a 43-ft (13.1-m) beam and a draught of 9.5 ft (2.9 m), their massive wooden hulls were fully clad along their length with 4.3-inch (10.9-cm) thick wrought-iron plate. Three of them, the *Devastation*, *Lavé* and *Tonnante*, received their baptism of fire in 1855, bombarding the five Russian forts of Kimbourn Kosa in the Black Sea. Firing their batteries of 16 50-pounder shell-guns from a range of 900–1,200 yards (820–1,100 m), they caused the forts to surrender in just over an hour and a half. Their armour easily withstood numerous hits by red-hot shot and bursting shells.

Elated by the success of their floating batteries, the French started work immediately on four ironclad warships, the *Gloire*, *Invincible*, *Normandie* and the slightly bigger *La Carrone*. The 5,617-ton (5,707-tonne) *Gloire* was the first to be launched, in 1859. These ships, which were infinitely more manoeuvrable and faster than the floating batteries (although they were classed as frigates because their guns were all mounted on a single gundeck), were truly the forerunners of the all-steel battleships that were to follow in the last quarter of the century. Britain, seeing her fleet of wooden ships likely to be made obsolete by the French ironclad frigates, replied with the *Warrior*, launched in 1860, and the *Black Prince*, launched 11 months later; their long, low profiles earned them the nickname, 'Black Snakes of the Channel'. The navies of the world now vied with each other to build the biggest and most powerfully armed ironclads.

The design of naval guns was also undergoing considerable change. Just prior to the Crimean War it had been discovered that by rifling the barrel of a gun, the shell could be made to spin in its flight, giving it a predictable trajectory through the air, greater accuracy and a longer range. To overcome 'windage', the gap necessary between the shell and bore of the gun to allow loading from the muzzle, gunfounders reverted to breach-loading. Following the Crimean War, guns grew enormously in size and weight. Then the largest smooth-bore gun had fired a 10-inch (25.4-cm) shell and weighed 4 tons (4 tonnes); by the early 1860s, they were firing 13-inch (33.0-cm) shells weighing a monstrous 600 lb (272 kg) from a 22-ton (22-tonne) gun. Rifled breach-loaders grew from 6.3 inches (16.0 cm) in calibre to 12.5 inches (31.8 cm). Barrels had to be strengthened by shrinking hoops of iron round them to cope with the increased power of the charges, and a new type of mounting had to be designed to absorb the recoil. The old wooden truck mounting with its four wooden wheels was hopelessly inadequate and was replaced by a wrought-iron slide mounting, with compressor systems to check the recoil. This led to the introduction of a revolutionary idea that was to play an important part in a whole new concept

---

STATISTICS OF THE *GLOIRE* AND THE *WARRIOR*

Both ships were constructed throughout of wrought iron (their armoured sides strengthened with teak) which allowed the introduction of watertight transverse bulkheads. At first they reigned supreme, the last word in naval warfare, immune to even the largest calibre shell-guns. Yet within months they were ousted by a new generation of vastly larger ironclads.

	Gloire	*Warrior*
Launched	1859	1860
Displacement	5,617 tons (5,707 tonnes)	9,000 tons (9,144 tonnes)
Length	252 ft (76.8 m)	365.5 ft (11.4 m)
Armour (Amidships)	4.7 inches (11.9 cm)	4.5 inches (11.4 cm)
Armament	26 50-pounders (Rifled, breach-loading)	26 68-pounders (Smooth-bore, muzzle-loading)
		10 110-pounders (Rifled, breach-loading)
		4 70-pounders (Rifled, breach-loading)
Speed	12 knots	14 knots

La Gloire, *the first ironclad warship built by the French in 1859.*

of naval gunnery and the design of warships – the revolving turret. In England, Captain Henry Cowper Coles had been working on the idea since 1855 and by 1862 a 3,880-ton (3,942-tonne) coastal defence vessel, the *Prince Albert*, had been laid down with four centre-line turrets, each mounting a 9-inch (22.9-cm) gun. The turrets were turned manually by rack-and-pinion gear and took over a minute to make one full revolution. Firing was slow and gunnery control primitive, and gunfounders and designers worked feverishly to be first with an efficient revolving turret.

First Ironclad Engagement

Simultaneously in the United States of America, John Ericsson, a Swedish engineer who had immigrated there in 1848, had the same idea, but he had the added stimulus of wartime conditions. The American Civil War, which erupted between the Northern and Southern States in 1861, found the United States Navy ill-prepared: it had a fleet of only 42 warships, none of them armoured. When, during its early success, the Confederate Army of the Southern States captured the main naval dockyard at Norfolk, Virginia, it found a brand-new wooden steam frigate that had been scuttled, the USS *Merrimack*. She was raised from the bottom; cut off flush, 3 ft (1 m) above the waterline; clad in 4-inch (10-cm) thick iron plates, which were bolted to the 2-ft (61-cm) thick timber hull; and armed. The Confederates pinned their hopes on the fact that ironclad warships would be able to withstand the heaviest shot of their vastly superior enemy. They renamed her the CSS *Virginia*, but she remained popularly known as the *Merrimack*.

Naval gunnery in North America, under the direction of Admiral Dahlgren, had taken a different turn to that of the European fleets. He advocated the use of monster smooth-bore, muzzle-loading guns of up to 15-inch (38-cm) calibre, which were known as 'soda bottles' because of their shape. These fired either a low-velocity spherical shell or solid shot. European navies had already turned to an elongated shell with a pointed nose cone that could penetrate existing armour.

Meanwhile, in answer to the Confederate *Merrimack*, the Northern Federal States were constructing the *Monitor*, a purpose-

built ironclad battery, which was designed to fight low in the water while offering the smallest possible target. She was the brainchild of John Ericsson, and was designed to carry a single revolving turret. This turret, set amidships, was turned by a steam engine housed below decks and mounted two 11-inch (28-cm) Dahlgrens. Although she eventually gave her name to an entire class of warships used for bombardment, at the time she was stared at in disbelief. One Southern naval officer described her as 'Such a craft as the eyes of a seaman never looked upon before – an immense shingle floating in the water, with a gigantic cheese box rising from its center'. These two ships, the *Monitor* and *Merrimack,* were to be the first ironclads to engage one another in a naval action. It took *Monitor's* gunners eight minutes to load, aim and fire; *Merrimack's* gunners five to six minutes.

On the 8 March 1862, the *Merrimack* went into action against the Federal fleet which was blockading the York and James Rivers at Hampton Roads. She rammed and sank the wooden frigate *Cumberland,* forced the *Congress* to strike her flag, and drove the *Minnesota* aground. Shells fired at her by the Northern ships and shore batteries were harmlessly deflected by the sloping sides of her armoured casement. All in all it was an auspicious start to her naval career, but a more worthy adversary, the *Monitor,* was steaming south from New York, towed by a steam tug, the *Seth Low.*

The sea was lapping over the *Monitor's* deck, a scarce foot above the water. A less seaworthy craft could not be imagined and, when she was hit by a northwesterly gale she all but sunk. Giant green rollers smashed against the 6-ft (1.8-m) high smoke-stacks of the wildly rolling ship and sent a cascade of water into the engine room. Dense clouds of smoke, steam and gas rolled through the ship below decks; half-suffocated, coughing and retching, the engineers and stokers staggered from the engine room – the water had stretched the fan belts used to operate the blower system and no fresh air was being sucked into the ship. Once the ventilation system was restarted, the engineers recovered and the *Monitor* sailed on.

The gale had blown itself out. The *Monitor* slipped into Hampton Roads on the evening of 8 March, and berthed alongside the *Minnesota.* The seasick aboard – and most of the crew had been sick – were sufficiently recovered to face an evening meal. The officers, according to Acting Paymaster William Keeling, sat down to '. . . a supper of soup, good beef steak and green peas, fruit, nuts and brandy'. At dawn the shrill whistle of the bosun's pipe roused the ship; from across the bay drifted the sound of fife and drum as the *Merrimack's* ships company was called to quarters. On the deck of the *Monitor,* Lieutenant John Worden, her commander, was staring through his telescope at the

Above: The USS Lehigh, *an early Union ironclad built in the style of the original* Monitor.

Opposite top: A watercolour of USS Merrimack *before she was scuttled and later converted by the Confederates into an ironclad.*

Opposite bottom: An 11-inch Dahlgren gun aboard a Union warship during the Civil War. It is positioned on a slide-pivot mounting.

THE FIRST BATTLE BETWEEN IRON SHIPS OF WAR.
The "Monitor" 2 Guns and "Merrimac" 10 Guns.
The Merrimac was crippled and the whole Rebel Fleet driven off.

Above: The Monitor *steers straight for the* Merrimack *to close the range.*

STATISTICS OF THE TWO IRONCLADS		
	USS Monitor	CSS Merrimack
Displacement	987 tons (1,003 tonnes)	4,500 tons (4,572 tonnes)
Length	172 ft (52.4 m)	263 ft (80.2 m)
Beam	34 ft (10.4 m)	51 ft (15.5 m)
Armour	3.25-inch (8.3 cm) hull	4-inch (10.2 cm) hull
	8-inch (20.3 cm) turret	
Armament	2 11-inch (28-cm)	
	Dahlgren	2 7-inch (17.8-cm) rifled
	(165-lb/75-kg shell)	2 6.4-inch (16.3-cm) rifled
	(168-lb/76-kg solid shot)	6 9-inch (22.9-cm) Dahlgren
Maximum Speed	9 knots	9 knots

Opposite top: The Monitor *closes with the* Merrimack *during the engagement. This romantic engraving has ignored the fact that the Confederate ship was much bigger.*

Opposite bottom: The sinking of the USS Cumberland *by the* Merrimack.

Merrimack slowly wallowing towards them through the early morning mist. Already the sun was beginning to break through – it was going to be a fine day. He ordered a course to intercept the enemy ironclad and took up his position in the forward pilot house.

As the iron turret hatch clanged shut above them, the *Monitor*'s gun crew looked nervously at each other. Would the turret armour keep out the *Merrimack*'s 9-inch (23-cm) shells? Sunlight, filtering through the grating above and battle lanthorns, provided what feeble light there was. At the order to fire, the Dahlgrens thundered out, one at a time – the ship shuddered along her full length. The gun's crew frantically cranked the turret round to reload, facing away from the enemy. The machinery for turning the turret mechani-

cally was no longer working – it had rusted up as a result of the soaking it had received during the gale.

Aboard the *Merrimack*, her captain, Commander Catheby ap Roger Jones, gazed in disbelief at the weird vessel steaming between them and the *Minnesota*. Deciding to ignore the approaching pygmy, whatever it was, he lay-to and commenced to pound the helpless *Minnesota* with shell, to which she replied with erratic volleys of her own. Both ships were firing 'line of sight', ricocheting their shells along the surface of the water to achieve greater accuracy. Caught between the two ships as she was, the *Monitor* was in considerable danger of being hit by the shells skidding past her from either side – in fact, during the action she was hit several times by the

Minnesota. By 0845 the Southern commander, realizing that his ship was being peppered with 11-inch (28-cm) shells, altered course to take on the strange craft.

The two ironclads slowly circled each other; the range closed to 100 yards, 50 yards, then they were almost touching. For two hours they blazed away at each other with little effect; at one point when the *Merrimack*'s pilot ran her aground, she was at the mercy of the Northern ship for a quarter of an hour. From point-blank range the *Monitor* registered hits with six salvoes, cracking the enemy's plates, but failing to penetrate them. After the initial fear, the

Northern gunnery crew got overconfident. As three of them were leaning against the turret wall, chatting, a 9-inch (23-cm) shell landed directly alongside them, causing a great dent. One of the gunners, thrown to the deck, leaped up immediately; another, thrown clean over both guns, remained unconscious for an hour; the third, whose head had been only inches from the point of contact, 'dropped over like a dead man' but on regaining consciousness, was found to be none the worse for wear. Indeed the only casualty on either side was Lieutenant Worden. He was peering through the observation slit in the pilot

Fast blockade-runners in St. George's harbour, Bermuda, wait to make their dash to Southern ports.

house, registering the fall of shot, when a shell crashed straight against it – his face remained permanently blackened by gunpowder and he lost the sight of one eye.

At 1210 the *Merrimack* hauled off – she had had enough. The battle between the two ironclads had lasted for well over three hours, and although battered and dented, neither ship had received any lasting damage. The gunnery was completely ineffectual: the *Monitor* registered 20 hits from the 41 rounds fired and she herself received 23 direct hits (three of them from the *Minnesota*). The Battle of Hampton Roads ended in a draw; apart from demonstrating

the need for armour-piercing shells, it had little influence on naval warfare, certainly not in the development of the battleships that were about to appear.

Blockade-Runners and Privateers

The Confederate States (the South) had little industry and, in order to survive, they had to import all their arms and ammunition from Europe and export their cotton to pay for them. The Federal Navy (the North) naturally imposed a tight blockade on Southern ports, which soon became a

The privateer with the most Union victims to his credit – 71 – Captain Raphael Semmes of the CSS Alabama.

matter of life or death for the Confederates to force. To run the blockade they employed fast, 17-knot grey camouflaged paddle steamers which burned anthracite coal and gave out very little tell-tale smoke; these paddle steamers could easily out-steam the Federal warships. Making port at night, they would hurriedly discharge their cargo, load up with cotton and slip away before first light. It was highly profitable, but at the same time, a risky business – a ship's captain could make as much as $5,000 a month as compared with his normal pay of $160. In the first two years of the war, Federal ships captured 850 blockade runners.

The South also built and bought, from the supposedly neutral British, armed steamers which were used as privateers to harry Northern merchant ships. The most famous privateer (whose name came up time and time again at the Neutral Commission that sat in Geneva after the war and awarded the United States of America, $15,000,000, which Britain had to pay) was Captain Raphael Semmes of the *Alabama*. At the outbreak of the Civil War Semmes held a commission in the United States Navy but, as his sympathies lay with the South, he resigned to become one of the Confederates' most able commanders. His first ship was the CSS *Sumter*, a converted packet boat whose boilers had been extended to provide space for more coal and which had been fitted with an 8-inch (20-cm) swivel-gun and four 24-pounders. For six and a half months he ranged the Atlantic, destroying 17 Federal merchantmen before steaming to Europe to pick up a brand new ship, the *Alabama*, which was destined to become the most famous privateer of the war, with 71 seizures to her credit. A three-masted barque with an auxiliary engine, the *Alabama*, built in England ostensibly for a neutral country, had a maximum speed of 13.5 knots and when armed in the Azores, turned into a formidable raider. Though deep-sea mariners to a man, her crew were a hard lot, drawn from ports bordering the Irish Sea, and it says much for Semmes's power of command that he turned such a mob into an efficient fighting unit. An entry in his diary for 1863 reads, 'September 19th – The men on shore leave are all drunk. Only a few have returned.'

After cruising the North and South Atlantic, the Indian Ocean and China Sea and increasing his score to 71, Semmes took the *Alabama* to Cherbourg for a refit. Immediately the telegraph lines began to hum. The United States Consul sent a message to the USS *Kearsage*, then at Flushing. As soon as she was loaded, she weighed anchor and made for Cherbourg. There she cruised up and down before the harbour entrance. Semmes, without hesita-

tion, issued a challenge to the commander of the *Kearsage*, Captain Winslow, and putting his collection of captured ships' chronometers into safe hands, sailed out to meet him on Sunday 19 June 1864. The coming fight had a holiday air about it – an English yacht, the *Deerhound*, turned up and a train brought 1,200 Parisians to view the spectacle from the cliffs.

Escorted out of territorial waters by a French warship, the *Alabama* was the first to open fire from a range of 2,000 yards (1,800 m). For an hour, the two evenly matched ships – *Kearsage* with seven slightly heavier guns, and the *Alabama* with eight – circled each other, pounding away as the range closed to 600 yards (500 m). The gunnery was hardly of the highest order – of the 370 shots fired by the *Alabama*, only 14 registered hits, and one of those failed to explode. Winslow had taken the precaution of hanging anchor chains along his hull, but Semmes had not and a chance 11-inch (28-cm) shell from the Federal ship put his engines out of action. With his ship rapidly going down by the stern, Semmes was forced to strike. He, with 40 of his crew, were rescued by the *Deerhound*; the remainder were captured and taken aboard the *Kearsage*, apart

The end of the Alabama, *when Semmes was forced to surrender to Captain Winslow of the USS* Kearsage.

USS ESSEX

from the 12 men who died during the action. The ship's doctor went down with the *Alabama*, refusing to leave the handful of grievously wounded seamen left aboard.

A Time of Experiment

The battle between the *Monitor* and *Merrimack* underlined the need for more efficient, accurate and penetrating weapons, and naval guns continued to grow in size over the next 30 years. The re-introduction of breach-loading increased the rate of fire by eliminating the need to bring the gun inboard to reload. Longer barrels and the advent of slow-burning gunpowder in 1870 increased the muzzle-velocity of the shell, giving it greater power of penetration. This, naturally, resulted in the use of heavier armour, and as shells reached 18 inches (45.7 cm) in calibre, it was made as much as 24 inches (61.0 cm) thick. Towards the end of this period more effective gunnery and gun design enabled the size of heavy armament to be reduced to a more or less standard calibre of 12 inches (30.5 cm), and the introduction of

hardened steel saw the armour reduced to a similar 12-inch (30.5-cm) thickness.

It was a time of experiment. Countries, forced to break away from tradition by the new problems imposed by the rapid development of guns, armour, engines and boilers, clamoured for 'battleships', capable of delivering heavy salvoes from revolving turrets. Yet conservative elements in the world's navies were reluctant to make the break. The Royal Navy clung to its masts and spars, the French to their barbettes rather than turrets. When HMS *Captain*, a battleship of 7,760 tons (7,884 tonnes), carrying nearly 26,000 square feet (2,418 sq m) of canvas on three masts, with a freeboard of only 6 ft 6 inches (1.98 m), turned turtle in the Bay of Biscay in 1870, she marked the end of sail-rigged capital ships.

The 9,390-ton (9,540-tonne) *Thunderer*, launched in 1872, and her sister ship *Devastation* were the first sea-going battleships to be built without rigging. They were followed by the French *Tonnerre* of 1875, a coastal defence ship mounting two 10.6-inch (26.9-cm) guns in a single turret. France, along with most other

Opposite top: The screw-driven steamer USS Essex of 1876.

Opposite bottom: In the gunnery conning tower of HMS Thunderer.

Below: HMS Devastation.

Opposite: On the
gundeck of USS
Marblehead during the
battle of Cienfuegos in the
Cuban War of 1898.

nations, had turned to turret-mounting for the main armament, using barbettes only for secondary armament. In the mid-1870s the Italian Navy created a panic among other European fleets when the *Dandoro*, *Duilio* and *Andrea Doria* were put into commission. The *Andrea Doria*, launched in 1885, displaced 11,200 tons (11,380 tonnes), had a speed of 16 knots and boasted four monster 17-inch (43.2-cm) guns. On both sides of the Atlantic, navies vied with each other to build bigger and more powerful capital ships, and by the end of the century the prototype of the classical battleship had evolved. Typical of these was the HMS *Revenge* of 1892; she and her six sister ships led the field at the time.

Within 15 years, the *Revenge* along with all other battleships, had been made obsolete by the launching of HMS *Dreadnought* – a devastating revolution in the design of capital ships had occurred.

HMS *Revenge*	
Launched	1892
Displacement	14,150 tons (14,376 tonnes)
Length	380 ft (115.8 m)
Beam	75 ft (22.9 m)
Draught	28 ft (8.5 m)
Speed	17.5 knots
Engines	2 triple expansion engines – 13,000 hp
Crew	710
Armament	4 13.5 inch (34.3 cm)
	12 6 inch (15.2 cm)
	16 6-pounders
	13 12-pounders
	7 torpedo tubes

Below: HMS Dreadnought
of 1875. Her heavy shells
were still muzzle-loaded.

Première année. — N° 2

Huit pages : CINQ centimes

Dimanche 5 Juin 1898.

LE PETIT MÉRIDIONAL

Supplément Illustré du Dimanche

ABONNEMENTS

SIX MOIS | UN AN

France, Algérie, Tunisie. 2 fr. | 3 fr. 50
Étranger (Union postale). 2 fr. 50 | 5 fr.

Direction, Rédaction, Administration : Rue Henri-Guinier, MONTPELLIER

ANNONCES

POUR LA PUBLICITÉ S'ADRESSER :
A Montpellier : Rue Henri-Guinier.
A Paris : Rue de la Bourse, 7.

Combat de Cienfuegos (Cuba)

Une batterie du navire américain « Marblehead » pendant l'action.

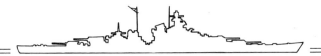

The Dreadnoughts

The Rising Sun in the East

As the navies of Europe and the U.S.A. vied with each other to build bigger and more powerful battleships, a force was rising in the East that was destined to upset the accepted balance of naval sea power.

At the turn of the 18th century, Japan was, to all intents and purposes, a medieval feudal power, isolated from the rest of the world and untouched by the Industrial Revolution which was sweeping Europe and North America. It was a visit to Japan by a squadron of American steam-powered warships under Commodore Perry in 1853 that triggered Japan's meteoric rise as an industrial power. Realizing that they were being left behind by the West, the Japanese leaders began to study Western ideas, and by the end of the 19th century, with the help of Britain, the country had acquired a small but powerful fleet, that was shortly to prove its worth in action.

Smarting under the humiliation of being forced to return Port Arthur to the Chinese, Japan was further angered by the concessions granted to Russia to use it as a naval base and to extend her Trans-Siberian Railway to the port of Niu-Chwang. Abruptly breaking off the talks that followed, the Japanese government ordered Admiral Heihachiro Togo to attack the Russian squadron at Port Arthur. There was no formal declaration of war, just a sudden, lightning attack on the port, an act of unheralded aggression that was to be repeated 37 years later at Pearl Harbor. The torpedo attack that took place on the night of 8 February 1904 caused much damage, but no ships were actually sunk. The world's major powers watched events with interest. It seemed that, for the first time, modern heavy capital ships would face each other in action, but the success of

the small torpedo boats also caused some concern. Although they had not been sunk, two battleships and an armoured cruiser were put out of action for some time.

The navy of the Czar was vastly superior to that of Japan, but it was unfortunately split into three more-or-less equal squadrons, two of them half the world away from Port Arthur. The Black Sea squadron was trapped in its inland sea by the London Treaty of 1870 which did not allow it to pass through the Dardenelles, and the Baltic squadron, even though it was allowed egress through the Skagerrak, was even further away. To the amazement of Western naval strategists, the Czar ordered Admiral Rojdestvensky, Commander of the Baltic Fleet, to sail his squadron 18,000 miles (28,800 km) to join up with the remains of Far East Fleet at Vladivostok. On 1 January 1905, before Rojdestvensky's fleet was halfway there, the Japanese captured Port Arthur, and what ships were not sunk by Japanese seige guns scuttled themselves – there was now no effective Russian Far East Fleet.

Meanwhile the Baltic squadron had sailed from its base on 14 October 1904. This star-crossed voyage was to underline all the drawbacks suffered by a large coal-fired fleet operating over such a distance. Without a single Russian base between the Baltic and Vladivostok, Rojdestvensky was forced to rely on a fleet of 70 German merchantmen to keep him supplied with coal. This meant trans-shipping thousands of sacks of coal, an activity which could only be carried out in a sheltered anchorage or in the very calmest of seas. In fact the Russian Admiral was the very first to load and reload coal while at sea. The air of 'fantasy' surrounding the enterprise was heightened when the Russian fleet fired on

a group of British fishing trawlers in the North Sea, believing them to be Japanese torpedo boats. One trawler from Hull was sunk with all hands, and only frantic diplomatic negotiations prevented the luckless Rojdestvensky having to contend with the Royal Navy – the British Press called for the destruction of 'the mad dog'. The fears of the Russian Admiral, who thought the expedition doomed to failure from the start, were partly realized during

this skirmish, as several of his ships were hit by shells fired by the others in his fleet. The four newly commissioned battleships with him had been hastily manned by untrained scratch crews – it was intended to train them during the voyage out.

It says a lot for Admiral Rojdestvensky's naval skill that he managed to bring his fleet the full distance to engage the Japanese off the island of Tsu-Shuma in the Korean Strait. However, officers and men

A fanciful Japanese interpretation of the Russo-Japanese War of 1904.

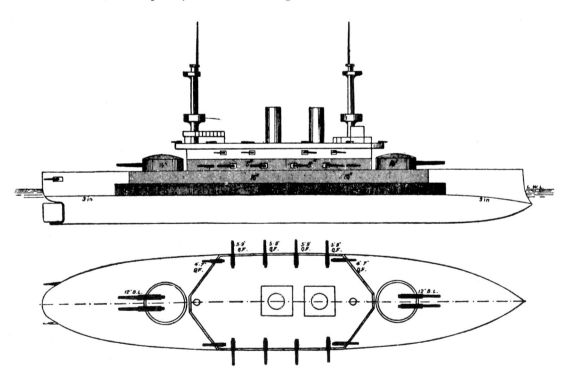

First-class Battleship "Tri Sviatételia." Also with modifications, the "Tavritchesky."

Displacement, 12,480 tons. **Speed,** 18 knots. **Normal Coal Supply,** 1,000 tons. **Armor:** Belt, 18 inches; gun positions, 16 inches; deck, 3 inches. **Armament,** four 12-inch B. L., eight 5·9-inch rapid-fire, four 4·7-inch rapid-fire, fifty-six small rapid-fire pieces. **Torpedo Tubes,** 6. **Complement,** 582. **Date,** 1893.
Five ships are building of the "Peresviet" type. These are improved "Tri Sviatetelias," of 12,674 tons and 18 knots with 9½-inch belts and armed with four 12- or 10-inch B. L. guns, eleven 6-inch rapid-firers, sixteen 3-inch, ten 1·8-inch and seventeen 1·4-inch rapid-firers.

DESTROYERS (HARD LYING)

With the development of the Whitehead torpedo – by 1870 it was 14 inches (35.6 cm) in diameter, carried a 33-lb (15.0-kg) warhead, travelled at 25 knots and had a range of 1,000 yards (900 m) – the major naval powers even began to have doubts about their heavily armoured capital ships. In 1894 one observer wrote '... when some high authorities are beginning to doubt whether the position even of the battleship in naval warfare of the future is not beginning to be imperilled by the development of vessels of the *Havock* and *Hornet* class regarded as sea-keeping torpedo-boats!'

The success of the torpedo depended on speed: the speed of its own approach and the speed of the craft that delivered it. Smaller navies, seeing a means of neutralizing the big ships of the major naval powers, began building fast steam launches. The British Admiralty might take the lofty view that the torpedo-boat was the 'weapon of the weaker power', but the more thoughtful saw a real danger and sought an answer to this novel means of attack. The British shipbuilders, Yarrow and Thornycroft, competed to produce small fast torpedo-boats, which were snapped up by foreign powers. The Admiralty, influenced by a statement in *The Times* following the 1878 Naval Review, ordered a dozen of these 'First Class' torpedo-boats.

'One of the features of the Review was the performance of two long double-funnel torpedo-boats, built by Yarrow, which have realized the extraordinary speed of 21 knots. The manner in which these malevolent-looking craft rushed up and down the lines and round the ships was the astonishment of all beholders.' *The Times*, 14 August.

At a lecture given to the Royal United Services Institute in 1885, Alfred Yarrow let out the astonishing information that whereas Russia had 115 torpedo boats and France 50, the Royal Navy had a mere 19. A crash building programme was introduced, particularly after First Sea Lord Northbrook wrote, that 'The torpedo would be the most powerful weapon of offence, and would be able to dispose of the most formidable ships in the service of this or any other country.' The first attempt to protect battleships against torpedo attack was to provide them with cumbersome metal anti-torpedo nets, draped round the ship on a series of heavy booms; these were intended either to stop the torpedo or to explode it prematurely. The resulting loss of speed through drag was eventually found to be unacceptable and new methods against torpedo attack were sought.

What was required was a larger ship, fast enough to overhaul a torpedo-boat and with a sufficiently powerful armament to destroy it. After a number of experimental craft had been tested, the first successful 'torpedo-boat destroyer', the *Havock*, appeared in October, 1895, to be followed by the *Hornet* in March, 1896. Sinister-looking craft, they were 180 ft (55 m) by 11 ft (3.4 m) with a 'turtle-back' forecastle. Displacing 240 tons (244 tonnes), they reached speeds of 27.6 knots under forced draught, 'the furnaces were of such dazzling white that coloured glasses were necessary when trimming.' They were armed with one 12-pounder, two 6-pounders and three 18-inch (46-cm) torpedo tubes, set one forward and two aft; their bridge structure was no more than a canvas screen; their armour on the conning tower, ½-inch (1.3-cm) plate.

The conditions for the crew of 42 were hard in the extreme. The unsynchronized engines set up a terrible vibration; they rolled appallingly, and the gunners suffered from the rush of wind through the sighting port in the gun shield. To keep up the high speeds, the stokers worked non-stop, shovelling in the ship's load of 94 tons (96 tonnes) of coal at the rate of 44.5 miles (71.6 km) per ton, at 10 knots. Conditions were, in fact, so bad that the Admiralty issued a special pay allowance for officers and ratings serving in the new 'destroyers' – 'Hard Lying' money. By the turn of the century, the destroyer had become an integral part of every navy; completely unarmoured, she relied solely on her speed for protection against attack. With the introduction of the Parsons steam

Admiral Rojdestvensky's flagship Czarevitch.

turbine engine, the destroyer became a force to be reckoned with – on her trials in 1899, HMS *Viper*, a destroyer of 325 tons (330 tonnes), reached a speed of 36.58 knots. The fuel consumption went down, but more important, the killing vibration was eliminated – but destroyer men still retained the 'Hard-Lying' money.

By the beginning of the First World War, destroyers of the 'Tribal' class were generating speeds of 33.5 to 34.8 knots, carrying a virtually useless 12-pounder, which was later replaced with a 4-inch (10-cm) gun. When the *Swift* class appeared, 345 ft (105 m) long, weighing 2,170 tons (2,200 tonnes), they mounted two 4-inch guns, two 18-inch (46-cm) torpedo tubes and had a top speed of 36 knots. The torpedo itself had become a lethal weapon, more than capable of sinking a battleship if it hit it in a vulnerable spot. The 18-inch torpedo now had a range of 4,000 yards (3,600 m) travelling at 44 knots, or 10,000 yards (9,100 m) at 28 knots, and destroyers with high speeds had become a menace to capital ships.

Vice-Admiral Sir Baldwin Walker laid down the role of the destroyer for the Royal Navy, which applied equally to other navies.

1. Screening the advance of a fleet when hostile torpedo craft are about.
2. Searching a hostile coast along which a fleet might pass.
3. Watching an enemy's port for the purpose of harassing his torpedo craft and preventing their return.
4. Attacking an enemy fleet.

The 'Tribals' of the 6th Flotilla, based at Dover, had an eventful war and stood up well to the strain of an arduous routine. For 17 days they had a full head of steam up, whether in habour or at sea, ready at a minute's notice to weigh and go into action. Then for three days they were laid up for boiler-cleaning, and every four months, they spent 20 days in dry dock for coating the ship's bottom and overhauling.

Between October and November, 1914, the Dover destroyers bombarded the seaward flank of the German army on the Flanders coast, on one occasion demolishing the Hotel Majestic at Ostende which was being used by the Kaiser's General Staff Officers. However, many of the most exciting actions in which destroyers were involved were against submarines, which, although as well-armed, lacked speed. A typical encounter occurred towards the end of the war. On a dark overcast spring night in 1918, the destroyer *Fairy*, together with an armoured whaler and six trawlers, was acting as escort to a convoy of 30 merchantmen off Flamborough Head. The sea was flat calm, and as senior escort ship, her commander, Lieutenant Barnish, had taken station 'to seaward and a little abaft the beam of the rear ship of the convoy'. In such shallow water no one expected a U-Boat attack, so it was with some surprise that *Fairy*'s Yeoman of Signals read off a flashing message, 'Merchantman torpedoed'. At almost the same instant a look-out reported, 'submarine on port bow' – it was a mere 300 yards (275 m) away on the surface. Turning his ship in a tight circle, Lieutenant Barnish signalled full-ahead on the engine-room telegraph, and the *Fairy*'s bow wave lifted, as she surged straight for the submarine – frantically flashing a recognition signal in case the submarine was British.

At point-blank range, the destroyer's crew could hear orders being shouted in German as she caught the U-Boat a glancing blow on the stern. Aboard the *UC.75*, the captain ordered 'abandon ship' as the small, 350-ton (360-tonne) destroyer raced in to ram again, wildly firing her 6-pounder. Far from attacking the convoy, the *UC.75* had, in fact, accidentally collided with one of the merchantmen, and was in the process of assessing the damage that had been done to the U-Boat. Charging flat out, the *Fairy*, crashed into the side of the German and came to an abrupt halt. The destroyer's bows crumpled back as far as the bridge. The U-Boat quickly sank in a pool of diesel oil, but the *Fairy* herself was rapidly going down by the head. An attempt was made to beach her stern first, but when her madly threshing screws surfaced out of the water, the crew took to the boats along with the crew of the *UC.75*, to be picked up by another ship.

Japanese battleships go into action at the Battle of Tscu-Shuma in 1905.

alike, doubtful of the outcome from the start, had been further demoralized by the seemingly never-ending voyage. At 1320 hours on 27 May 1905, Japanese Admiral Togo took his six battleships, followed by six armoured cruisers, across the course of the Russians who were approaching line ahead, thus 'Crossing the "T"', which allowed him to bring all his heavy guns to bear; the enemy, on the other hand, could only reply with his forward guns. Nelson had deliberately put himself in Rojdestvensky's position at Trafalgar, but naval gunnery had advanced out of all recognition since then, and salvoes of 12-inch (30.5-cm) shells, fired at 6,000 yards (5,500 m) and under, could have a devastating effect. So it proved. The Japanese gunners soon found their aim with disastrous results: six of the eight Russian battleships were sunk; the other two surrendered. Of the 37 Russian ships that faced the Japanese at Tsu-Shuma that afternoon, 22 were sunk or went aground, six were captured and six reached a neutral port where they were interned. Only three managed to escape to Vladivostok – a cruiser and two destroyers. One important fact emerged from this engagement; in a major naval action, only big guns counted, the 8-inch (20-cm) and 6-inch (15-cm) supplementary armament was useless. Among the foreign observers who watched with more than usual interest was the Royal Navy; it had already come to this conclusion, and had a revolutionary, all-big-gun battleship about to go on the stocks at Portsmouth, HMS *Dreadnought*.

The 'All-Big-Gun' Ship

Urged on by the First Sea Lord, Sir John Fisher, a man of demonic energy and iron will, Portsmouth Dockyard beat all previous records for speed in shipbuilding. Laid down on 2 October 1905, the *Dreadnought*, who gave her name to a whole generation of battleships, slipped down the launchway just four months later on 10 February 1906. By commandeering gun turrets destined for other battleships, she was completed, ready for sea, by Christmas 1906. It had taken only 14 months to build her, a record that has never been broken. Fisher, fearful of the growing might of the Imperial German Navy, clamoured for more monsters of this size.

The *Dreadnought* was, in every way, a revolutionary ship that made all other capital ships obsolete. At the time of her completion, the standard battleships of all the world's navies were steel-built, weighed around 17,000 tons/17,300 tonnes (full load displacement) and mounted four big guns of 12-inch (30.5-cm) calibre in two centre-line turrets. They also carried a secondary armament ranging from 9-inch (23-cm) to 3 pounders. Powered by triple-expansion engines, they could reach a top speed of 18–19 knots, and were protected by 12-inch (30.5-cm) steel armour. With most of these 'mixed-armament ships' offering much of the same performance in speed, armour and firepower, it became a race between navies to exceed each other in numbers. Britain, by 1900, had a 'two-power' standard of naval strength, her fleet equalling in numbers the combined fleets of any two other countries.

Despite the numerical superiority of the Royal Navy, the Admiralty was impressed by an article written by Italian warship designer Vittorio Cuniberti in 1903, under the title, 'An Ideal Battleship for the British Navy'. He put forward an argument for a 17,000-ton (17,300-tonne) battleship, protected by 12-inch (30.5-cm) armour and mounting 12 12-inch (30.5-cm) guns, which could reach a speed of 24 knots. Fisher, who had experimented with long-range firing and more accurate gun-control, was fascinated with the possibility of delivering such a potentially destructive weight of shell at ranges in excess of 8,000 yards (7,300 m), and badgered the Admiralty to commission HMS *Dreadnought*. Naturally reluctant to introduce a new concept that would probably cause them to scrap most of their existing capital ships, many of the Admiralty strategists and naval commanders turned a jaundiced eye on the new ship, anxious to find a major fault that would make it a non-feasible proposition.

By 1914 the food aboard ship had definitely improved – no longer did this 18th-century ballad apply:

'THE SAILORS LAMENT'
or
'The True Character of the Purser of a Ship'

As his name foully stinks, so his butter rank do smell,
Both hateful to sailors, scarce good enough for hell:
The nation allows men what's fitting to eat,
But he, curse attend him, gives us musty meat,
But bisket that's mouldy, hard stinking Suffolk cheese,
And pork cut in pounds, for to eat with our pease.

At last the Admiralty took note of Samuel Pepys's remark, 'Englishmen, especially seamen, love their bellies above everything else. . .' and in 1906, laid down a daily 'standard ration'.

Bread – 10 oz or Biscuit – 7 oz or flour – 10 oz

Fresh meat – ½ lb of beef or mutton – pork two days per month.

Potatoes or fresh vegetables – 1 lb

Butter – 1 oz

Sugar – 2 oz

Tea – ½ oz or Coffee – 1 oz

Chocolate – ½ oz or Coffee – 1 oz

Condensed milk – ¾ oz

Jam, marmalade or pickles – 1 oz

Preserved meat or salmon – 4 oz – 1 day a week in harbour; 2 days a week at sea, as a supper ration.

Many a labourer ashore would have thought these rations princely.

In the event, the *Dreadnought* was a complete success, fully vindicating Fisher's faith in her. The first battleship to be powered with Parsons turbine engines, she could make 21 knots, giving her a 3-knot advantage over any of her rival battleships, yet still allowing her the protection of 11-inch (28-cm) steel armour. Her ten 12-inch (30.5-cm) guns were arranged in five turrets, to fire six forward, six aft and eight on the beam. Displacing 22,000 tons/22,350 tonnes (full load), she easily overshadowed any existing battleship, and her stark superstructure, uncluttered by secondary armament, was a complete break with tradition, as was her huge tripod mast, set between two funnels. One defect, however, was the placing of the tripod mast behind the forward funnel as the smoke from the funnel at times obscured the gun control perched at the top. This was overcome in later versions by introducing two tripod masts fore and aft of the two

Opposite top: By 1892 the officers' wardroom had begun to take on a more modern appearance. The wardroom of the battleship HMS Resolution.

Opposite below: The midshipmen's mess, the Gun Room, aboard HMS Caesar in 1856.

Below: 'Rum Up.' Serving grog aboard the battleship HMS Glory, 1899.

Building the all-big-gun
battleship HMS
Dreadnought. *The point of
her construction reached by
3 October 1905.*

funnels. Fisher was so delighted in proving the many critics of the *Dreadnought* to be wrong that he headed an official paper he submitted to the Admiralty:

NEW NAME FOR THE
DREADNOUGHT
The *Hard-Boiled Egg*
Why? Because she can't be beaten.

Autocratic, unable to suffer fools gladly, this flamboyant character was to come into contact with an equally flamboyant character eight years later, when Winston Churchill became First Lord of the Admiralty.

HMS *Dreadnought* – 1906

Length	561 ft (171.0 m)
Beam	82 ft (25.0 m)
Draught	27 ft (8.2 m)
Speed	21 knots
Armour	11-inch (27.9-cm) steel
Armament	10 12-inch (30.5 cm);
	24 12-pounders;
	5 Maxim machine guns;
	5 18-inch (45.7-cm)
	torpedo tubes
Complement	729

Taken by surprise, the Germans immediately suspended the building of the *Deutschland* class battleships of 13,400 tons (13,600 tonnes) with a top speed of 18 knots and began a programme for the *Nassau* class, mounting ten 11-inch (28-cm) guns and with a speed of 20 knots. To put these ships on the stocks called for a vast programme of reconstruction, which the Kaiser immediately sanctioned. To take their warships from the Baltic through into the North Sea, the Germans had just completed the Kiel Canal, but as it took ships of up to 16,000 tons (16,260 tonnes), it had to be widened and deepened. It also meant enlarging dockyards and reconstructing existing dry docks. Once the concept of the all-big-gun battleship had been accepted, the increase in size grew dramatically in a very short space of time. By 1914 battleships were displacing 28,000 tones (28,450 tonnes) and a year later, more than 30,500 tons (31,000 tonnes).

Another innovation of Admiral Fisher's fertile brain was the battle-cruiser. He believed that the future of naval warfare lay with the big heavy battleship, the destroyer and the submarine and he could see no role for the cruiser. Instead he favoured a *Dreadnought* armoured-cruiser which was later called a 'battleship cruiser' and was eventually shortened to battle-cruiser. In theory it would make the conventional armoured cruiser obsolete. Its displacement would be much the same as that of a battleship, but it would be armed with only four twin 12-inch (30.5-cm) turrets, and carry only a 6-inch (15-cm) steel armoured belt, to allow a top speed of 25½ knots. With her turn of speed and heavy guns, she would be able to hunt down and sink any

CRUISERS

Although the world's navies concentrated most of their attention on building bigger and better capital ships, a certain amount of thought was given to the design of fast armoured cruisers and even faster light cruisers. During the 18th and 19th centuries, a 'cruizer' was any ship that operated independently – it was not a class of ship; this only came later as its role began to change. The early 'cruizers' were usually fast frigates who protected merchantmen against privateers, attacked enemy shipping themselves and scouted for the fleet.

It was during the 1880s that they began to become a definite class of ship. Smaller than a battleship, they had to be fast enough and sufficiently heavily armed to catch and destroy commerce raiders, and themselves prey upon enemy shipping. Armour was sacrificed for firepower and speed as a cruiser was never intended to be a ship of the line. Naval history, however, is full of instances where cruisers fought alongside battleships.

With the introduction of steam turbines and later, oil-fired boilers, cruisers became faster with a far greater cruising range, a deadly menace to marine commerce.

Below: With a speed of 21.85 knots, HMS Dreadnought *was the first battleship to be fitted with Parsons steam turbines.*

Bottom: The Dreadnought *nearing completion, 11 June 1906.*

marauding armoured cruiser harrying the trade routes, and act as a scout for the main battle fleet. The theory was sound enough, providing that other navies did not build battle-cruisers, which of course they did.

Outbreak of the First World War

Britain and Germany, locked in a race to increase their numbers of capital ships, were heading for war, – it began on 4 August 1914. The capital ships of the two sides were, in the main, designed for different purposes. Great Britain with her widespread Empire had to be able to deploy her ships over vast distances, which called for more spacious living accommodation; the Germans, on the other hand, designing their battleships for more localized warfare, had a spartan attitude towards living conditions. The battleships of the Royal Navy, designed to bring the German High Seas Fleet to a pitched battle, concentrated on gunpower and speed at the expense of armour – the 12-inch (30.5-cm) gun had given way to a 13.5-inch (34.3-cm) gun in 1910, and the 15-inch (38-cm) gun by 1915. The Germans, seeking to even up the British superiority in numbers of battleships by using torpedo boats and submarines, despite what was said at the time, aimed to avoid such an engagement. The German Navy's role was more defensive. This meant that speed and gunpower had to be sacrificed – it was only with reluctance that they turned to the 12-inch gun from the 11-inch (28-cm) gun – to incorporate heavier armour.

Opposite top: An early cruiser, HMS Blenheim of 1907, from a painting by Norman Wilkinson.

Opposite bottom: British battleships in the Solent, 1914.

THE NUMBER OF CAPITAL SHIPS IN SERVICE AT THE OUTBREAK OF THE WAR

Pre-Dreadnoughts (1893–1908)		Dreadnoughts	Battle-cruisers
Great Britain	40	22	9
France	17	4	Nil
Italy	8	3	Nil
Japan	16	2	6
	81	31	15
Germany	23	15	4
Austria-Hungary	12	3	Nil
	35	18	4

Below: The First World War German battleship Bismarck, under construction in 1900.

Coronel and the Falklands

Vice-Admiral Maximilian Graf von Spee, commanding the German East Asiatic Squadron, found himself surrounded by heavy enemy units when the war broke out. On receiving a wireless message from Berlin, 'Imminent danger of war with Great Britain, France and Russia', he had hastily sailed from the German base at Tsingtau in China and lay anchored with his six ships at Pagan Island in the Marianas. With Japan likely to enter the war at any moment on the side of the Allies, he realized that the chance of his squadron operating with any success in the Indian and Pacific Oceans was virtually nil. Without bases, his coal-fired cruisers would be forced to coal from German merchant ships in lonely anchorages, constantly on the look-out for patrolling Allied warships, who were only too well aware of all the likely spots. His orders from the Kriegsmarine, emphasized by the Kaiser who saw himself as no mean naval strategist – he even attempted to design warships himself – were quite clear. '. . . The aim of cruiser warfare is to damage enemy trade; this must be affected by engaging equal or inferior forces, if necessary. . . . The conduct of naval war in home waters must be assisted by holding as many of the enemy's ships as possible in foreign waters.'

After a conference with his captains, von Spee decided that the best chance of effecting his orders was to take his ships to the west coast of South America to disrupt the considerable British mercantile trade along that coast. One cruiser might well be able to operate alone in the Indian Ocean to good effect, so he despatched the 3,600-ton (3,660-tonne) Emden, a light cruiser. She did, in fact, create havoc there, sinking or capturing 23 ships in 70 days, before she was beached and made to surrender on 9 November 1914. He turned east into the Pacific with his remaining ships: the Scharnhorst, his flagship, an 11,400-ton (11,600-tonne) armoured cruiser completed in 1908, with a top speed of 23 knots; her sister ship, the Gneisenau; and the slightly faster light cruisers – the Dresden, 3,600 tons (3,660 tonnes); the Nurnberg, 3,400 tons (3,450 tonnes); and the Leipzig, 3,200 tons (3,250 tonnes) and somewhat slower. Noted for its gunnery – the Scharnhorst had won the Kaiser's gunnery prize two years running – it was a powerfully-efficient squadron, capable of taking on any equivilent force.

He arrived off the coast of Chile at Coronel on 1 November, where he met the cruiser squadron of Rear-Admiral Sir Christopher Craddock. The British Admiral had with him: two antiquated armoured cruisers – his flagship, the Good Hope, built in 1902, 14,100 tons (14,330 tonnes) and the Monmouth, 1903, 9,800 tons (9,960 tonnes); an armed merchant cruiser, the Otranto; and the light cruiser Glasgow, 4,800 tons (4,880 tonnes), the only

modern warship in his force. As von Spee took the precaution of transmitting all his wireless signals through the *Leipzig*, Craddock believed that he was steaming to do battle with a single light cruiser. Warned well in advance by a wireless message from the *Glasgow* scouting ahead, the British Admiral still decided to attack, despite what he knew to be hopeless odds. The heaviest guns he could muster were two 9.2-inch (23.4-cm), against von Spee's 16 8.2-inch (20.8-cm) guns, worked by superbly trained gunners, the best in the Imperial German Navy. It was soon all over. The Germans opened fire at 1900 hours and, by 1957 hours, a shattered *Good Hope* went down with all hands including Kit Craddock. The *Monmouth*, whose 6-inch (15-cm) guns hardly ever got within range, sank less than an hour later. The *Otranto* and *Glasgow* escaped, the latter to fight again at the Falklands.

When news of this defeat reached the Admiralty in London, immediate action was taken to send out a force strong enough to wipe out the Germany cruisers. The thought of the damage that von Spee could wreak if he took his ships into the Atlantic threw the place into a panic. Fisher and Winston Churchill, now First Lord of the Admiralty, quarrelled over who should command the British squadron, but the latter finally had his way, and Vice-Admiral Sir Doveton Sturdee was soon steaming south with a powerful squadron. His flagship, the *Invincible*, and her sister ship,

the *Inflexible*, were 17,250-ton (17,530-tonne) battle-cruisers, mustering between them 16 12-inch (30.5-cm) guns, with a top speed of 25 knots. In support were the armoured cruisers *Carnarvon*, *Cornwall* and *Kent*, and the light cruiser *Bristol*. Although von Spee's cruisers would be no match for Sturdee's force, it would be no easy task to run him down in the vast wastes of the Atlantic. As it turned out the German squadron saved them the trouble.

After his victory at Coronel, Vice-Admiral von Spee was advised by the Kriegsmarine to return home across the Atlantic. Violent storms held up his progress, and it was 1 December before he rounded Cape Horn and headed north. By 8 December he was off Port Stanley in the Falklands; Sturdee's squadron had arrived the day before. Von Spee now made a fatal mistake. Confident after his victory and following an inaccurate intelligence report that there were no British warships in the area, he decided to attack Port Stanley, destroy the wireless station and set fire to the coal dumps. Bitter opposition from three of his captains, Maerker of the *Gneisenau*, Ludecke of the *Dresden* and Haun of the *Leipzig*, who begged him to give the islands a wide berth, were swept aside. At 0900 hours on 8 December they were ten miles (16 km) away from Port Stanley, the *Gneisenau* and *Nurnberg* steaming ahead to carry out the intended operation. A signal lamp flashed from the gunnery control position on the foremast of

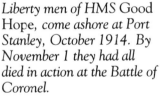

Liberty men of HMS Good Hope, *come ashore at Port Stanley, October 1914. By November 1 they had all died in action at the Battle of Coronel.*

the *Gneisenau*; Korvettenkapitan Busch had sighted four triangular masts in the harbour – British battleships, or still worse, battle-cruisers.

Orders were flashed from the flagship to alter course to the southeast in the hope of running into mist. Von Spee was not to know it, but had he pressed on, he would have caught the British coaling. As it was, the enemy, led by the battle-cruisers, were in hot pursuit by 1000 hours. Outgunned, five knots slower, von Spee had no choice. Ordering his light cruisers to, 'Leave line and try to escape', the German Admiral turned his armoured cruisers towards the enemy. At 1247 hours Sturdee's 12-inch (30.5-cm) guns opened up – so confident was Sturdee that he had given orders for the crews of his ships to have a midday meal before opening the action.

The German gunnery lived up to its high reputation; twice when he got within range of their 8.2-inch (20.8-cm) guns, Sturdee was forced to turn away to open the range. But the odds were even more telling than at Coronel. At 1617 hours the *Scharnhorst* went down taking Maximilian von Spee with her; at 1800 hours the *Gneisenau*

sank, followed an hour and a half later by the *Nurnberg* and *Leipzig* – the latter's crew, lining the rails, sang the 'Song of the Sea' as she went down. Only the *Dresden* escaped, making her getaway in a sudden squall that blew up.

Probing Actions

In the first months of the war, the British Grand Fleet at Scapa Flow and the German High Seas Fleet at Wilhelmshaven eyed each other with caution. On the one hand, the British Commander, Admiral Sir John Jellicoe, was very much conscious of being, as Winston Churchill put it, 'the only man on either side who could lose the war in an afternoon', and was naturally cautious. On the other hand, the Kriegsmarine were anxious to lure part of the Grand Fleet into battle on favourable terms. To this end the German battle-cruisers under Admiral Hipper carried out a series of raids on the east coast of England, bombarding Yarmouth and Scarborough. In every case they evaded the battle-cruisers of Vice-Admiral Sir David Beatty that had to steam from Scapa Flow. Public opinion, incensed by

The cruiser HMS Kent raised steam quickly by burning the wardroom furniture, to head for the Battle of the Falklands.

the fact that the Germans were able to shell the English coast with impunity, forced the Admiralty to base some units of the Grand Fleet at Rosyth in the Firth of Forth.

The first real 'big ship' clash occurred in January 1915. Hipper came out with three battle-cruisers, the *Seydlitz*, *Moltke* and *Derfflinger*; the armoured cruiser *Blücher*; four light cruisers; and a destroyer flotilla. A harassed Admiralty had set up a chain of radio listening-posts along the east coast, and as the men in the Admiralty had a copy of the German Navy's code, they not only knew that Hipper's squadron was out, but could roughly determine the course it had set. Beatty and four battle-cruisers raced from Rosyth to intercept. Initially accompanied by the Fourth Cruiser Squad-

ron, Beatty picked up light cruisers and destroyers on the way.

Contact was made when the cruiser *Kolberg* fired on the light cruiser *Aurora*, having failed to answer a recognition signal. Hipper, uncertain of the strength of the force against him, turned for home, chased by Beatty who was determined to bring the German to action before he reached port. Squeezing every ounce of speed from his battle-cruisers – at times they did 29 knots – Beatty brought the slower German ships within range of his 13.5-inch (34.3-cm) guns off the Dogger Bank and opened up. As hits registered on the *Seydlitz*, her two after-turrets were set ablaze and only prompt action on the part of her gun crews, who flooded the magazine, saved her from going up. Beatty,

The chase begins; the British battle-cruisers begin to overtake the slower German cruisers in the Falkands.

aboard the *Lion*, suffered a similar fate and had to transfer his flag to a destroyer. Then, as a result of sloppy, imprecise signals from Beatty, his ships turned from the fleeing German battle-cruisers and concentrated on the *Blücher*, the weakest ship in the squadron.

What could have been a successful British battle-cruiser action turned into a messy affair, with both sides dissatified with the result. The British gunnery was inadequate – the battle-cruiser *Tiger* had not scored a single hit during the whole engagement – and, not for the first time, the signalling proved faulty. Notwithstanding the damage done to the *Seydlitz*, Hipper considered himself lucky, and set about improving the fire precautions in the main turrets, reducing the number of cordite

Vice-Admiral Sturdee, the victorious British commander at the Battle of the Falklands.

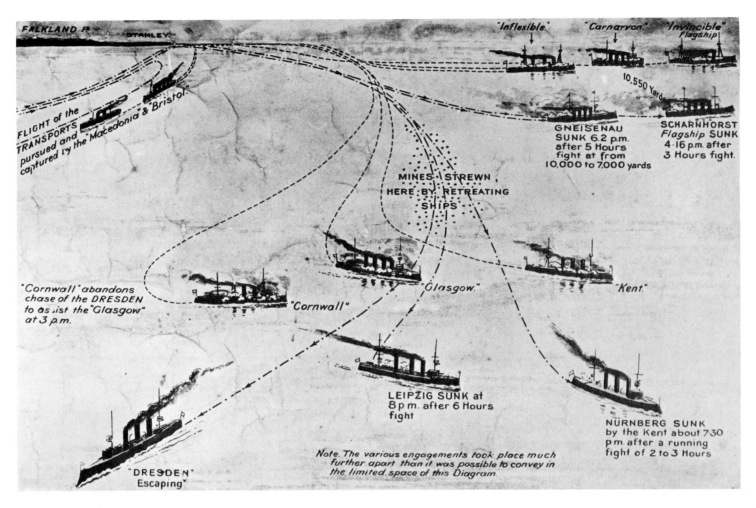

An artist's diagram of the Battle of the Falklands.

charges stored there during action. The British, blissfully unaware of the narrow escape of the *Seydlitz* and not knowing that their own cordite might 'flash off' instead of just burning, did nothing.

The Battle of Jutland

When Vice-Admiral Reinhard Scheer was given command of the High Seas Fleet in January 1916, he brought a new spirit of aggression to the German Navy. In Britain, following the withdrawal from the Dardenelles, Fisher and Churchill left the Admiralty, and the capital ships deployed there returned to the Grand Fleet. Jellicoe now had under his command: 24 Dreadnoughts mounting 12-inch (30.5-cm) or 13.5-inch (34.3-cm) guns, four super-Dreadnoughts with 15-inch (38-cm) guns, nine battle-cruisers, eight armoured cruisers, 26 light cruisers and two seaplane carriers. Scheer could muster: 15 Dreadnoughts, seven pre-Dreadnought battleships, five battle-cruisers, 11 light cruisers and 62 destroyers. This was the complement of the two fleets in the spring of 1916.

With the German armies locked in a costly stalemate before Verdun, the High Command decided it was time to mount an offensive at sea. Scheer devised a plan to use Hipper's battle-cruiser squadron to

draw out part of the Grand Fleet and lead them into a trap. Firstly, U-Boats were sent to lay mines along the course likely to be taken by the Grand Fleet from Scapa Flow and Rosyth. Then the German commander led the whole of the High Seas Fleet from Wilhelmshaven into the North Sea. Even before he sailed, however, the Admiralty had intercepted a radio signal from the German High Command, '31 Gg 2490', and although Admiralty specialists were unable to decipher it, they correctly assumed that the High Seas Fleet had put to sea. Beatty was ordered to weigh immediately and steam for the Skagerrak with six battle-cruisers and four *Queen Elizabeth* class, 15-inch (38-cm) gun super-Dreadnoughts. The Grand Fleet under Jellicoe sailed south from Scapa Flow to join him there. The scene was set for the greatest battleship action of all time.

Admiralty officials began to have doubts about their interpretation of the intercepted signal when their radio-directional stations began to pick up radio messages from Scheer's flagship, the *Friedrich der Grosse*, coming from the Jade River. To mislead British Intelligence, the German Admiral had exchanged call signs with a shore station. For his part, he had no idea that the whole of the Grand Fleet had put to sea four hours before he had himself.

The signal '31 Gg 2490' had informed all naval units that Secret Order 2490 would be put into operation on 31 May. Hipper's squadron consisted of six battle-cruisers (*Lützow*, his flagship, *Seydlitz*, *Derfflinger*, *Moltke* and *Von der Tann*) accompanied by four light cruisers and three destroyer flotillas. Heading north from Jutland into Norwegian waters, the plan was to lure part of the Grand Fleet out so that it could be picked off by the main High Seas Fleet in support 50 miles (80 km) to the south southeast.

On the course he had set, Beatty would cross Hipper's squadron to the south, trapping the German Admiral between himself and Jellicoe who was steaming southeast. Scheer, still unaware that the British were already out in full force, would steam flat out to support Hipper, only to be faced by the whole of the Grand Fleet. Barring a miracle he would be drawn into a trap himself. Then, by one of those curious imponderables that decide battles, light cruisers from both squadrons changed course to investigate a Danish steamer.

As soon as they spotted each other through the afternoon haze, the light cruisers, *Elbing* and *Galatea* closed the range, their wirelesses crackling. So far there had been no advance intelligence: the submarines of neither side had radioed any worthwhile reports, and the Zeppelins had been useless. Within minutes of receiving the message from *Galatea*, seaplane No. 8359 was swung outboard from the converted cross-Channel packet *Engardine* and was taking off across the still water. Hardly was she airborne than she was down again with engine trouble. Aloft once more, her observer, Assistant Paymaster Trewin, tapped out at 1530 hours, 'Three enemy cruisers and five destroyers, distance 10 miles (16 km) bearing 90°, steering course to N.W.'. Aircraft had been used in a naval battle for the first time. Beatty, on an easterly course, was intent on cutting off Hipper from his home bases; the German squadron had turned-about to the southeast to draw the British towards the main units of the High Seas Fleet. Beatty's look-outs, perched high up the tripod masts, had already sighted the Germans at a range of 24,000 yards or almost 14 miles (22 km). Beatty kept his battleships over the horizon, out of sight, so as not to deter Hipper from giving fight. Both Admirals believed they were driving the other into a trap.

The opposing squadrons were on a converging course when at 1546 hours, the *Lützow* opened fire on the *Lion* at 18,000 yards (16,500 m). The Battle of Jutland had begun. Fire gongs rang throughout the *Lion* as she began firing 20 seconds later. Signalling errors – they had learned little since the Dogger Bank action – caused the *Lion* and the *Princess Royal* to fire on the same ship, leaving the *Derfflinger* free to

The British battleships steam line ahead at the Battle of Jutland.

Opposite top: German
capital ships steam into
action, photographed from
the cupola of a Zeppelin.

Opposite bottom: A German
battleship in action at
Jutland.

close and fire at will. As the range closed to 12,000 yards (11,000 m), cordite fumes, and smoke from the racing destroyers drifting across the target, made gunnery difficult. Nonetheless, with the sun behind them, the German battle-cruisers were firing well; after three minutes they had made eight hits on the *Lion*, the *Tiger* and the *Princess Royal*. Seven minutes passed before the British scored a hit, but by then the *Queen Mary* had turned her guns on the *Derfflinger*, firing with 'fabulous rapidity' according to an observer on the German ship.

At 1600 hours an 11-inch (28-cm) shell from the *Lützow* landed close to the magazine and knocked the *Lion*'s 'Q' turret amidships. Only the presence of mind of a mortally wounded Royal Marine officer, Major Marvey, who flooded the magazines, saved the flagship from blowing up – he was posthumously awarded the VC. With fires raging from a further six hits, the *Lion* pulled out of the line of battle. At 1603

hours the *Von der Tann* landed three shells on the stern of the *Indefatigable*. As she pulled out, belching smoke, a further two 11-inch (28-cm) shells crashed into her forward turret; in a sheet of vivid orange flame her magazine exploded, tearing the ship apart. Debris was flung high into the air as she turned-turtle and rapidly sunk, shrouded in brown cordite smoke. A German destroyer picked up two survivors; the rest of her crew – nearly 1,000 men – went down with the ship. When the *Queen Mary* 'opened out like a puffball' spewing metal everywhere, Beatty remarked to his flag-captain, 'There seems to be something wrong with our damn ships, Chatfield'. There was – insufficient armour to protect their magazines – a fault that was to repeat itself in the Second World War when the 'Mighty Hood' blew up. The *Tiger*, after swinging away to miss the sinking *Queen Mary*, picked up her survivors, nine out of a complement of 1,285.

Reduced to four battle-cruisers, and

Above: Dreadnoughts HMS Revenge and HMS Hercules deploy into position at Jutland.

Below: The main armour of a British battleship swings onto target during the First World War.

facing an apparently undamaged enemy, Beatty found things beginning to look desperate when the 15-inch (38-cm) battleships began firing salvoes at an incredible 19,000 yards (17,400 m). The *Barham*, *Valiant*, *Warspite* and *Malaya* had been steaming for an hour to reach the action, and their salvoes, far more accurate than those of the battle-cruisers, were soon crashing into the German ships whose 11-inch (28-cm) guns were out of range and could not hit back. Now hopelessly out-gunned, it was Hipper's turn to be worried, but he continued to engage the enemy, anxious to hold on until the arrival of the High Seas Fleet. The German destroyers, racing for a torpedo attack, were counterattacked by British destroyers, and a dis-

orderly action broke out, with the big ships adding to the confusion by opening up with their secondary armament. Weaving in and out of the columns of water flung up by shells and obscured by billowing smoke, the destroyers pressed home their attacks on the capital ships and fought among themselves. Not a single torpedo found its mark, but the *Nestor* sank two German destroyers, before being hit herself and going down along with the *Nomad*.

The *Lion* was frantically flashing the squadron to break off the action and run north. Scheer had arrived with his battleships and Beatty intended to lead him towards Jellicoe's Grand Fleet which was steaming south. Yet again the signalling on the bridge of the *Lion* was at fault, and it

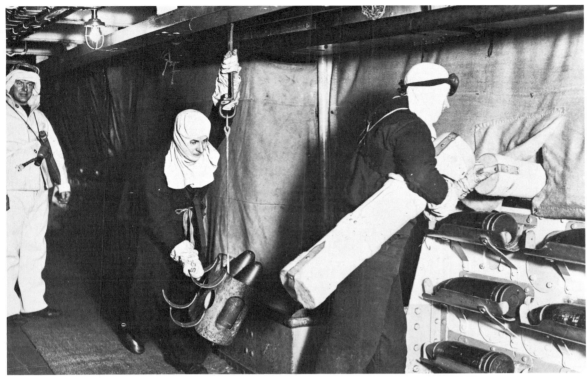

was some time before Rear-Admiral Evan-Thomas, commanding the four battleships, became aware of Beatty's manoeuvre. As his ships ponderously hauled round to head north, they came within range of the guns of the High Seas Fleet. The *Barham* and *Malaya* were soon hit by the concentrated fire and suffered considerable casualties, but their return fire had hit the leading German battleships, the *Grosse Kurfürst* and *Markgraf*. Dodging and weaving, steering by 'the last enemy salvo', the British battleships needed all their superior speed to escape. Confident of his superiority over the enemy, a jubilant Scheer ordered a general pursuit. Jellicoe, aware of the action, sent three battle-cruisers of the *Invincible* class on ahead to join Beatty. They arrived at 1726 hours, just as he had stopped his 'run to the north', to re-engage the German battle-cruisers in an effort to stop them seeing and reporting the imminent arrival of the Grand Fleet. Now it was the turn of Beatty's battle-cruisers to inflict damage on the enemy: the *Lützow* and *Derfflinger* were badly hit; fires were raging on the *Seydlitz*; and all the *Von der Tann*'s 11-inch (28-cm) guns were out of action.

Although gaining further successes, Scheer realized the growing danger of his position. Ahead of him the Grand Fleet steamed across his van in a single line that stretched for nine miles (4 km), each end disappearing in the mist; Jellicoe, the best naval tactician of the day, had completely out-manoeuvred him. Crashing broadsides from the extended line of British battleships tore into a van of the High Seas Fleet; the *Lützow* was crippled and other battle-

cruisers were heavily damaged. It was small consolation to Scheer that the battle-cruiser *Invincible*, silhouetted against the lowering sun, took a salvo on her midships turrets and blew in two, her two halves standing up on the shallow Jutland Bank 'like gravestones to her 1,026 dead' – there were only five survivors. The armoured cruiser *Defence* went down at about the same time. An anxious Scheer ordered a 'battle turnaway', the only way out of the trap, and one by one the German battleships made a complete 180°-degree turn to head south under cover of a smoke screen laid down by the destroyers.

Anticipating this move, Jellicoe swung the Grand Fleet to starboard at 1856 hours, taking up a southerly course that would put him between Scheer and his bases. At that point Scheer 'went against all the rules' as the official history of the German Navy put it. Altering course, he not only brought his fleet within 10,000 yards (9,000 m) of the enemy, but allowed Jellicoe to 'Cross the "T"' once again. In desperation, with British shells tearing into his leading ships, he ordered a second 'battle turnaway', and with clockwork precision, his fleet took up a reciprocal course, this time saved by Hipper's battle-cruisers. Led by the *Derfflinger*, they began their 'death ride', following Scheer's order to 'Charge the enemy. Ram. Ships denoted are to attack without regard to consequences'. Fifteen-inch (38-cm) shells tore away the *Derfflinger*'s after-turrets; the *Von der Tann*, her control-turret blown apart, had only one gun still firing. Hipper ordered in his destroyers for a torpedo attack from 7,000

The damaged battle-cruiser Seydlitz in Wilhelmshaven harbour after the Battle of Jutland.

yards (6,400 m), and although not one of the 28 torpedoes found its mark and six destroyers were put out of action and a seventh was sunk, they caused the British battleships to change course away from Scheer. This gallant action saved the High Seas Fleet. The German Admiral's second 'battle turnaway' had gone unnoticed in the gathering gloom, the billowing gun-smoke and the screen laid down by the destroyers.

By 2035 hours the fleet engagement was over. Jellicoe had no intention of fighting a night action and the fleeing German battleships were allowed to fight their way through the screen of British light cruisers and destroyers that harried them through-out the night. They got back safely to harbour with only the loss of the old pre-Dreadnought battleship *Pommern*, sunk by a torpedo, and the battle-cruiser *Lützow*. The Germans made port first and were quick to claim a 'Great Naval Victory'. They had lost only one antiquated battle-ship, one battle-cruiser and four armoured cruisers, whereas the British had lost three modern battle-cruisers and three armoured cruisers. Germany had lost 2,551 men and the British had lost 6,094 men. Yet many of the German ships had been badly dam-aged, and their Admiral, twice out-ma-noeuvred, had to run for home. As one wag put it:

'The Germans cried aloud "We've won!"
But surely 'tis a curious view
That those are conquerors who run
And those the vanquished that pursue.'

The High Seas Fleet never again put to sea in force, but the Grand Fleet was equally tied up at Scapa Flow, watching in case the High Seas Fleet ever should. The best officers and ratings from the High Seas Fleet were transferred to the U-Boat Arm in an all-out effort that very nearly brought the Allies to their knees. Morale plum-meted as the German battleships swung about their buoys in harbour, and when Hipper, newly appointed as Chief of Naval Staff, tried to get them once again to sea, the crews mutinied.

On the British side there was much heart-searching. Deck armour around the turrets of capital ships was strengthened; the manufacture of cordite was examined, and more attention was given to the quality control of shells – many had exploded prematurely at Jutland before they had pierced the German armour.

The Underwater Menace

It was during the 16th century that naval strategists first seriously considered the notion of an underwater ship, a ship that could creep up on an enemy fleet unseen, deliver a lightning attack and disappear again under the waves. William Bourne, an Elizabethan interested in, among other things, ships and their design, turned his attention to 'submersible' ships. He wrote in his *Inventions and Devices* of 1578, '. . . also it is possible to make a ship or boat that may goe under the water unto the bottome, and so come up againe at your pleasure'. His design never got off the drawing board, but it is quite clear from his drawings and notes that he had stumbled onto the successful basic principle of underwater craft that has since developed over the years into the present day nuclear submarine, '. . . that anything that sinketh, is heavier than the proportion of so much water, and if it be lighter than the magnitude of so much water, then it swimmeth or appeareth above the water'.

His 'submersible' boat, designed in the form of the hull of an Elizabethan galleon, had two leather ballast tanks which allowed sea water in below the waterline, causing the boat to sink. Buoyancy was restored by the submariners in the flotation chambers turning screw presses that forced the water out again. Sound though the theory was, Bourne gave no indication how his 'submersible' would be propelled underwater. Also, although he provided a hollow mast for admitting air into the boat, subsequent efforts in the use of manpower in propelling underwater craft would seem to indicate that his operators would soon have been exhausted by their efforts.

This was confirmed some 40 years later in the oar-powered 'submarine' of Cornelius van Drebbel, a Dutch inventor. Discarding Bourne's principles of buoyan-cy, he designed an underwater craft that was ballasted until it lay awash, then forced under and propelled by oars. Van Drebbel was sufficiently persuasive to convince King James I of its value, and demonstrated his invention before him on the River Thames in 1620. According to record, it travelled at a depth of between 12 and 15 ft (3.7 and 4.6 m) from Westminster to Greenwich, a distance of nearly 4 miles (6 km). This is hardly likely as there was no provision made for replacing the air that the rowers breathed.

Further attempts to build submarines followed, with varying degrees of success; like the early 'birdmen' who took to the air, many of the early submariners often paid with their lives, either drowning or suffocating to death – fears that have remained with submariners through the ages. The first real submarine was built by a Frenchman. de Son, in 1653. An ambitious craft, made of wood covered with greased leather, it was 72 ft (22 m) long, contained enough air to keep a man alive for three hours and was fitted with a paddle wheel driven by a clockwork motor, the first submarine to be propelled by mechanical means. De Son's claims for it were no less ambitious, 'he doeth undertake in one day to destroy a hondered Ships, can goe from Rotterdam to London and back againe in one day, and in six weeks to goe to the East Indiens, and run as swift as a bird can flye, no fire, nor Storme, nor Bullets can hinder her, unless it please God'. Unfortunately its clockwork motor was too weak to move it through the water, and on its trials it remained motionless. The lack of a suitable propulsion unit was to restrict the development of the submarine throughout the 17th and 18th centuries. One ill-fated attempt was made by a Plymouth ship's carpenter, Day, in 1773. By attaching

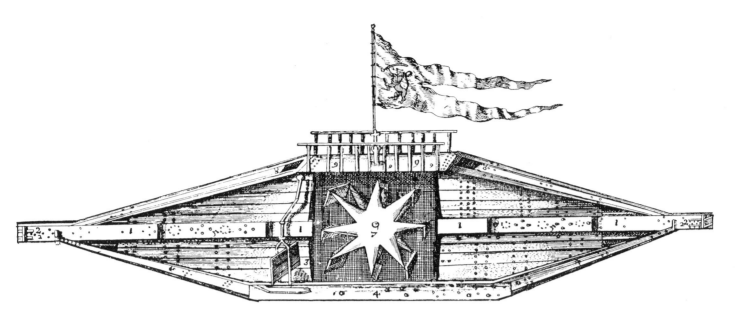

De Son's submersible, built in 1653. His claims for her performance were more than ambitious.

heavy rocks to his submarine he was able to sink it to a depth of 30 ft (9 m) in Plymouth Sound, and raise it to the surface by releasing the rocks by means of a mechanical contraption inside the boat. On his second attempt the mechanism failed to work and Day and his submarine sank 132 ft (40 m) to the bottom, where the pressure of the water crushed the boat.

As ever, it was the needs of war that brought about the more startling developments in submarines. Young David Bushnell, a graduate of Yale University and an ardent Republican, sought a new weapon with which to break the stranglehold of the British fleet blockading the Atlantic seaboard of America. With just a handful of hastily converted merchantmen to combat the strength of the Royal Navy, he reasoned that only a craft that could approach the blockading ships unseen would have a chance of doing any real damage. He came up with the *Turtle*. Later, in 1778, Bushnell wrote to Thomas Jefferson, 'The external shape of the sub-marine vessel bore some resemblance to two upper tortoise shells of equal size joined together: the place of entrance into the vessel being represented by the opening made by the swell of the shells at the head of the animal. This inside was capable of containing the operator, and air, sufficient to support him thirty minutes without receiving fresh air.'

This curiously shaped craft was held upright by a 700-lb (318-kg) keel, 200 lb (91 kg) of which was detachable in an emergency. Inside the *Turtle*, the operator was presented with a most complex set of controls: a foot-operated push valve to flood the ballast tanks; two hand-operated pumps to force out the sea water; a rudder-bar crank; a propeller-operating crank; an

ascent and descent propeller; and the all-important bomb-release screw. The bomb, a 150-lb (68-kg) charge of gunpowder in an oak container, was attached by rope to the bomb-release screw, which would, all being well, be embedded in the enemy's keel – the bomb, lighter than the water it displaced, would float upwards to nestle against the keel of the ship. After a series of highly successful trials, on the night of 6 September 1776, the *Turtle* was towed down the Hudson River by two rowing boats. The tow was then slipped to allow the tide to carry her down to the British blockade ships, anchored off Plateau Island. Inside the *Turtle*, Sergeant Ezra Lee cranked desperately to get her back on course as she was swept past her target by the over-strong tide. Ringing wet with sweat from his efforts, Lee at last manoeuvred the *Turtle* directly below the hull of Lord Howe's flagship, the 64-gun *Eagle*. Bushnell had considered every point bar one: he had not taken into account that British ships serving abroad were copper-sheafed against the Toredo worm, and although Lee tried in several places, he was unable to screw through to attach the bomb. With the rapid approach of daylight, he had to give up the attempt, and surfacing, was carried upstream by the incoming tide. A guard boat spotted him and gave chase, but he deterred them by releasing the fused bomb – the resulting explosion was sufficiently violent to suggest that had it gone off under the *Eagle*, she would have gone down. Other attempts made were frustrated by the good look-out maintained on the ships. Bushnell's *Turtle* itself may have been unsuccessful, but she set a pattern that would be put to good effect by the manned torpedoes of the Second World War.

The Submarine Begins to Take Shape

A fellow American, Robert Fulton, constructed a model of an underwater craft that began to take on the shape and attributes of a modern submarine; it had an ellipsoid shape, flooding valves, a conning tower and diving planes. The 21-ft (6.4-m) *Nautilus*, constructed of copper over an iron frame, was designed to operate at a depth of 25 ft (7.6 m) carrying a crew of three. Not fitted with a periscope, it was proposed that she would rise sufficiently out of the water to be able to take sightings through the thick glass scuttles set into her hemispherical conning tower. Her underwater power came from a hand-cranked screw, but on the surface, assisted by a retractable sail, she could make from 2 to 3 knots, given a favourable wind. Her attack weapon was an explosive charge trailed at the end of a line, which was to be attached to an enemy's hull by means of a spike rather than a screw.

Fulton, another convinced Republican, offered *Nautilus* to France for use in her war against Britain. Also a convinced capitalist with an eye for business, he asked to be paid 4,000 francs for every gun on any ship that his submarine sank – in the case of a first-rater, this would have amounted to 400,000 francs in gold (at least £4,000,000 in modern terms). Although interested, this was too much for the impoverished French Directory and, after some haggling, it turned Fulton's offer down, as did other European governments. By 1800 he was back in France, where Napoleon, the newly elected First Consul, realized the submarine's potential and granted Fulton 10,000 francs to build a full-scale model.

On a full trial in Brest harbour, *Nautilus* blew an old schooner sky high, much to the consternation of the French admirals, who saw in Fulton's infernal machine a weapon so terrible that their conscience would not let them agree to its use. By then Napoleon had lost interest and the *Nautilus* was finally rejected in 1804. Disillusioned, Fulton offered his submarine to Britain (which he was able to do with a 'clear' conscience after the Peace of Amiens). The Prime Minister, William Pitt, was more than interested and authorized a demonstration in which a target brig, the *Dorothy*, was blown in two off Walmer in Kent. A powerful committee, set up to

The unsuccessful attack on HMS Eagle *by USS* Turtle.

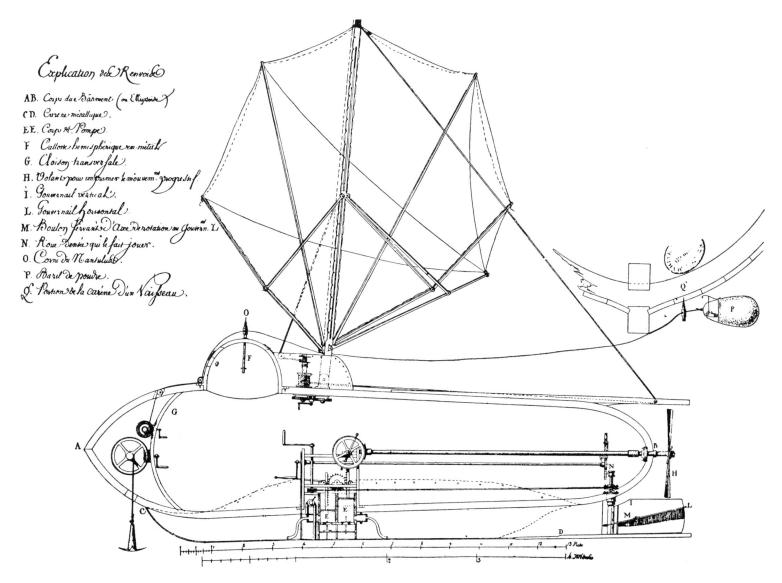

Robert Fulton tried, with little success, to interest both France and Great Britain in his submarine, Nautilus.

observe the demonstration, was so appalled at the result that it refused to have anything to do with Fulton's invention. Reluctantly, Pitt had to give up the idea, particularly after Admiral Lord St. Vincent had written, 'Pitt was the greatest fool that ever existed to encourage a mode of warfare which those who commanded the seas did not want, and which, if successful, would at once deprive them of it.' Fulton returned to the U.S. to run a successful steamship line and plan an 80-ft (24-m) long steam-driven submarine, the *Mute*, but he died during her trials in 1815 and she never went into commission.

After being sent to St. Helena, Napoleon once again showed an interest in submarines, this time as a means of escape. Friends of Bonaparte approached a daring, resourceful and completely unscrupulous Englishman, Thomas Johnson, the famous 'Hampshire smuggler', and offered him £40,000 to rescue the erstwhile Emperor and take him to the United States. Realizing that the Royal Navy would be on the watch for any surface ships approaching the island, Johnson set his fertile brain to

design a submarine. The plan might well have worked had not Napoleon died before the 100-ft (30.5-m) submarine was completed. Later, Johnson built his underwater craft and carried out trials in the Thames. During one trial he all but lost his life when his boat fouled an anchor cable, trapping him below for an hour or more.

The First Underwater Escape

A Bavarian artillery sergeant, Wilhelm Bauer, gained the unenviable distinction of making the first underwater escape from a submarine which was lying crippled on the sea bed. In 1851 he built a submarine called the *Seetaucher* in German or *Le Plongeur Marin* in French, which translates as 'Sea Diver' in English. This was the first underwater craft to submerge by diving at an angle under forward propulsion. Built of sheet iron, she had a double bottom to which water was admitted to give her negative buoyancy. Once awash, a heavy weight was moved backwards and forwards by means of a big wheel which caused her to dive bows first in a series of dips. As in the earlier submarines, forward motion was achieved by hand-cranked propeller. Although of limited attack value, she was successful in causing the Danish fleet blockading the German coast to keep a respectful distance.

During an exercise in Kiel harbour in February 1851, Bauer and two of his assistants accidentally took the 'Sea Diver' down to 60 ft (18 m). The pressure at that depth was too great for the thin iron plates; ominous creaks turned into a loud crack as the plates buckled and jets of water shot through the seams. By sheer willpower, Bauer convinced his two panic-stricken assistants that their one slender hope of survival lay in flooding the boat to equalize the pressure. Slowly the boat was filled with water while the crew gasped in the remaining air trapped in the top of the submarine. The hatch was opened and all three men shot to the surface. Whether his two companions remained submariners after that experience is unknown, but Bauer went on to build a submarine for the Russian Navy, *Le Diable Marin* or 'Sea Devil'. He made 134 successful dives in this 52-ft (16-m) long submersible, built at Leningrad (St. Petersberg) in 1855. Czar Alexander II held a naval review in Kronstadt harbour to celebrate his coronation at which Bauer caused a sensation by diving

with a small orchestra aboard. At the royal salute, the submerged band struck up 'God Preserve the Czar', the Russian national anthem. This made a marked impression on the ships at the review, who could hear the music drifting through the water.

'Davids'

To combat the Federal blockade during the American Civil War, the Confederate Navy built a series of semi-submersible torpedo boats which they christened 'Davids', an allusion to the fact that they saw themselves as 'giant killers' opposing Federal 'Goliaths'. The submarine had begun to take on a cigar-shaped hull, which offered better underwater performance and overcame the chief limitation of previous designs by incorporating a steam engine as a power unit. The 'Davids' were not, in fact, submarines. They could only be trimmed down until they were awash; their narrow superstructure containing the hatchway and the funnel remained above the surface of the water. The danger of this was underlined when the very first model (actually named *David*) was swamped during her trials by the wash of a passing steamship and sank like a stone. Despite this castastrophe, volunteers came forward to man her once she had been salvaged, and under the command of Lieutenant

A confederate David torpedo boat, aground in Charleston harbour during the Civil War.

Glassell, she made a torpedo attack on the Federal ironclad *New Ironsides*. Although she damaged the ironclad by blowing a hole in her side, the *David* herself was swamped by the explosion which occurred only 20 ft (6 m) from her bows, and sank – only Glassell and two members of the crew managed to escape.

The barrel of gunpowder used by Bushnell and Fulton was considered too crude, so the more sophisticated spar torpedo had been developed (though it is doubtful whether the two former designers would have regarded such a suicidal weapon as an improvement). The spar torpedo consisted of a copper case filled with 134 lb (61 kg) of gunpowder carried at the end of a 30-ft (9-m) spar attached to the bows of the submarine. Reverting to manpower, Captain Horace L. Hunley designed a true submarine which, using a stern propeller cranked by eight men, could travel on the surface at a speed of 7.5 knots, providing the sea was dead calm. Tapered ends containing ballast tanks were added to an existing cylindrical iron boiler to form the 30-ft (9-m) hull of the submarine, which held enough air to last the crew for two or three hours. She had two hydroplanes forward to keep her below the surface, and a conning tower from which the commander could steer the boat. Built at Mobile,

Alabama, she was shipped by rail to Charleston for her trials. These proved disastrous. On 5 October 1863, water thrown up by a passing ship flooded into her open hatch and took her down with the whole of her crew including Hunley. Undeterred, the Confederates salvaged her and again put her into commission, naming her the CSS *Hunley* after her designer. Surprisingly enough there was no difficulty in raising a crew of volunteers to man her, and under the command of Lieutenant George E. Dixon of the 21st Alabama Infantry Regiment, she was prepared for action.

On the moonlit night of 7 February 1864, the *Hunley* slipped silently out of Charleston harbour; Dixon steered her towards the blockading Federal sloop *Housatonic*, which was anchored in 28 ft (8.5 m) of water at the channel entrance. At first the look-outs mistook the *Hunley* for a floating log, but as the supposed log continued to come straight at them, they realized their mistake. Frantic orders were shouted to slip cable but it was too late. The submarines redoubled their efforts at the cranking handles and the *Hunley* shot forward, smashing her spar torpedo into the side of the Federal ship. The violent explosion which followed tore a great hole in the *Housatonic* and she rapidly sank, taking the

The CSS Hunley, *before her ill-fated attack on the* Housatonic.

The Locomotive Torpedo

Naval cadets at torpedo drill with a Whitehead torpedo aboard HMS Drake.

Hunley down with her. No one aboard the sloop was drowned, but the whole crew of the submarine perished. Some years later while examining the wreck of the *Houasatonic*, divers discovered the hull of the *Hunley* with nine skeletons aboard.

The attack may have ended in disaster for the *Hunley*, but it confirmed what many naval observers had believed for some time, that the submarine was a weapon with a terrible destructive potential. Naval strategists listed the points they considered necessary to make the submarine a wholly effective weapon of war:

1. A powerful engine to drive her on the surface.
2. A separate engine to drive her underwater.
3. A means of conning whilst underwater.
4. A method of escape for the crew should the vessel be sunk.
5. An adequate supply of air.

The Locomotive Torpedo

However, most important of all, they sought a torpedo that could be fired at a distance, preferably from underwater. This torpedo was not long in coming. In 1865 Austrian artilleryman Captain Luppis invented a clockwork-driven craft (with an explosive charge) that could be guided by lines attached to its rudder. From this primitive device, Robert Whitehead, the English manager of a Fiume engineering works, devised the 'locomotive torpedo', the weapon that was to turn the submarine into so deadly a menace. Cigar-shaped, with a gun-cotton warhead, it was powered by a compressed-air motor that drove a rear propeller. Constant depth was maintained by a depth-keeping mechanism, and its course maintained by two fixed rudders. In 1877 the Whitehead torpedo had a range of 1,000 yards (900 m) and a speed of 7 knots. Rapid development in speed and reliability and an increase in range followed. By the turn of the century it was a very powerful naval weapon, difficult to evade. Running silently below the surface like a giant grey shark, the 'fish', as it became nicknamed, could only be detected by the wake of bubbles sent up by its compressed-air motor.

Experiments in Propulsion

The next 30 years saw remarkable developments in submarines; every country was now anxious to provide its navy with this most formidable underwater weapon – no longer were fleet admirals bothered by conscience. The increased efficiency of steam engines and the invention of the internal-combustion engine solved the problem of surface propulsion – speeds of between 12 and 16 knots were achieved. The problem of propulsion below the surface was solved by using a battery-operated electric motor which gave speeds of up to 8 knots and which did not use up any precious oxygen when running. Among the designers who added most to the increased efficiency of the submarine were Holland and Lake of the United States, Nordenfelt of Sweden, Goubet of France and Garrett of Britain. Submarines began to take on a more sleek, yet somehow more sinister, shape as designers sought to eliminate underwater resistance and drag by giving them either a single hull with saddle ballast tanks, or a double hull with internal saddle tanks.

In 1887 the combined efforts of Garrett and Nordenfelt produced a submarine that made its debut at the Royal Naval Review to celebrate the Golden Jubilee of Queen Victoria. The *Nordenfelt No. 2* was 125 ft (38 m) long and 12 ft (3.7 m) in diameter. Its maximum surface speed of 14 knots was provided by a steam engine, which also gave it an underwater speed of 5 knots. The hull, generally constructed of $^5/_{16}$-inch (8-mm) plate with 1-inch (2.5-cm) plate on the top side for protection against smaller weaponry, had taken on the fish-like shape that was to become so familiar in the two World Wars of the following century. But *Nordenfelt No. 2* had two serious drawbacks. Try as they might, the two designers had been unable to achieve reliable depth-keeping; once a torpedo had been fired there was no compensation for the resulting change in weight. This was a design fault that would eventually be corrected by a more efficient distribution of the ballast tanks. A more serious drawback was underwater propulsion. The *Nordenfelt No. 2* had an underwater range of only 20 miles (32 km) and by the end of the run, the temperature in the engine room had risen to an unbearable 150°F (40°C).

The answer to this major problem – an engine that could operate without drawing oxygen from the atmosphere of the boat – came from an unlikely source. While the more powerful navies of Britain, France, the U.S.A. and Germany were persevering with, and improving upon, the Garrett-Nordenfelt designs, a young Spanish naval lieutenant, Isaac Peral, was building an electric-powered submarine that could cruise below the surface as long as the air in the boat lasted. Powered by two 30 hp electric motors driven by 450 accumulator batteries, it had a maximum surface speed of 11 knots and a submerged speed of 8 knots. Three smaller auxiliary motors provided the power to pump out the ballast tanks. Fitted with a periscope which allowed the commander to con below the surface and armed with a single torpedo tube, it had all the makings of a powerful weapon, despite its depth-keeping problems. The Spanish Government, however, harping on its drawbacks rather than its merits, refused to allow Peral to build an improved version of his 'boat'. It was only when the Spanish cruisers were being sunk with impunity at Manila during the Spanish-American War of 1898, that the government began to regret its hasty decision. The American Admiral Dewey had no such doubts when he wrote, 'If they had had two of those things [Peral's submarines] at Manila, I could never have held it with the ships I had.'

Once it was realized that the battery-driven electric motor was the key to underwater navigation, France took the lead in the design of both the electric motors and the submarines themselves. France's most successful designer up to this time had been Gustave Zedé. After building three small submarines, 60 ft (18.3 m) long, all versions of the *Gymnote* (Eel), he constructed a much larger boat, 159 ft (48.5 m) in length, carrying three 17.7-inch (45.0-cm) torpedoes fired from a bow tube. By the time all the snags resulting from her size had been ironed out, the *Gustave Zedé* and her successor, the *Morse*, were outdated by a craft which was being built as the result of an open competition. The French Government was looking for a 200-ton (203-tonne) submarine with a surface range of 100 miles (160 km) and a submerged range of 10 miles (16 km) – a seaworthy, hard-hitting boat with good depth-keeping qualities. The winner was a Frenchman, Maxime Laubeuf, whose *Narval* of 1899 was the true forerunner of the modern submarine. What made Laubeuf's design unique was the introduction of two separate propulsion units for surface and underwater operation, and a double hull to provide ballast tanks and fuel storage. The surface engine, an oil-fired steam engine realizing a speed of just under 10 knots, was also used to power a dynamo used to recharge her batteries – underwater she could make 5.3 knots. She was far stronger than her predecessors; she had an outside hull of ¼-inch (6.4-mm) steel plate and an inner one of ½-inch (12.7-mm) plate. Armed with four torpedoes, the *Narval* had only one serious drawback. The need to shut-down her boiler before submerging meant that she took 15 minutes to dive and during that time she was completely vulnerable to attack by surface ships.

The United States Navy, following the tradition set by Bushnell, Fulton, Hunley and others, also began to take a particular interest in submarines, seeing them as a valuable addition to a growing fleet. Their two chief designers, Simon Lake and John P. Holland, competed for a government contract. Although Holland won it, Lake's boat was stronger, sounder and more ad-

John Philip Holland, 1840–1914.

vanced in design. By adding two hydroplanes – one pair forward and one pair aft – Lake demonstrated that it was possible to keep a submerged boat on an even keel, even at the lowest speeds. He lost the contract simply because he failed to realize the attack potential of a submerged warship. Lake saw the role of the submarine as a purely defensive one: laying on the bottom she could send out a diver to cut underwater telegraph cables and disrupt enemy minefields, moving along the sea bed by means of a set of retractable wheels. Thus Holland's more aggressive design was accepted, not only by the U.S. Navy, but by most of the other navies of the world.

By the end of the 19th century, the submarine was accepted as an established part of all the world's major fleets, with the notable exception of Great Britain – but even she was forced to undertake a submarine programme in 1901. In 1903 France led the field with ten boats in service and 33 near completion, virtually as many as the rest of the world's navies put together. Great Britain had nine, the United States eight, Russia nine, Germany four, and Italy six. But the race was on and, once it committed itself, the Royal Navy

Below: Lake's submarine, surfaced in calm water.

Bottom: HMS Holland I with her crew, in 1901.

instigated an intensive building programme that was to give it a vast superiority in numbers at the outbreak of the First World War. However, two significant events occurred before then: the Germans built their fast 'Unterseeboot', the U.1, and in January 1904, the French put a diesel engine into the submarine *Aigrette*. The concept of a dual propulsion system was now an established fact, as was the use of electric engines for running submerged. Where navies differed was in the choice of a surface engine. France favoured steam until 1905, while the British favoured petrol-driven internal-combustion engines till as late as 1907. The first made diving a slow, tedious and potentially dangerous business; the other presented the danger of petrol fumes being ignited by an electric spark which would cause an explosion within the boat. Both dangers were eliminated by the introduction of the new diesel internal-combustion engine which ran on oil, a far less volatile fuel than petrol. Strangely enough, the Imperial German Navy, that was, in the future, to exploit the potential of submarine warfare far more than any other fleet, was among the last to adopt the diesel engine, even though a German invented it. In the last few years before war broke out, there was a frantic scramble among the major world powers to strengthen their navies, including the submarine arm.

Outbreak of the First World War

When the First World War finally broke out in 1914, the Allies – Great Britain, France, Italy and Russia – had 168 submarines to the 35 U-Boats of Germany and Austria.

NUMBER OF SUBMARINES AT THE OUTBREAK OF WAR

Gt. Britain	77 boats
France	45 boats – 25 being built
America	35 boats – 6 being built
Russia	28 boats – 3 being built
Italy	18 boats – 2 being built
Germany	29 boats
Austria	6 boats – 1 being built

At the beginning of the First World War, neither side fully realized the potential of the submarine as a naval weapon; both rather saw it as a short-range reconnaissance tool, useful for reporting the movement of enemy surface ships. Both were equally reluctant to make a direct attack on an enemy vessel, warship or mechantman. Such an act of ruthless aggression, delivered with complete surprise, could only lead to all-out total war. Then on 6 August 1914, the U-Boat Arm of the Imperial German Navy went over to the offensive. Intended to test their reliability and range of operation as much as anything, ten U-Boats were ordered to patrol as far as the Orkneys – far, far further than any had travelled during peacetime. Ostensibly they were to bring back information concerning the disposition of the British Grand Fleet. This operation led to the loss of two boats. U.15 was rammed by the *Birmingham* as she lay on the surface, immobilized by engine failure, the sharp prow of the cruiser slicing through the submarine like butter. U.13, on the other hand, simply failed to return – 'reported missing' was to become a common term. U.9 broke down on the second day and was forced to return to her base at Kiel, but this boat was to play an important part in the all-out U-Boat campaign that was about to open.

In London, the Admiralty, while applauding the action of the cruiser *Birmingham* in sinking the U.15, was disturbed by the fact that a German submarine could operate so far from her base. The erstwhile inviolate base at Scapa Flow in the Orkneys was now at risk. Panic measures were taken to scatter the heavy units of the Grand Fleet round other bases as a temporary measure until the defences of the main base could be strengthened by sealing its entrance channels with anti-submarine nets and blockships. In fact two German U-Boats did later penetrate the base, but both were sunk. If the British were worried, the Germans were delighted. Overnight they found themselves holding a weapon of undreamed potential; the naval planners in Berlin began to consider how to use it.

The U-Boat Menace

The U-Boat that came into service in the middle of 1914 was a hard-hitting fighting ship with little thought given to comfort and living conditions while at sea. Crammed with machinery and instruments, engines and batteries, torpedoes, ammunition and food supplies, ballast and fuel tanks, there was little room left for the 35 officers and men. Conditions after a few days at sea were far from pleasant. A U-Boat could now cruise for 4,440 miles (7,100 km). It could stay under for 80 miles (128 km) at a stretch, which at a speed of 5

PERISCOPES

VENTILATION SHAFTS

METAL TAIL FLAG

WHEEL FOR STEERING
WHEN ON THE SURFACE

MAIN
HATCH

COMPASS. The Needle
Points are reflected to
the interior of Boat
by a number of mirrors

CONNING
TOWER

TORPEDO
HATCH

EXHAUST PIPE
FROM ENGINES

WATER LINE

LIFE SAVING
HELMET

AIR
PUMP

LOCKERS

COMPRESSED
AIR
CHAMBERS

AIR LOCK
END
REMOVED

18'? WHITEHEAD
TORPEDO

WHITEHEAD
TORPEDO

AIR
COMPRESSORS

DECK

OIL & BALLAST
TANKS

knots, could mean 16 hours without fresh air before the boat could surface, usually at night in areas where there were unlikely to be any enemy warships. The conning-tower hatch would be thrown open and the diesel engines ignited; falteringly at first in the stale air, they would soon mount into a thudding rhythm, drawing blessed clean air throughout the boat. The constant damp air and unsanitary conditions did little for the health of the crews, and respiratory diseases were all too common. On the surface the boats rolled badly in a heavy sea; many of the crew, especially the new hands, were seasick – another stench to permeate the boat and mingle with the smell of sweat, cooking and diesel oil. With only room for look-outs on the bridge, a good captain saw to it that as many hands as possible shared look-out duty, and whenever possible the engineers left their reaking engine room, in turn, to breathe in some fresh air.

Clothes tucked away in kit bags became covered in mould. Bedding was less likely to suffer as it was always kept warm – in these cramped conditions, the off-watch crew flopped into recently vacated beds as soon as the new watch turned out. Food, particularly the bread taken aboard, also quickly got mouldy, but the U-Boat crews were always given the best food available at the start. As the war went on, the Germans became aware that their best chance of bringing Great Britain to her knees lay with the U-Boat Service. U-Boat morale was high due to their startlingly mounting successes, and the cream of the officers and men of the High Seas Fleet began to be

transferred to the 'Unterseeboote'. The officers lived in much the same fashion as the men, eating the same food, cooked in a minute galley; their wardroom was a passageway for all and sundry on watch; their bunks were cut off only by a curtain. This made for a close-knit unit. Although the rigid protocol of the surface ships had, by necessity, to be relaxed, a U-Boat's ships company was a highly disciplined body that went into action like a well-oiled machine. U-Boat commanders were picked for their initiative, daring and quick reactions, but even more important was their ability to handle and get the best results from their crew. For the good of the whole, they had to be ruthless at times – for example, they would have to shoot anyone who became hysterical during a depth-charge attack or when trapped on the sea bed. Forced upon them, this attitude towards their own men goes some way to explain the ruthlessness they later showed towards the enemy.

At this time these 750-ton (762-tonne) U-Boats were 212 ft (64.6 m) in length with a 20-ft 9-inch (6.3-m) beam, and usually cruised at 8 knots on the surface, with a maximum speed of 5 knots submerged. They were armed with two 20-inch (51-cm) torpedo tubes in the bow (this was later increased to four) and two in the stern; they also carried a 4.1-inch (10.4-cm) deck gun, to be used mainly for surface attack against merchantmen.

As the war progressed, the German Navy, whose ships were pinned in their own bases, came to rely more and more on the U-Boat Arm, and gave priority to

Opposite: An artist's cut-away impression of a British submarine.

Below: Cut-away drawing of a German First World War U-Boat.

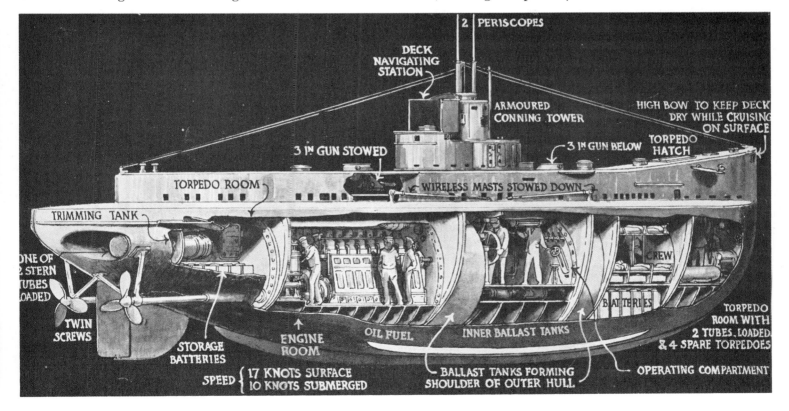

German submariners photographed aboard their UC.1-class U-Boat in the First World War.

improving U-Boat design and increasing its efficiency. By 1915 a standard boat had been adopted which, apart from minor adjustments, was to remain the German's general service U-Boat throughout the war. The 'Mittel-U' class, from U.57 upwards, displaced 750 tons (762 tonnes) on the surface and 830 tons (843 tonnes) submerged. They were faster and more reliable than the early boats, reaching speeds of between 15.5 and 17.5 knots on the surface from twin diesels, and 8 to 9 knots from twin electric motors when submerged. The performance was hardly bettered by the standard U-Boats in service during the Second World War. Once it was realized that they were involved in a war of attrition and that they were saddled with a surface fleet that at best could have only a nuisance value, the planners in the German Navy placed orders for two new types of U-Boats: the 'UC'-type minelayers and the little 'UB'-type coastal submarines, which, however, were later developed into larger boats and became the blueprint for the Second World War generation of U-Boats. The early types of this class, UB.1 to UB.17 were only 92 ft (28.0 m) long, displaced 143 tons (145 tonnes) submerged, had a cruising range of 1,600 miles (2,560 km) at a surface speed of 16.5 knots and one submerged of 5.5 knots. From UB.48 onwards, the displacement had reached 657 tons (668 tonnes) submerged, the range had increased to 8,500 miles (13,600 km) and the speeds to 13.5 and 7.5 knots respectively.

The first act of outright aggression occurred when the U.21 sank the British cruiser Pathfinder at the entrance to the Firth of Forth in September 1914. This boat was to gain even more fame in the Mediterranean under the command of Kapitän-Leutnant Hersing, one of the many U-Boat 'aces' to emerge from the First World War. Later in the month, another U-Boat ace, Kapitän-Leutnant Otto Weddingen, first sank the 12,000-ton (12,200-tonne) heavy cruiser Aboukir off the Dutch coast and then, in quick succession, the Crecy and Hogue, a total loss of 11,000 seamen. The cruisers had nick-named themselves the 'Live Bait Squadron', but they had expected to draw out only surface ships. When, three weeks later, Weddingen sank the cruiser Hawke off Aberdeen, with a loss of 500 officers and men, it brought home to Admiralty officials that they had an unexpected problem on their hands.

Defensive Strategies

Although, in itself, the loss of the old cruisers had little effect on the offensive power of the Grand Fleet, it nonetheless forced the various navies to set into motion defensive tactics to deal with this silent underwater menace. At first there was little that could be done to counter a U-Boat attack. Unless she surfaced, when she could be sunk by gunfire or rammed, the U-Boat was undetectable. The only answers appeared to be to screen battleships and heavy cruisers with a flotilla of fast destroyers whose bows had been strengthened for ramming or, if a tell-tale periscope were spotted, to outrun it – most capital ships could work up to 25 knots or more compared to a U-Boat's underwater speed of 5 knots. Ships also began to adopt zigzag courses which, although it made watch-keeping difficult, made it even more difficult for a U-Boat commander to calculate the run of his torpedoes. Under any circumstances, with a target running away from him at up to 30 knots, his calculations had to be swift and accurate.

While laying-to or at anchor, most of the larger ships were protected by anti-submarine nets which were sometimes fitted with small mines. The mine, once Britain had perfected a dependable one, became an effective weapon against the U-Boat menace. Sprinkled round the approaches to Britain's own naval bases and along the enemy coast, they accounted for one in four of the U-Boats lost during the First World War. However, without doubt the *unterseeboote* had the upper hand until the middle of 1916. Then two anti-submarine innovations came along that tipped the scales in favour of fast, manoeuvrable submarine killers such as destroyers and motor-torpedo boats. The depth-charge, a 300-lb (136-kg) bomb that could be pre-set to explode at any given depth by means of a hydrostatic device, could shatter a submarine's plates and send her to the bottom if it exploded close enough – particularly if it exploded beneath her. The force of an explosion in water is over twice as powerful as the equivalent explosion in air. Coupled to this, British scientists came up with an underwater listening device, a hydrophone which was capable of detecting the sound of an underwater electric motor and its direction.

All-Out U-Boat Warfare

For the first months of the war, the navies of both sides felt themselves bound by the Hague Convention and International Law. The harrying of merchant shipping carrying vital supplies was the job of the cruiser;

The beginning of the all-out U-Boat campaign in the First World War – the sinking of the Lusitania.

she would stop a merchantman, examine her papers, then either take off her crew and sink her by gunfire, or sail her home with a captive crew. Several events occurred that changed this, and by the middle of 1915 both sides were drifting towards total war. Great Britain relied on her maritime commerce for survival. By disrupting this, the Germans believed that they could bring the country to its knees. However, eight out of her nine cruisers operating outside the North Sea had been sunk or were firmly blockaded, without having done any appreciable damage to British shipping. The German Navy turned to the U-Boat Arm. When, in October 1914, *U.17* stopped, searched and sank the *Gitra*, her commander, Kapitän-Leutnant Feldkircher, opened up a devastating new form of naval warfare (even though a submarine had to surface to carry out such an attack, leaving herself highly vulnerable to surface gunfire and ramming). On 4 February 1915 Germany declared that the waters surrounding the British Isles were now a war zone – any of her ships found in this area would be sunk without warning. It was also added that it 'would not always be possible to identify neutral ships' which in consequence might inadvertently be attacked. Other factors mitigating against a neutral ship being recognized as such were the slow speed of submarines under water and the inadequate viewing of shipping through a periscope, especially in a heavy sea. U-Boat commanders had to make attack decisions quickly, sometimes in seconds, and the chance of viewing error was high.

Allied shipping losses grew alarmingly from 47,900 tons (48,700 tonnes) in January 1915, to a peak of 185,800 tons (188,800 tonnes) in August of that year. By the end of the war they had lost 12,850,814 tons (13,056,427 tonnes) – 5,531 ships. At one point the U-Boats came close to winning the war for Germany – a lesson well learned by naval planners of the future. But with the advent of the new anti-submarine weapons and the introduction of the convoy system, U-Boat losses became crippling. During the war the German Navy lost nearly 50 per cent of her submarines – 178 boats, representing 5,364 officers and men or 40 per cent of her U-Boat crews.

On 7 May 1915, during the build-up of submarine warfare, *U.20* torpedoed and sank the British passenger liner *Lusitania* on her way from New York to Liverpool, with 159 American nationals on board. World opinion was outraged by this unheralded attack on civilians, and it did much to make American opinion favour the Allies. It was the first inkling of the 'frontline' role that was to be played by civilians in future wars. The facts of the attack have never been fully clarified – claims and counter-claims have obscured the incident. A press release, issued by the German Embassy in the United States and printed in the New York newspapers, warned Americans of the possible danger of travelling on a British ship. Was the *Lusitania* armed? Was she carrying a large cargo of high explosives? Kapitän-Leutnant Schweiger, the U-Boat commander, put down a second explosion that occurred 'to the liner's boilers blowing up, or possibly coal or munitions'; the laconic entry in his log in no way suggests that he was surprised by the fierceness of the explosion. What evidence there is, seems to preclude the *Lusitania* being armed or carrying munitions.

When Schweiger brought up the *U.20* to periscope depth off Kinsale in Southern Ireland, he saw what he at first took to be a line of destroyers. Gradually, as the faster ship closed, he recognized her as the four-funnelled British liner *Lusitania*. In his report of the attack he claimed he had been warned to be on the look-out for troopships from Canada, and he had no hesitation in manoeuvring his boat bows onto the liner's beam and firing a bow salvo. The tell-tale trail of the torpedo was spotted by the masthead look-out aboard the *Lusitania*, but travelling at 40 knots, it hit the liner before she could swing away, and she began to sink by the bows. Passengers scrambled aboard the lifeboats and those that could not, jumped into the dead calm sea. However, many did drown and among their number were several Americans. Schweiger's attack had turned into a major political blunder.

At the end of the First World War, the major Allied navies, in no doubt as to the value of the submarine as a deadly military weapon, scrambled to get their hands on their share of the surrendered U-Boats. Basing their designs on these, they began building bigger cruiser submarines, particularly the American and Japanese navies. However, largest of them all was the giant French *Surcouf*. Displacing 4,304 tons (4,373 tonnes) submerged, she was 361 ft (110 m) long, with a surface speed of 18 knots and an underwater speed of 8 knots. She carried two 8-inch (20.3-cm) guns (the largest that could be mounted on a submarine under the Washington Disarma-

The French Surcouf, *the biggest submarine built between the Wars.*

ment Treaty of 1922), mounted in a single turret; eight 21.7-inch (55.1-cm) torpedoes; and four 15.7-inch (39.9-cm) torpedoes. She also had an aircraft hanger abaft the conning tower to house a spotter float-plane.

The Germans, although banned from having submarines under the Treaty of Versailles, kept abreast of current development by building submarines for other countries, and when Hitler repudiated the Treaty on coming to power, German shipyards were in the position to mount a major U-Boat programme. Basing their designs largely on First World War models, they eventually produced the Type VII U-Boat, which became the standard design for the U-Boat of the Second World War.

Type VII U-Boat

Displacement	769 tons (781 tonnes) (surfaced)
Length	220 ft (67 m)
Speed	17 knots (surfaced), 7.5 knots (submerged)
Armament	five 21-inch (53-cm) torpedo tubes – 14 torpedoes carried
Range	6,500 miles (10,400 km) at 12 knots (surfaced)

Even by submarine standards, the living conditions were primitive and the quarters cramped; German U-Boat crews looked with envy on what they considered to be the spacious conditions enjoyed by British and American submariners. At the outbreak of the Second World War, Germany had 56 modern U-Boats in commission with six more nearly completed – Britain had 38. Submarines by now had become more reliable and efficient, but it still took a particular type of courage to serve on one – accidents could always happen, even in peacetime.

A Peacetime Tragedy

On 1 June 1939, with war clouds gathering on the horizon, HMS *Thetis* chugged away from the docksides of her shipbuilders, Cammell Laird of Liverpool, for her first diving trials in Liverpool Bay. It was a glorious sunny day as Britain's latest 'T' class submarine cut through the calm, sparkling waters of the bay, towards the position of her first dive which was to be made in only 137 ft (42 m) of water. On the bridge, her captain, Lieutenant-Commander 'Sam' Bolus, was faintly uneasy; he could not rid his mind of Robert Ostler's words, 'I wish you didn't have to go, sir'. Ostler had such a strong premonition of doom that he had asked to be transferred to another boat. Bolus shook off his gloom. What could possibly go wrong during a shallow dive on such a beautiful day in a dead flat calm?

Below decks the off-watch crew and the 50 passengers aboard picnicked on beer and sandwiches. As well as her complement of 53 officers and men, *Thetis* had aboard Admiralty officials from London who had come to witness the trials, Captain H.P.K. Oram who was the flotilla commander, a number of submarine officers from other boats and a group of men from the shipyard who would operate the machinery under the direction of naval officers (the normal routine until a boat was taken into commis-

sion). There were 103 in all, far too many for an already cramped boat – but after all, it was only a day's outing.

Just before 1330 hours, Bolus gave the order 'Prepare to dive'. The bridge was cleared and then the command came, 'Flood ballast tanks'. Thousands of gallons of sea water surged into the submarine, but nothing happened. Making nearly 10 knots, she was hardly going under at all – 30 minutes later her conning tower was still halfway out of the water. Carrying no torpedoes, the weight of the *Thetis* forward should have been compensated by flooding 5 and 6 – the bottom two tubes. Bolus ordered his torpedo officer, Lieutenant Woods, to the forward torpedo space to investigate. Hurrying through the torpedo-stowage space, he stepped over the sill of the collision bulkhead's watertight door to

The cramped quarters of a First World War submarine.

join Torpedo Gunner's Mate, Chief Petty Officer Mitchell, and Leading Seaman Hambrook who were already there – the door itself was clamped open which was normal diving procedure. He opened the test-cock to number 6 tube and a few drops of water slopped out which indicated that it was partly full; no water at all seeped from number 5 – it had to be empty, its bow cap closed to the sea. Ordered to open the rear door of number 5 tube, Hambrook pulled on the door lever but it would not budge. Wood added his weight and with a crash the door flew open, flinging the two men against the collision bulkhead as the water roared into the boat. Unable to close the watertight door, they staggered up the already sloping deck of the torpedo stowage-space and slammed shut the door to the electric motor room behind them – if the salt water had reached the batteries the Thetis would soon have been filled with deadly chlorine gas. Despite blowing all ballast tanks, the bows of the boat dropped alarmingly as she dived to the bottom and sunk deep into the mud. The boat was kept at a 40-degree angle by the air in her ballast tanks. Racing her engines astern had no effect and when fuel and water were pumped out, the angle steepened to 60 degrees and 18 ft (5.5 m) of her stern protruded above the water. The air in a 'T' class submarine was estimated to last 36 hours with a crew of 53, but with 103 aboard, it was anyone's guess how long it would last. Bolus, however, was not over-concerned; with her attendant tug Grebe-cock somewhere in the area, it would not be long before they got out.

But a sequence of tragic accidents followed. When the Thetis dived, the Grebe-cock had steamed away in the direction the submarine should have taken, and at 1600 hours, with still no sign of the Thetis, her commander anxiously sent off a message to the Royal Navy submarine base at Gosport, 'How long should Thetis remain under water?' The radio on Grebecock, however, could only reach as far as a station in the North of England; from there it went by regular Post Office telegram service to Gosport. Here, the boy delivering it by bicycle had a puncture and stopped to mend it. Thus it was not until 1815 hours that the Chief of Staff, Submarines, received it. He immediately sprang into action. Eight 'Tribal' class destroyers anchored in Weymouth Bay weighed and made for Liverpool flat out. Aircraft from an airfield 150 miles (240 km) away arrived on the scene at 2100 hours, but it was getting dark and they were forced to return to base.

By 2400 hours the men in the Thetis were desperately sucking in the already foul air, sprawled about the wildly sloping deck, eyes watering, many of them being sick. At 0730 hours it was decided to send up two men, wearing Davis Breathing Apparatus, from the stern escape chamber – Captain Oram and Lieutenant Wood. On the latter's arm was tied the Engineering Officer's

No one could guess the dreadful fate that was, within weeks, to overtake Britain's newest submarine, HMS Thetis.

Top: *The rescue ships arrive too late to save the crew of the doomed* Thetis.

Above: *All rescue attempts were to no avail.*

Report in case they drowned on the way up: 'From *Thetis*. On the bottom. Depth 157 feet (47.9 m). Tube space and stowage space full of water. Number five bow cap and inside door open to the sea. Air must be pumped into the submarine to save her. A diver must close the hatch to the deck more closely, or the air will escape. Look out for men escaping through the stern escape chamber.'

At 1000 hours two more heads bobbed to the surface, Stoker Arnold and Frank Shaw, a Cammell Laird man. In a desperate state themselves, barely able to speak, they whispered the dreadful story of the conditions aboard the submarine. Many had died in their own vomit, choking for air; others had drifted off into a final

sleep. Four had drowned in the escape chamber when one of them had panicked and pulled the face masks off the others. No one else escaped. One last attempt was made at 1500 hours; the wrong door was opened and the sea rushed into the engine room but most of the crew were already dead.

The cause was never fully determined. One suggestion was that fresh paint had found its way into the test-cock, preventing it from working. One of the many questions asked was why Lieutenant-Commander Bolus had not ordered the torpedo tubes to be flooded immediately. The *Thetis* was later raised and renamed the *Thunderbolt*, but she was sunk by an Italian corvette off Sicily in 1943.

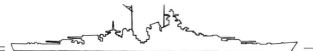

Floating Airfields

From the time that cannons were introduced into naval warfare in the Middle Ages, the fighting potential of a ship began to be measured in terms of the number of guns she carried and the weight of shot she could deliver. Over the years these guns became bigger and more accurate and had a greater range, until at the beginning of the First World War the ultimate in sea power was the armoured battleship displacing up to 30,000 tons (30,480 tonnes), whose guns ranged from 11-inch (28-cm) to 15-inch (38-cm) calibre, with a range of over 20,000 yards (18,300 m). Doubts, however, were beginning to creep in, and a handful of far-sighted naval strategists saw in the Whitehead torpedo, a menace that could put an end to the dominance of these great floating batteries. They were already at risk from unseen attack from below the waterline – and with the advent of the aeroplane came a danger that would ultimately put an end to their usefulness. However, the aeroplane and its threat lay far into the future; few at the time of its invention realized the potential of aircraft as naval weapons.

Aircraft at Sea

From the novelty of the flimsy flying machines of the Wright brothers, aircraft began to develop at an alarming rate, and their inventors and champions saw in them the weapons of the future. Yet even the most far-seeing naval officers regarded them as purely defensive weapons, faster, more efficient scouts that could detect an enemy far more quickly than cruisers and destroyers.

One such officer, Captain Sueter, Director of the newly formed Royal Navy Air Department, defined their role to the Admiralty:

1. Distant reconnaissance work with the fleet at sea.
2. Reconnaissance work off enemy's coasts, working from detached cruisers or special aeroplane ships.
3. Assisting destroyers to detect and destroy submarines.
4. Detecting minelayers at work or mines already laid.
5. Locating hostile craft in waters which have to be kept clear for our war and merchant vessels.
6. Assisting submarines in their lookout for vessels to attack.
7. Screening our fleets and harbours from observation by hostile aircraft by attacking the latter.
8. Preventing attacks on Dockyards, Magazines, Oil Storage Tanks, etc., by hostile aircraft.

When he referred to 'hostile aircraft', Sueter had in mind the enormous gas-filled dirigibles the Germans had put into production at the beginning of the century.

Since 1900 Count Zeppelin had been improving on his early dirigibles, 420-ft (128-m) long monsters, powered by two diesel engines driving four propellers, which could travel at 16 mph (26 km/h); by 1914, his 'Zeppelins' had reached speeds of up to 60 mph (96 km/h) and could carry a substantial bomb load. The German Navy saw them rather as reconnaissance aircraft, but when used in a major sortie of the High Seas Fleet, the one that ended at Jutland, they proved ineffective. Nonetheless, they were a potential menace that led to arming aeroplanes to deal with them.

As early as 1903 navies were experimenting with the possibility that observation from the air could give prior warning to an approaching enemy, but no one had seriously considered the rickety 'heavier-

Overleaf: War from the air was introduced against British ships by Zeppelins; here they can be seen bombing cruisers.

than-air' machine for naval reconnaissance duty. The most likely answer had seemed to be an airship which was equipped with one of the new-fangled wireless sets – huge manned kites towed behind fast ships had already been tried. When the Royal Navy's first rigid airship, the *Mayfly*, broke her back in bad weather, the Admiralty turned its attention to manned observation balloons, leaving the Germans to develop the dirigible. The French, Russians and Americans, quick to see the naval possibilities of 'heavier-than-air' machines, were investigating the possibility of their use in conjunction with ships.

Then in 1910 there came the major breakthrough: an aircraft took-off from a ship. For some time the German Hamburg-American Steamship line had been interested in the idea of launching an aircraft from a ship to provide an express ship-to-shore mail service, but the company's own pilot had insufficient experience to make the attempt. It was left to the Americans to supply a civilian pilot and Eugene Ely, flying a Curtiss Model D called the *Albany Flyer*, carried out the experiment. A platform with 5 degrees of slope was erected on the bows of the USS *Birmingham* which was anchored in Norfolk harbour, Virginia. It was 83 ft (25.3 m) long by 24 ft (7.3 m) wide, giving the *Flyer* a bare 57 ft (17.4 m) once it was positioned for take-off. At 1516 hours on a misty afternoon in November 1910, Ely revved the engine of his flimsy machine and careered down the first-ever flight-deck. As a safety precaution should she hit the water, the *Flyer* had been fitted with a bag of corks attached to the keel and canister floats beneath the wings. Unable to gain enough speed for a clean take-off, the Curtiss dropped the 37 ft (11.3 m) from the cruiser's bows to the surface of the water, submerging floats, wheels and the tips of the propeller. For agonizing seconds it looked as if the flight would end in failure, but struggling with the controls, Ely managed to lift the nose of the aircraft and become airborne. History had been made.

It was reasoned that if an aircraft could take off from a ship, it could also land on one, so by the following January, the armoured cruiser USS *Pennyslvania* had been fitted with a 720-ft (219.5-m) long and 32-ft (9.8-m) wide flight-deck, built over its stern and after gun turrets. At 1000 hours on 18 January 1911, watched by a fascinated ships company hanging from every vantage point including the yards and after funnel, Ely manoeuvred his air-

Eugene Ely takes off from the deck of USS Pennsylvania in his Curtiss Pusher aircraft.

Looking aft as Ely makes the first-ever deck-landing on the Pennsylvania, on 18 January 1911.

craft to come in from the stern at 40 mph (64 km/h). Every precaution had been taken to ensure a safe landing; the flight-deck sloped upwards towards its extremity and the superstructure and ship's sides had been festooned with canvas to act as safety nets. A crude deck-landing system was devised by stretching ropes across the platform; raised above the deck by timber sleepers and weighted down each end by 51-lb (23.2-kg) sandbags, they acted as 'arrester wires' for the grapnel hooks slung below the aircraft. Other ingenious systems followed, but in essence this remained the basic principle of deck-landing until the coming of the 'Vertical Take-Off' aircraft. Ely landed successfully, 50 ft (15 m) from the after superstructure, then took-off again and returned safely to base. Although slow to start, the Royal Navy began to show an interest in the military use of the aeroplane at sea, and a significant step forward was taken by Commander Sampson when he flew a Short hydroplane from the bows of the battleship *Africa* while she was steaming into the wind at 12 knots. The same year, 1912, the United States Navy, unhappy at cluttering the stern of a warship and losing the use of her after guns, began to experiment with a steam catapult

to save space. Yet none of these innovations was pursued by the other navies of the world, who were still obsessed with battle-ships and failed to appreciate the significance of these achievements. They were now beginning to accept the concept of aircraft at sea but believed the future lay with the seaplane which could be lowered over the side for take-off and recovered by crane.

In 1913 the Admiralty authorized the conversion of the 5,700-ton (5,790-tonne) armoured cruiser *Hermes* to take three float-planes – one of them a Short Folder – strictly for reconnaissance purposes. Wireless communication between aircraft and ship proved to be so successful that orders were given for the acquisition of an 'Aviation Vessel'. A cargo vessel with five holds was chosen and these holds were to be turned into hangers and workshops to accommodate ten seaplanes. But by mid-1914, war looked inevitable and other means had to be found to get aircraft to sea quickly. Three cross-Channel ferries, fast enough to keep pace with a fleet, were taken over and fitted with a large hanger aft and with handling cranes, but not with a flight-deck. These strange-looking craft, the *Engadine*, *Empress* and *Riviera*, soon found themselves in action once the war started. An aerial bomb had been devised and a few days before the outbreak of war, Flight Lieutenant Longmore made the first aerial torpedo 'drop' from a Short seaplane; this opened up a new role for naval aircraft, despite the 'big ship' fixation of senior naval commanders.

On Christmas Day 1914 the seaplane carriers, *Engadine*, *Empress* and *Riviera*, steamed into the North Sea from Harwich, protected by light cruisers and destroyers. The plan was to bomb the Zeppelin sheds at Cuxhaven at the mouth of the River Elbe, in the hope of luring units of the High Seas Fleet out of their harbour and into a submarine trap. It was a beautiful sunny day as the ships steamed deep into the German Bight; the sea was calm, perfect for a seaplane take-off and strike. Of the nine aircraft in the operation, only seven became airborne and they, losing their way in dense fog over the German coast, failed to locate the Zeppelin sheds and jettisoned their bombs. Only two made it back to the carriers; the others, running out of fuel, were forced to 'ditch' in the sea, where the crews were picked up by various ships. As the unsuccessful force scurried back to base, it was bombed by German aircraft from the mainland who were more successful in finding their targets. The Royal Naval Air Service or R.N.A.S., as it had come to be called, learned a lot from this disastrous venture, and when the newly commissioned 'Aviation Ship' *Ark Royal* sailed for the Dardenelles in 1915 with another seaplane carrier, the *Ben-my-Chree*, they put the lessons learned to good use.

The First Torpedo Attack

It was the *Ben-my-Chree* that first went into action in the Dardenelles campaign. The German U-Boats sent to assist the Turks had already sunk two old battleships and the *Ark Royal*, considered too slow and vulnerable to operate in the forward areas, was pulled back to the safer waters of the fleet base at Imbros. The converted Channel packet *Ben-my-Chree*, on the other hand, was fast enough to outrun a submarine and her loss would not have been as disastrous as that of the specially converted *Ark Royal*.

In August 1915 a Short 184 seaplane was cranked over the side, her engine started up and her crew (pilot and observer) clambered aboard. Below her was slung a 14-inch torpedo. The seaplane was now a more substantial affair with a

The Ark Royal, later renamed Pegasus, in Mudros harbour in 1916.

The first effective torpedo attack was made in a Short 184, lowered over the side of Ben-my-Chree.

fuselage and cowled engine – no longer was it a flimsy contraption of string and wire. The Short 184 lumbered forward, gaining speed as her large wooden floats churned through the water; then, as the pilot eased back on the joy stick, her nose went up and she became airborne. Gaining height painfully slowly, she flew over the peninsula in search of prey. Sighting a Turkish supply ship, her pilot brought her in low on the beam, closer and closer, letting the torpedo go at less than a quarter of a mile (400-m) range. It ran true and crashed into the supply ship, tearing a gaping hole below the waterline and within minutes the Turkish ship had sunk to the bottom. The R.N.A.S. had discovered an effective new weapon. Two other seaplanes were equally successful in attacking their targets a few days later, but although the enemy ships were damaged, they did not go under: a torpedo with a more powerful warhead was obviously necessary.

The Coming of the Aircraft Carrier

The R.N.A.S., convinced of the potential of the new form of attack, clamoured for a more imaginative approach to getting an aircraft at sea airborne. Only under ideal weather conditions could the seaplanes take-off and land; once the sea became choppy or developed a swell, the aircraft were useless. What was needed was a form of flight-deck from which to fly off and land faster, *wheeled* aircraft and a greater range from which to make a torpedo attack. Firing torpedoes from close-in was all very well for attacking unarmed merchantmen, but lumbering in against a warship, the seaplanes would be blown out of the air before they ever got within attacking range. The naval planners at the Admiralty, ever cautious and conservative, were slow to recognize the potential and by and large stood by the policy of lowering seaplanes over the side for take-off, but they grudgingly acknowledged the need to investigate deck take-offs. The *Campania*, an ageing Cunard liner which was still capable of 22 knots, had a 200-ft (61-m) long sloping deck added forward; this deck was used to fly-off seaplanes but there were no deck-landing facilities, so the seaplanes still had to land alongside and be craned aboard.

An ingenious device, the Gregory-Riley wheel gear, was the next invention developed to facilitate take-off. A Heath Robinson affair, it nevertheless proved highly successful in getting seaplanes airborne from a deck. A cross-axle was attached below the seaplane's floats with two ordinary aircraft wheels fitted either side. A pair of springs, mounted each end of the axle and which forced the undercarriage off once the seaplane was clear of the deck, were held rigid by two pins which the pilot could release by pulling on two wires leading up to the cockpit.

After the Battle of Jutland, Jellicoe, conscious of the lack of accurate intelligence during the engagement, clearly saw the need for reliable aircraft to scout ahead of the fleet, and pressed for a viable Fleet reconnaissance system. The seaplane, subject as it was to the vagaries of the weather, was obviously not the answer, and clearly the aircraft themselves must be freed from temperamental breakdowns. For example, in the middle of spotting for a battle-cruiser squadron, Seaplane No. 8359, after radioing information of the enemy's movements, had to break off reconnaissance because of engine trouble. Her pilot reported on landing: 'At 3.45 p.m. (GMT) a petrol pipe leading to the left front carburetter broke and my engine revolutions dropped from 1,200 to 800 and I was forced to descend. On landing I made good the defect with rubber tube and reported to the ship that I could go on again. I was told to come alongside and be hoisted in. I was hoisted in at about 4.0 p.m. (GMT).' By this time the battle-cruisers were hammering away at each other and there was no need for aerial reconnaissance. The Zeppelins, out in force spotting for the High Seas Fleet, did little better, as they were frustrated by the haze in the battle area.

Under pressure, the Admiralty gave way to the clamour for an 'aircraft carrier', a vessel capable of flying fast, wheeled aircraft and allowing them to land back on her while under steam. The Conte Rosso, a liner being built in Britain for Italy, was taken over for conversion and work commenced to turn her into a floating aerodrome, capable of housing 20 aircraft in below-deck hangers. She was to be called Argus, 'He who sees all' – hardly a name that suggests an attacking role. However, she was destined to become the world's first true aircraft carrier with a clear flight-deck. Her purpose-built lines were totally unlike anything seen at sea before, but were soon to become commonplace as the basic pattern for all aircraft carriers. She carried no funnels, the exhaust gases being discharged through two ports aft, and her pilot house was mounted on an elevator.

HMS *Argus*

Displacement	15,775 tons (16,027 tonnes)
Length	565 ft (172.2 m)
Length of flight deck	550 ft (167.6 m)
Speed	20.7 knots
Number of aircraft	20
Armament	6 4-inch (10-cm) anti-aircraft guns

In 1917 the Royal Navy converted the liner Conte Rosso *into an all-clear flight-deck aircraft carrier.*

Opposite: The heavy cruiser
Furious *was converted into*
an aircraft carrier in 1918.

Unfortunately she would take at least 18 months to commission and the need for naval aircraft was urgent. Interim measures had to be devised. Oddly enough it was 'Jackie' Fisher's removal from power after the Dardenelles Campaign that supplied the answer. To lend heavy-gun support for a major landing in the Baltic where the depth of draught of battleships precluded them from operating inshore, he had pushed through a programme to build three curious 'tin-clads', facetiously nicknamed, '*Spurious*', '*Curious*' and '*Outrageous*'. It was the last of this trio, HMS *Furious*, a 786-ft (239.6-m) long cruiser displacing 22,000 tons (22,350 tonnes), with a speed of 32.5 knots and mounting two monster 18-inch (46-cm) guns, that the Admiralty eagerly seized for conversion on Fisher's downfall. When she joined the Fleet in 1917, her forward 18-inch (46-cm) gun had been replaced by a hanger and take-off deck which sloped downward towards the bow (later a landing-on deck was added abaft

the funnel) and she could accommodate up to 30 aircraft.

There was no shortage of naval pilots prepared to experiment with deck-landings, flying the latest and fastest fighters and fighter-bombers. Land-based aircraft were now flying at speeds in excess of 100 mph (160 km/h), and it was often a hazardous business landing them on a ship steaming into the wind. The Sopwith Pup with a top speed of 110 mph (177 km/h) was among the first seaborne aircraft; soon it was followed by the Sopwith 1½-Strutter with a top speed of 106 mph (170 km/h) and the Sopwith Cuckoo, a purpose-built torpedo strike aircraft with a top speed of 105 mph (167 km/h) – the Fairey Swordfish, used by the Fleet Air Arm for much of the Second World War, only had a top speed of 139 mph (222 km/h). It was with such wooden-framed, fabric-covered aircraft as those in the table below that naval airmen pioneered deck take-offs and landings.

Aircraft	Wing Span			Length			Maximum Speed		Ceiling		Armament
	ft	in	m	ft	in	m	mph	km/h	ft	m	
Sopwith Pup	26	6	8.1	19	3	5.9	110	176	17,000	5,200	1 MG*
Sopwith 1½-Strutter	33	6	10.2	25	5	7.7	106	170	13,000	4,000	2 MG 2 bombs
Sopwith Camel	27	0	8.2	18	9	5.7	125	200	17,000	5,200	2 MG 2 bombs
Sopwith Cuckoo	46	8	14.2	28	6	8.7	105	168	12,000	3,700	1 18-inch torpedo

*machine gun

Below: A Sopwith 1½-
Strutter.

One of the first launching
trials of a Sopwith Camel.

The first successful deck-landing ever was made in August 1917 on HMS *Furious*, which had just come into commission. Squadron Commander Dunning, piloting a Sopwith Pup, had to swerve her round the ship's bridge to land on the 200-ft (61-m) long sloping deck; a deck-crew rushed forward to assist at the final touchdown by hanging on to straps attached to the aircraft. With the *Furious* steaming into the wind such flimsy machines might well be blown overboard. On his second attempted landing, Dunning successfully sideslipped round the bridge, but as he touched down a tyre burst; the Pup veered madly to starboard and skidded over the side before the deck-crew could reach her. Plunging into the water, the aircraft was hit by the ship and forced under, drowning Squadron Commander Dunning – the first, but not the last, victim of a deck-landing. Following Dunning's fatal accident, a landing deck was added abaft the funnel. It was fitted with ropes athwartships, similar to the method used by Ely. Wires ran fore and aft should the aircraft veer either side on touching down. Violent eddies of wind created by the ship's superstructure, however, made deck-landing a very hazardous operation and it was finally abandoned as impractical.

Meanwhile Commander Sampson, who had made the successful take-off from the battleship *Africa*, was working on a parallel idea, the High Speed Sled. His plan was to use a flat-bottomed barge fitted with a 58-ft (17.7-m) long flight-deck which would be towed into the wind at 32 knots by a destroyer. A Sopwith Camel, equipped with a quick release mechanism, was secured at one end of the barge, and when the breeze plus the speed of the ship reached the flying speed of the aircraft, she took off. This experiment, although quite successful (one pilot launched in this manner did, in fact, shoot down a reconnaissance Zeppelin over the North Sea), was, however, not really a permanent answer to operating aircraft at sea.

Before her short career as an aircraft carrier was finished, the *Furious* did fly off one successful strike in July 1917. Zeppelin activity had increased, but with limited success, and little damage had been done to the ships they had bombed. Nevertheless, navy personnel resented this attack from the air and means were sought to fight back using aircraft which, by this time, were developing into efficient fighting machines. Seven Camels, armed with small bombs, took off from the *Furious* as she cruised off the German coast and flew towards the Zeppelin sheds at Schleswig – the Royal Navy had decided to attack the source of menace. Small though the bombs were, they tore through the flimsy roofs and two Zeppelins went up in flames; the raid was a great success, but at a cost. The seven Camels managed to steer safely through the anti-aircraft flak and avoid patrolling enemy fighters, but five of them ditched into the sea because of engine failure or lack of fuel and the *Furious* failed to retrieve the two that did return.

American Tests

The war came to an end without a successful answer to operating aircraft at sea being found, but the potential was recognized. The launching of the *Argus* towards the end of 1918, too late to be of any use, led to a close evaluation of her faults which would be rectified in the aircraft carriers *Hermes* and *Eagle*, by then under construction. A setback occurred when the R.N.A.S. lost its individual identity and was combined with the Royal Flying Corps to form a single command, the Royal Air Force. For years she became the poor relation in the postwar scramble for aircraft and development estimates.

Among the staunch advocates of naval aviation at the end of the war was American Brigadier General 'Billy' Mitchell of the U.S. Army Air Force. At an early stage he had become aware of the potential of attacking warships from the air, and sinking them using aircraft alone. Experience gained by Britain and other major powers during the war showed that aircraft attacks on capital ships were of limited value and the more conservative naval planners on both sides of the Atlantic turned to bigger and better battleships as the lynch-pin of their naval strategy. Aircraft were still only seen as useful adjuncts to surface ships, invaluable for reconnaissance, but only of marginal value as attack weapons. This was the popular opinion of the day despite Admiral Sims, the commander of U.S. naval forces during the war, championing the cause of naval aviation and persuading the Navy Board to recommend that six aircraft carriers with unrestricted flight-decks of 700 ft (213 m) and capable of 33 knots should be built. At the end of hostilities these plans had been hastily put into abeyance.

Flying in the face of entrenched opposition from senior United States commanders, Mitchell badgered the authorities to

Commander Dunning successfully landing his Sopwith Pup on the Furious. *On his second attempt a wheel burst, the aircraft went over the side and he drowned.*

allow him to carry out bombing trials off the Virginia Capes in 1921. He was convinced that the heavily armoured battleship was an anachronism, a thing of the past that was all too vulnerable to attack from the air – a prophecy that was proved to be true later, but at the time was difficult to establish conclusively. With the scant experience of the First World War to guide them, loaded up with small and not very powerful bombs, his pilots took off to sink a number of anchored ex-German warships.

In hindsight it was hardly a fair test, given the strength of the opposition to his ideas, but the trials were watched with interest, not least of all by the Imperial Japanese Navy, with a hungry eye on the Pacific. The aircraft attacked in perfect flying conditions, aiming to drop their bombs close alongside to rupture the ships' plates causing them to take in water and sink. The first two targets, a U-Boat and a destroyer, were easily disposed of; a light cruiser proved more difficult; but it was when his pilots tried to sink the battleship *Ostfriesland* that they ran into trouble. After two days of bombing, she finally did go down, but this caused unfavourably disposed U.S. naval observers to point out that all that had been achieved was to demonstrate that a battleship could be sunk from the air – provided it was stationary and in no position to fire back. Mitchell,

HMS Eagle, *taken from the air.*

for his part, was convinced that he had proved his point. But support for his ideas was to come from an entirely different source – the Washington Disarmament Conference.

Meanwhile Britain, who had led the field in naval aviation at the end of the war, was using the *Argus* with its 549-ft (167.3-m) clear flight-deck to gain experience operating with fighter aircraft and torpedo bombers, experience which was fed into the two new aircraft carriers under construction, *Hermes* and *Eagle*. The 22,500-ton (22,860-tonne) *Eagle* began her trials in 1920, but at the leisurely pace that was to mark aircraft-carrier development in most countries. France showed no interest at all, apart from a half-hearted conversion of the battleship *Bearn*, which was never a success. Italy was not concerned either as she saw her role as limited to the Mediterranean, which she could easily cover with land-based aircraft. Germany, of course, restricted by the Treaty of Versailles, was forbidden an interest. It was four years before the *Eagle*'s trials were completed, the experience gained during them being incorporated into the 10,900-ton (11,100-tonne) *Hermes*, commissioned in 1923. One point established was that a bridge and flying control should be placed on the starboard side, a basic layout that has been generally accepted ever since.

The Growth of the Japanese Carrier

The other country to show an interest in naval aviation was Japan. Anxious to maintain her position as a world-class naval power that she had gained in the First World War, she saw in aircraft the means of delivering a swift blow anywhere in the vast Pacific. In 1922 the *Hosho*, although small (she displaced only 7,000 tons/7,100 tonnes), was the first purpose-built aircraft carrier to go into service, and she incorporated many of the innovations introduced into the British aircraft carriers. Even so, the main efforts of the Imperial Japanese Navy were directed towards building large 43,000-ton (43,700-tonne) capital ships, mounting 16-inch (41-cm) guns. American and Japanese interests had clashed towards the end of the war. When the United States Navy had proposed to fortify it naval base at Cavite in the Philippines, the Japanese saw it as another 'Port Arthur' on their doorstep.

The Japanese shipbuilding programme had not gone unnoticed in the U.S.A., so, in order to protect their interests in the

Below: An aircraft touches down on USS Langley.

Bottom: Aircraft stacked on the hangar deck of USS Saratoga.

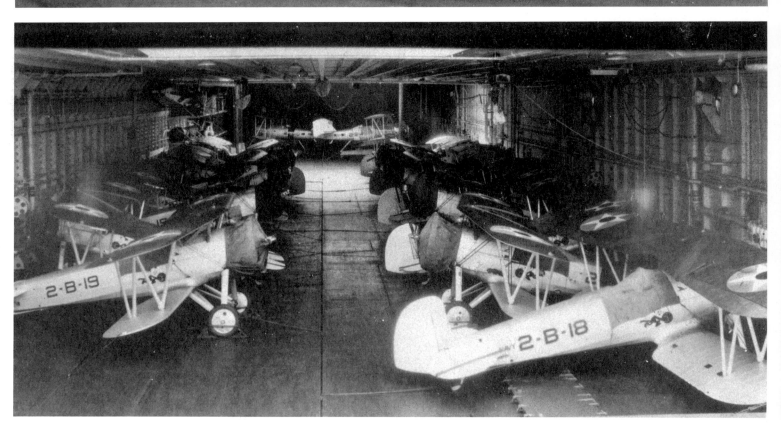

Pacific, they laid down capital ships of equivalent weights. Britain, not to be outdone and still seeing herself as *the* major naval power, provided for a class of 48,000-ton (48,800-tonne), 16-inch (41-cm) gunned battle-cruisers in the 1922 estimates, to be followed by 43,500-ton (44,200-tonne) battleships armed with nine 18-inch (46-cm) guns. With Britain allied by treaty to Japan, the 'Big Navy' lobby in the American State Department demanded a navy powerful enough to engage the combined fleets of these two nations, should the need arise. These frenzied rearmament programmes in countries bled white economically by the First World War were sheer madness and could not continue. The only solution was to get the major naval powers around the negotiating table.

At the invitation of President Harding, delegates from the U.S.A., Italy, Japan, Great Britain and France met in Washington on 21 November 1921 for a conference on the limitation of armament. After much spirited wrangling, the Washington Treaty (Treaty for the Limitation of Armament) was signed of 6 February 1922. Work was stopped on all but six capital ships; many were scrapped. Few if any at the Conference considered naval aviation a serious threat, as the tonnage allocated to

each country clearly indicates. Great Britain and the United States had 135,000 tons (137,160 tonnes) each at their disposal; Japan, 81,000 tons (82,300 tonnes); and 60,000 tons (61,000 tonnes) each for Italy and France. A 'Scrap or Convert' clause in the Treaty made available a number of large capital ship hulls that could easily be converted into aircraft carriers. Unwittingly, the Washington Conference had set into motion a train of events that would bring about the fall of the battleship they so much feared.

Virtually overnight and at enormous cost the aircraft carrier grew to a monstrous size, able to house 70 to 80 aircraft. The U.S. *Langley* of 1922 which displaced 12,700 tons (12,900 tonnes) was followed five years later by the *Saratoga* and *Lexington* which were 33,000-ton (33,500-tonne) monsters, 890 ft (271 m) long, armed at heavy cruiser strength with eight 8-inch (20-cm) guns and 12 5-inch (13-cm) guns, and able to reach a speed of 35 knots. The Japanese, following suit, converted a battleship and a battle-cruiser into the *Kaga* and *Akagi* which were slightly smaller and 2 to 4 knots slower than their American counterparts. Whereas the U.S. Navy followed the British example of installing an island structure on the starboard side,

Japan built her first clear-deck aircraft carrier, the Hosho, in 1934.

with a huge funnel, the Japanese reverted to earlier designs, maintaining a completely clear flight-deck. Another feature of Japanese aircraft carriers was that the flight-deck ended well short of the bows, allowing the lower hanger deck to continue forward on to the forecastle through large doors. The upper hanger deck, also fitted with doors at the forward end, extended midway between the two other decks, in theory allowing take-off from three levels. But this ambitious concept was never a practical proposition. Later, small island structures were added, portside on the *Akagi*, starboard on the *Kaga*. Great Britain, too, was extending her range of aircraft carriers, but without reaching the proportions of the American and Japanese carriers. Nevertheless, at the outbreak of the Second World War she had a substantial carrier force.

Deck Landings

Considerable thought had been given to increasing the safety of deck-landings and this became more and more necessary as the speed of aircraft more than doubled. The old systems soon proved to be completely inadequate, even when supplemented by a series of transverse wooden

The Royal Navy aircraft carrier Courageous *with the* Glorious *in the background.*

flaps that were raised when the aircraft came into land. In theory the aeroplane would be slowed down as it knocked down the flaps; in practice knocking down these flaps caused endless damage that kept the workshops constantly overloaded with repair work. Unbelievably, nothing came along to replace this short-lived innovation; for the next five years aircraft came in to land without the benefit of arrester gear. It was not until 1931 that a system of transverse wires which led over braked drums was used for deck-landings on the 22,000-ton (22,350-tonne) *Courageous*. This system was the forerunner to the hydraulically arrested wires that have been used ever since.

The hydraulically controlled arrester wires coupled with the introduction of wheel brakes on aircraft, and later, retractable hooks, made deck-landing considerably less hazardous; at the same time it allowed the development of faster aircraft for naval aviation. Eventually every two sets of arrester wires had their own hydraulic arrester unit. As the landing hook caught onto the arrester wire, it drew it out from its drums, causing a piston to force hydraulic fluid along a cylinder through a small hole into a pressure tank filled with air. The aircraft, racing across the deck,

would continue to pull out the arrester wire, freeing more and more fluid into the tank and compressing the air. Once the hook was released after landing, the compressed air forced the hydraulic fluid back into its cylinder, returning the arrester wire to its normal position wound round the drum.

This led to the introduction of the LSO, the Landing Signals Officer or 'Batman', who became the most important man on the flight-deck once the aircraft were coming in to land. With the dramatic increase in speeds, deck-landing became an exact science, a methodical procedure in which the LSO played a major part. No longer was it a haphazard affair left mainly, if not entirely, to the pilot. Now, once the 'Affirmative' flag had been hoisted – a white cross on a red ground – the pilot came under the control of the LSO. Pilot training became more thorough and intense. Constant practice ashore on simulated flight-decks accustomed pilots to come in at the right heights and pre-tested speeds, and it was then up to the LSO to get them down safely, often on a heaving deck. Later, the skill of these officers was tested to the full when it came to landing Seafires on the short flight-decks of 'Woolworth' carriers – converted merchant ships.

Standing on a small deck-level platform at the after port side of the flight-deck, a safety net beneath him in case of a wayward aircraft, the LSO would bring in the pilot at the correct height, line and speed, by a series of hand signals, using two paddles shaped like table-tennis bats. Ideally, the pilot approached directly from astern with plenty of revolutions, nose well up, the

Left: A Landing Signals Officer or 'Batman' bringing in a Swordfish.

Landing Signals Officer's Flag Signals

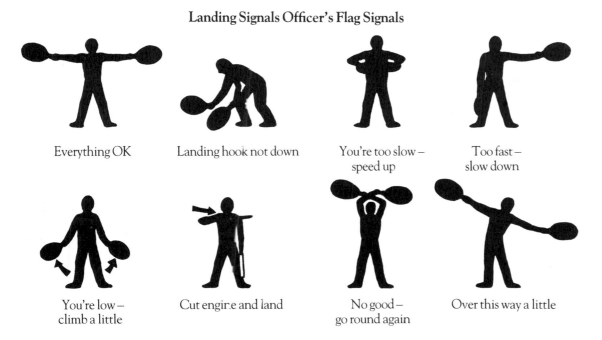

Everything OK Landing hook not down You're too slow – speed up Too fast – slow down

You're low – climb a little Cut engine and land No good – go round again Over this way a little

aircraft hanging from its propeller, arrester hook down, slowly sinking towards the deck. If the pilot was coming in on a true course, the LSO held his bats straight out, and as the aircraft reached the edge of the flight-deck, he would put his right-hand bat across his chest as a signal to cut the engine and land. Should a pilot cut his engine too high above the deck, the aircraft would most likely bounce, soar above the arrester wires and finish up in the crash barriers – sets of wires positioned a few feet above the deck. Most likely the propeller would be mangled and often the aircraft would turn over. Pilots, unfortunate enough to zoom over the crash barriers, usually landed in the sea, where, if they avoided being run down by the ship, they had to struggle to get out of the aircraft before it went down – in the nose-heavy Seafire it became literally a matter of seconds.

Aircraft Used at Sea

Parallel to the development of the aircraft carrier was the development of the aircraft that flew from her. By and large, most navies concentrated on the design of reconnaissance planes, fighters, bombers and torpedo aircraft. By the Second World War the aerial torpedo had come a long way since its successful use in the Dardenelles, and although it was still not completely reliable, it was extremely effective when it was. The optimum height for dropping was about 50 ft (15 m) – too high and it was liable to break its back, too low and it would skip along the surface. Often the delicate guiding mechanism would be damaged by the shock of impact with the surface of the water which would cause the torpedo either to veer wildly off course or to dive straight to the bottom. In some cases the 'exploders' added to the nose of the 'fish' failed to detonate the warhead, rendering a potentially damaging hit ineffectual.

While aircraft carriers were in their formative years between 1918 and 1922, there was little development of carrier-borne aircraft. The main types used in deck-landing experiments to test emerging naval aviation techniques were designed towards the end of the First World War. The aircraft which dominated this era were the tried and trusted Sopwith Camel, Sopwith 1½-Strutter, Sopwith Pup and Parnell Panther; relative newcomers were the Sopwith Cuckoo torpedo bomber and the Nieuport Nightjar. With speeds hovering around 100 mph (160 km/h), they were ideal aircraft with which to experiment and to solve the problems of a young, potentially powerful naval strike weapon.

The Washington Treaty and expansion in aircraft-carrier construction did not bring the changes in naval aircraft that might have been expected. These developments were to come between 1928 and the mid-1930s. True, planes were becoming faster and more reliable. The Fairey Flycatcher, the most successful naval fighter of its day, had a maximum speed of 133.5 mph (213.6 km/h), and the American Curtiss F6C-2 had achieved 159 mph (254.4 km/h), but they were still based on the traditional lines of First World War fighters. Great strides were made in the development of naval aircraft in the late 1920s and mid-1930s for this was the

golden era of flying. Charles Lindbergh flew solo from New York to Paris, followed a few years later by Amelia Earhart, the first woman to fly the Atlantic solo. General Italo Balbo led a mass flight of 12 Savoia-Marchetti flying boats from Rome to Brazil in 1931. Air races were introduced and record after record was broken to win the coveted Schneider Trophy; engines and airframes, in fact, the whole design of aircraft, made great advances.

Great Britain and the United States led the field in the design of naval aircraft, their planes reaching a speed threshold of 200 mph (320 km/h), but Japan was rapidly catching up, her own designs entering into close competition with the West's. The American aircraft companies – Boeing, Curtiss and Grumman – produced a stream of snub-nosed, tubby naval aircraft, fighters and torpedo bombers, ideal for operating from aircraft carriers. Some of the more successful were the Boeing F4B-4, Curtiss Goshawk and F11C-3, and the Grumman fighters that led up to the single-wing Grummans of the Second World War. The Grumman FF1, the first of the company's naval planes to introduce a retractable undercarriage, had a top speed of 207 mph (331 km/h), and by 1934 a further development, the F3F-1, flew at 231 mph (370 km/h). Britain stuck to more traditional designs, although the Hawker Nimrod of 1932 had a maximum speed of 205 mph (328 km/h) and the Gloster Gladiator, the last Fleet Air Arm biplane, was considerably faster. The Japanese, studying the advances being made by American designers, produced the 200-mph (320 km/h) Nakajima A2N, which was to be the last of

The launching catapult on the forecastle of the battleship USS Arizona, 1931.

their naval biplanes. Japanese designers concentrated on manoeuvrability at the expense of armour and airframe.

From the mid-1930s to 1939, there was frenzied activity to produce fast, manoeuvrable, powerfully armed naval fighters, bombers and torpedo bombers and their design took a dramatic leap forward. By 1939 the biplane had totally disappeared, with two notable exceptions: the Fleet Air Arm still clung to the Fairey Albacore and the Swordfish – the archaic, lumbering, but so manoeuvrable 'Stringbag', whose deadly accurate torpedo attacks produced such crippling results. The nations of Europe looked on anxiously as the Fascist and National Socialist dictatorships of Italy and Germany got into their stride. The more far-seeing statesmen and military leaders believed war to be inevitable. Neither Germany or Italy had a naval air force but their fast, modern surface craft and submarines posed a threat that called for a strong naval air force. Inter-service rivalry between the Kriegsmarine and Göring's Luftwaffe prevented the completion of two Graf-Zeppelin-class *Flugzeugtrager*. Half-cruiser, it carried 16 6-inch (15-cm) guns and 12 4-inch (10-cm) AA guns, and half-carrier, it housed 12 Messerschmidt fighters and 28 Junkers 87 dive-bombers. With a maximum speed of 34 knots, it would have proved a nightmarish commerce raider if it had ever come into commission. The U.S.A. was also concerned. Military campaigns in China and Manchuria had brought home to her the rising ambitions of a cadre of Japanese militarists with designs on the Pacific. Despite strong anti-war sentiment, the United States Navy accelerated the provision of a strong naval air arm. At the commencement of the Second World War, Great Britain, the United States and Japan all had naval aircraft of high-performance which improved as the war went on.

Swordfish in formation.

NOTABLE NAVAL AIRCRAFT IN WORLD WAR II					
	Maximum Speed		Ceiling		
	mph	km/h	ft	m	Armament
GREAT BRITAIN Fairey Swordfish – torpedo/reconnaissance	140	224	10,500	3,200	1 MG 1 Lewis Gun 1 18-inch (46-cm) torpedo or bombs
Fairey Albacore torpedo bomber	161	258	20,000	6,100	3 MG 1 torpedo
Supermarine Spitfire fighter/bomber	342	547	43,000	13,100	4 20-mm cannon 3,500 lb (1,589 kg) bombs
UNITED STATES Grumman Avenger torpedo bomber	260	416	24,000	7,300	4 MG 1 torpedo
Grumman Hellcat – fighter	371	594	37,000	11,300	6 0.5 MG
JAPAN Mitsubishi A6M5 (Zero) fighter	351	562	38,520	11,740	2 2.7 MG 2 20-mm cannon
Nakajima B5N2 (Kate) torpedo bomber	235	376	27,000	8,230	1 MG 1,764 lb (800 kg) bombs 1 torpedo

Grumman Hellcat
production line.

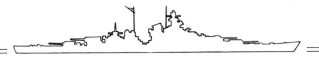

The Second World War

After the Washington Conference of 1922 the capital strength of the major naval powers had undergone a startling change.

Country	Ships Retained	Ships to be Scrapped	Ships converted to Aircraft Carriers	New Ships
Great Britain	22	22	—	2
U.S.A	15	15	2	3
Japan	9	9	2	1
Italy	10	—	—	—
France	10	8	1	—

The Soviet Union had retained only two old battleships from the Czarist Fleet, and in view of the problems the country was experiencing after the Revolution and Civil War, Lenin decided not to embark on a shipbuilding programme. The German Navy, which had been allowed to keep eight old pre-Dreadnoughts at the end of the First World War, was not represented at the conference. The might of her High Seas Fleet and U-Boat Arm had surrendered and scuttled themselves, and the Treaty of Versailles limited the size of any proposed German warship, to replace the pre-Dreadnoughts on a ship-for-ship basis, to 10,000 tons (10,160 tonnes). Germany was forbidden to build submarines altogether. The Allies, however, had not reckoned with the ingenuity of the German shipbuilders and designers – already they were seeking ways to capitalize on these restrictions.

Pocket Battleships and Giants

In 1929 they had laid down a revolutionary new type of ship that obeyed all the restrictions imposed by the Treaty of Versailles (though not exactly as the new ships displaced 11,700 tons [11,900 tonnes]) but which posed a new threat to the navies of the rest of the world. Traditionally, armoured cruisers of around 10,000 tons (10,160 tonnes) mounted nothing bigger than 8-inch (20-cm) guns. However the new German 'Panzerschiff' (or 'armoured ship') carried six 11-inch (28-cm) guns. It had never occurred to the Allies when they laid down the maximum weight of 10,000 tons (10,160 tonnes) and maximum gun size of 11-inches (28-cm), that the two would be combined in one ship. To the delight of the German people, wallowing in a fervour of nationalism under their newly elected Chancellor, Adolf Hitler, and the astonishment of the rest of the world, the *Deutschland* appeared in 1933 – she was soon dubbed a 'Pocket Battleship'.

Deutschland

Displacement	11,700 tons (11,900 tonnes) – fully loaded 16,200 tons (16,460 tonnes)
Maximum Speed	28.5 knots
Armament	6 11-inch (28-cm); 8 6-inch (15-cm); 6 4.5-inch (11.4-cm); 8 37-mm; 6 20-mm
Armour	2¼ to 3¼-inch (5.7 – 8.26-cm) sides; 5½-inch (14.0-cm) turrets
Reconnaissance Seaplane	1

On paper she was a formidable proposition, a commerce raider with the fire power of a battleship. In practice, however, the 'pocket battleship' was a failure; she was over-gunned for a commerce raider, did not have the speed to catch armoured cruisers and was under-gunned and insufficiently armoured to take on a capital ship. This was soon discovered early in the Second World War, but, initially, the appearance

The German battleship
Tirpitz, *sister ship to the*
Bismarck, *in a Norwegian
fjord.*

struction and building programme to enlarge its fleet to be able to compete with the
navies of Britain and the U.S.A. Japan had
given two years' notice of her intention of
withdrawing from the 1930 Naval Treaty
that was to expire in 1936, but had agreed
to abide by the 'spirit' of the 1936 Treaty,
although reserving the right to build battleships of up to 45,000 tons (45,720 tonnes).
These restrictions were disregarded as it
became clear that Japanese shipyards would
never be able to compete in numbers with
those of Britain and the United States.
What was required were ships of maximum
size and fire power backed up by a massive
submarine fleet. To a large extent the size
of American battleships was governed only
by the size of ship that could pass through
the Panama Canal. To meet the require-
ments of the Japanese Navy for bigger and
more powerful battleships than the Ameri-

Yamato: completed December 1941
Musashi: completed August 1942

Displacement	72,000 tons (73,150 tonnes) – full load
Length	862 ft (263 m)
Maximum speed	27.5 knots
Armament	9 18-inch (46-cm); 12 6-inch (15-cm); 24 5-inch (12.7-cm) AA guns; 147 25-mm AA; 4 12.7-mm AA
Armour	15.75-inch (40.01-cm) belt; 7.8-inch (19.8-cm) decks; 19.75 to 25.5-inch (50.17 to 64.8-cm) turrets

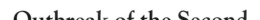

Outbreak of the Second

ron based at the Falklands under Commodore Harwood, was alerted. The ocean was scoured for the two commerce raiders. The *Deutschland*, evading the Allied patrols, made her way home to Wilhelmshaven by 15 November. Meanwhile, the *Graf Spee* marauded ships in the Indian Ocean before returning to hunt once again in South American waters.

Sinking of the *Royal Oak*

The *U.47* had been launched on 29 October 1938; less than a year later she was chugging away on her diesels out of Kiel, bound for her first wartime mission. Rumours were rife among her crew of 39

before she slipped her mooring wires; everyone had noticed that only 12 torpedoes had been shipped instead of the normal 14. A U-Boat's tour of operation usually lasted four or five weeks, so why only enough supplies for two weeks? Why had they only partially fuelled? Why had the number of bottles of lemonade been cut so drastically? None of the wildest guesses that were being bandied about came anywhere near the truth. The Kriegsmarine wanted a quick, spectacular success. The U-Boat Arm was chosen to provide it and *U.47* was selected to carry it out. Called to Berlin, the commander of *U.47*, Kapitänleutnant Gunther Prien, was presented with a breath-taking proposition – attack

Above: The German pocket-battleship Graf Spee.

Opposite: Kapitänleutnant Gunther Prien.

the British Fleet at anchor in Scapa Flow. It was not a new idea; it had been tried twice before in the First World War and both U-Boats had been sunk. Apart from the harbour patrols, anti-submarine nets and blockships, the tides and currents, racing through the narrow sounds leading into Scapa Flow, were fatal for submarines.

Travelling only at night on the surface in a mounting sea through squally wet weather, *U.47* spent the daytime mercifully motionless on the sandy bed of the North Sea. The younger submariners on their first long voyage in cramped conditions aboard a bucketing boat were nearly all seasick. Flung from side to side – crockery issued at the beginning of each tour usually lasted about two weeks – subjected to the stench of diesel oil coupled with the smell of cooking and stale air, all but hardened submariners were sick. Lying on the bottom everything was still and then the whole crew could enjoy beef, pork, veal, smoked eel, bacon or chicken, followed by fresh or tinned fruit, washed down with beer – nothing was too good for the crew of a U-Boat, and they earned it.

The crew, mustered in the forward torpedo space, were informed of their mission as they lay on the sea bed on their third day out. Until then it had been kept a closely guarded secret – only Prien and First Officer (*Oberleutnant zur See*) Englebert

Endrass knew where they were going. Crammed together, crouching on bunks, squatting on torpedoes, the crew – all 39 of them – listened with growing horror as Prien explained in detail how he intended to get *U.47* into Scapa Flow and then attack the British Fleet. Few sitting silent under the harsh light of the unshaded lamps shared his enthusiasm. He promised to sink 'aircraft carriers, battleships, cruisers', and staring at each man in turn, he promised to get them back home. Unconvinced by Prien's dramatics, the crew sat silent over their 'Hangman's' meal, the best the boat could offer, sipping the two bottles of beer with which they had been issued, together with a large slab of chocolate and 25 cigarettes. To a man they were convinced that they were on a one-way trip. By tradition, 19-year-old torpedo-man Herbert Hermann, as youngest aboard, had to serve the officers and petty officers their meal before sitting down to his.

The crew spent the rest of the day preparing for action. In the forward torpedo space the bunks, never cold as they were used turn and turn about, were clipped back against the bulkhead; the deck plates were opened and the four spare torpedoes hoisted up from below and secured on their rails ready for rapid reloading. The after torpedo tube, set between the electric motors was checked, ready for

66587 to.

U.47 *returns to port.*

firing. At 1857 hours the shout, 'Battle stations! Battle stations!, over the voice pipe had the crew racing for their action stations, like a well-oiled machine; within seconds the U-Boat was ready to attack. In the control room the bright lights had been replaced by an eerie red glow. The order was given, 'Stand by to surface'. The three look-outs were poised beside the conning tower ladder, ready to clamber up to the bridge as the submarine broke surface – for the last ten minutes they had been wearing red glasses to accustom themselves to the darkness outside.

'Periscope depth' came the call from Prien and the boat began to rise; the engineer officer chanted out the changing depth by metre. 'Up periscope' and Prien, cap pushed back, eyes glued to the view-finder, swung it rapidly through 360 degrees. 'Surface – down periscope'; he was satisfied that it was safe to go up – all noise in the boat was drowned by the hiss of compressed air and the roar of water being driven out of the ballast tanks. The boat began to roll as they neared the surface, but it was nowhere near as violent as before, for the weather had eased. Seaboots clanged on the iron rungs as the look-outs, led by Prien, scrambled up the ladder to the bridge. Surface water and bitterly cold air rushed in as the bridge hatch was unclipped

and was sucked into the boat by the thudding diesel engines to replace the stagnant, clammy air that had been deteriorating during their day on the sea bed.

As the look-outs reported 'nothing' starboard, port and aft, Prien peered dead ahead through his binoculars. The order, 'Both engines full ahead', was given, and the bow wave of U.47 lifted as she worked up to 17 knots, heading for the coast clearly silhouetted against the night sky. The sea had dropped since the previous day; no longer was it smashing against the bridge – now it was merely uncomfortably choppy. The sky was alight with dramatically changing colour as the Northern Lights, or *aurora borealis*, threw the British naval base of Scapa Flow on their starboard bow into sharp relief. Sensing the anxiety of his crew, Prien kept up a running commentary through the voice pipe. His voice echoed hollowly through the boat, '. . . it's like day, but the shadows being cast are a nuisance. South Ronaldsay is on our port side, beyond I can see Ward Hill, the highest point in Scapa Flow.' Below in the control room, the navigator followed the commentary on the chart – they would soon be coming up to Kirk Sound, their way in. He understood now why they were carrying only a part load for even at high tide there would be only a foot or so clearance under the keel – it would be touch and go.

The hand at the echo-sounder droned out the depths: '. . . 2 metres, 1 metre, half metre,. . .' the boat juddered as she crunched into the sand and shingle of the sea bed. 'Hard a starboard, full ahead.' The navigator stared at the chart: either it was wrong, or they were in the wrong place. They had, in fact, strayed into the shallow Skerry Sound. Smoke streamed from the racing diesels as the engineers sprayed the shafts to lessen the friction – for agonizing seconds the boat hung there, motionless; then it began to edge forward. '1 metre, 2 metres, 3 metres, . . .' – they were in clear water. Seeing St. Mary's village through his binoculars, Prien turned the boat to starboard, heading for Kirk Sound – it was 0015 hours. He felt the boat yawl as she was caught in the fierce current racing into the narrow channel. Ahead lay the block-ships – old, unattended sailing vessels, anchored to close the entrance. The unlit

houses of St. Mary's village lay no more than a stone's throw away. Headlights swept across the U-Boat as a car turned the bend into the village, but carried on to the north – it seemed that they had not been spotted. The heavy, penetrating thud of the diesels gave way to the thin, hardly discernable whine of the electric motors as Prien gave the order, 'Stop diesels. Half ahead, group up'. 'I'm going between the two northern blockships.' He struggled to keep the excitement out of his voice. The boat yawled to starboard and a loud clang ran down the length of the boat followed by a scraping noise that went on and on – they had fouled the anchor cable of one of the blockships. Silence – they held their breaths. 'We're through' – Prien definitely sounded excited.

Scapa Flow seemed empty. Where were the aircraft carriers and other heavy units? In fact, they had sailed only the day before. *U.47* began an agonizing search for a

Crewmembers of U.47 were given heroes' welcomes when they returned to their base.

target. Prien's voice suddenly came over the voice pipe, 'Single-funnel battleship ahead, 3,000 metres [3,280 yards]'. A hasty search through the recognition chart silhouettes confirmed it was a battleship of the *Royal Sovereign* class, probably the *Royal Oak*. 'Prepare for surface firing, – 'Fire one.' One by one the torpedoes cut through the water at a depth of 7 metres (23 ft); three of them had fired; the fourth had jammed. Prien swung *U.47* through 180 degrees and fired the stern torpedo. Endrass, watch in hand, timed the contact; three minutes went past and nothing – misfires, or had they missed completely? Only one hit had registered, and that only on the anchor chain of the battleship. Aboard the *Royal Oak*, a forecastle party had gone forward to find out why the anchor cable had gone crashing back into the locker. The last thing the *Royal Oak's* crew had in mind was a torpedo hit – Scapa Flow was impenetrable.

Prien, ordering course for Kirk Sound, was persuaded by Endrass to try another salvo. Frantically the torpedo-men reloaded, manhandling the torpedoes into the tubes for there was no time for cranking them in. Within two minutes, three deadly 'fish' were on their way towards the old battleship, set to explode below her armoured blister. *U.47* was already making for Kirk Sound at 17 knots when Prien shouted down the voice pipe, 'One, two, three flashes, we've got her.'

The sleeping men aboard the *Royal Oak* leapt from their hammocks as the battleship, shaken by three explosions in quick succession, heeled over to starboard in a 30-degree list. Tragically, the two massive main deck hatches, situated fore and aft of the main 15-inch (38-cm) gun turrets, had been closed down against aircraft attack – no one at the Admiralty had even considered the possibility of a torpedo attack by a U-Boat. Desperately the crew hauled on the pulley chains to raise the hatches but to no avail; the ship listed to 80 degrees, then rolled over, her barnacled keel uppermost, and quietly slipped under, taking 833 of her crew with her. The 300 survivors (crammed aboard the near-capsizing *Daisy*, a tiny fishing trawler that had been acting as the ship's liberty boat) heard a dreadful rumbling from within the *Royal Oak* as the 15-inch (38-cm) projectiles, each weighing over a ton, rolled from the shell bins and smashed their way through the stricken ship. It had taken less than eight minutes for the warship to go down. For fear of sinking herself, the *Daisy* was forced to pull away, leaving shrieking men struggling in the icy water. Eventually, rescue boats dragged a pitiful few of the survivors aboard who were suffering from shock and exhaustion, were wet, frozen and dripping fuel oil.

The base had been completely unaware of the attack; *U.47* had got in and out of the supposedly impenetrable Scapa Flow undetected. Dr. Goebbels's Ministry of Propaganda claim that the U-Boat fought her way out under continuous depth-charge attack from destroyers was totally untrue – it was an hour or so before the British Fleet knew it had been attacked. This successful and daring exploit, coming so early on in the war, did much to raise the morale of both the German people and the U-Boat Arm. In Britain all was gloom. Following close on the sinking of the aircraft carrier *Courageous* by *U.29* in September, *U.47's* success had once again demonstrated only too well just how vulnerable Britain's capital ships were to submarine attack.

The Expansion of the U-Boat Arm

As in the First World War, the U-Boat campaign soon got underway. The Kriegsmarine, rectifying its initial mistake, gave priority to submarine production. Eventually submarines were coming off the stocks at a rate of 200 a year and, by 1941, there were 249 U-Boats in service. As more and more U-Boats went into action, the tonnage of British merchant shipping sunk rose alarmingly. Between themselves alone, Gunther Prien (*U.47*), Joachim Schepke (*U.100*) and Otto Kretschmer (*U.99*) sank more than 500,000 tons (508,000 tonnes) of Allied shipping before meeting their end within ten days of each other in March 1941. (Other U-Boat aces emerged, but they never reached the figures of Kretschmer – 350,000 tons/355,600 tonnes.) *U.47* was sunk by the destroyer *Wolverine* on 8 March, *U.100* was rammed on 17 March by the destroyer *Vanoc* and Kretschmer was captured when *U.99* went down the same day.

The three U-Boat aces had been attacking a strongly escorted convoy 300 miles (480 km) west of Scotland. Between them they had sent a number of merchantmen to the bottom, when *U.47* met her fate. Depth-charged, she had disappeared with all hands. A week later *U.99* and *U.100*, in company with *U.557* (commanded by Lemp, the man who had commenced the U-Boat campaign by sinking the liner

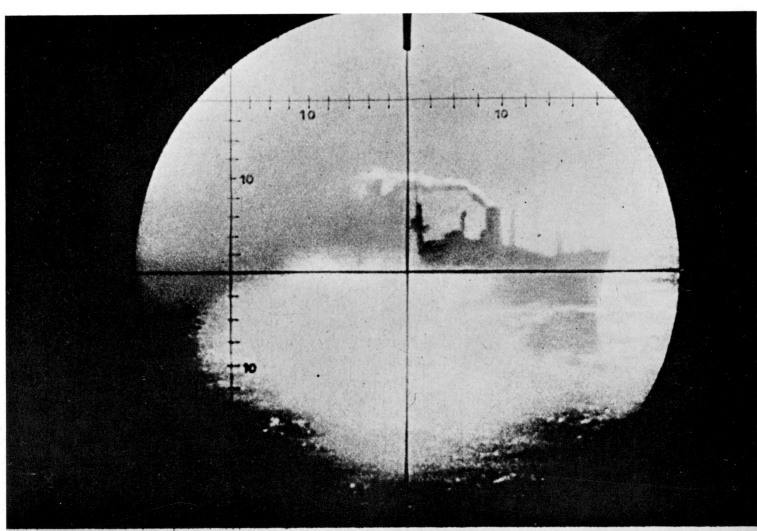

Englischer Frachter durch das Sehrohr eines deutschen Unterseeboots beobachtet
(unmittelbar nach Abschuß des Torpedos aufgenommen)
Torpedotreffer auf englischem Frachter

Athenia just after the war had started), attacked Convoy HX.112, a convoy of 41 ships from Halifax, Nova Scotia. Schepke's *U.100* was rammed by the *Vanoc* which had stopped to pick up survivors, guarded by the destroyer *Walker*. Having spotted *U.99* making off, the *Walker* left in pursuit. Luck had run out for Kretschmer, who had broken all previous records for a single attack by sinking six merchant vessels, totalling 59,000 tons (59,900 tonnes). Depth-charged by the *Walker* and badly damaged, he was forced to surface and surrender, but not until he had ordered his boat to be scuttled – the only casualty was the engineer officer detailed to set the scuttling charges, who was unable to get off in time and went down with her. Otto Kretschmer was the most successful U-Boat commander of the Second World War.

As the U-Boat war progressed, the attitudes on both sides hardened. Admiral Dönitz, under extreme pressure from Hitler, ordered his commanders not to pick up survivors. The Allies ordered, 'If you see a submarine, kill it, even if it is picking up survivors'. The tonnage of Allied merchantmen sunk rose at a near-crucial rate to a peak of 650,000 tons (660,400 tonnes) a month. This was rapidly approaching the figure of 800,000 (812,800 tonnes) a

Opposite: A U-Boat periscope view of a British freighter, and a photograph of another being sunk.

Above: Looking aft from the prow of an American battleship.

Left: The U-Boat of Kapitänleutnant Schultze returns to base after a successful mission.

month, calculated by Dönitz as being necessary to starve Britain into surrender. However, with the strengthening of the convoy system by, amongst other things, the addition of continuous air cover and with the increased efficiency of U-Boat hunting methods, the U-Boat campaign swung just as dramatically the other way. The spring of 1943 saw the monthly tonnage sunk decreasing and the number of U-Boats destroyed going up.

Monthly Tonnage Sunk – 1943

	tons	tonnes
April	245,000	248,900
May	165,000	167,700
June	118,000	119,900
July	123,125	125,000
	651,125	661,500

Number of U-Boats Destroyed

April	15
May	40
June	17
July	37
	109

In all, over 200 U-Boats were sunk in 1943, crippling losses that could not be replaced. In spite of the introduction of new types of U-Boats the losses continued to rise. An underwater breathing system, the 'schnorchel', that allowed the boat to run on diesels underwater was tried. Although it allowed a submarine to run continually at periscope depth, it was easily detectable from the air. Methods of giving false ASDIC echoes were introduced and experiments carried out with the Walther closed-circuit steam turbine engine.

Had the Walther propulsion system come out at an earlier stage, it might have had some bearing on the issue. As it was, it appeared towards the end of the war and there was not sufficient time to develop its full potential. It made a U-Boat capable of reaching 25 knots submerged, but there were a number of serious drawbacks. By burning an oxidant called 'Perhydrol' (a concentrated form of hydrogen peroxide) with fuel oil, the Walther turbine dispensed with atmospheric oxygen, but this combined fuel called 'Ingolin' was difficult to manufacture and store. Unless it was carried in clinically sterile tanks (synthetic rubber was discovered to be the best material with which to line the tanks), this highly unstable fuel was liable to decompose, which could lead to spontaneous combustion. Not only was Ingolin ex-

Below left: A U-Boat commander lines up on target.

Below right: The torpedo space of a U-Boat.

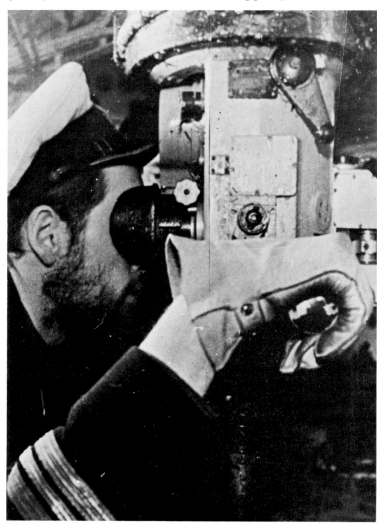

A U-Boat look-out at sea.

pensive to manufacture – costing eight times as much as conventional fuel oil – but vast amounts were used up at high speed (which, after all, was the whole point of the Walther system) giving the submarine a cruising range of only 80 miles (128 km). A more likely submarine to win the war for Germany was the Type XXI U-Boat. It was, in fact, a conventionally propelled submarine, but it was streamlined to minimize underwater drag and possessed mechanically operated torpedo-loading systems which allowed a U-Boat to carry up to 17 spare torpedoes that could be loaded far more quickly. By trebling the electric battery capacity, the Type XXI could increase the underwater speed of a U-Boat from 9 knots to 15.5 knots. Even though its production was given top priority, the Type XXI was not ready for operation until two weeks before the end of the war, too late to have any effect on its outcome.

The Turn of the Tide

Once the number of U-Boats destroyed passed the production replacement figure, and the loss in submarine crews had to be made up by transferring Army and Luftwaffe personnel into the Service, the underwater campaign was doomed. Surface attacks at night on shipping, first devised by Kretschmer, were countered by Allied surface search radar that could pick up a conning tower at a distance of 3 miles (4.8 km). The *Rüdeltaktik* or 'Wolf-pack tactics', whereby a number of U-Boats attacks the same convoy, relied on radio communication between the U-Boats. The introduction of High-Frequency-Direction-Finding ('Huff-Duff') into escort vessels pin-pointed U-Boat signals to within a quarter of a mile (400 m), allowing an accurate depth-charge attack. The aerial reconnaissance service provided to U-Boat groups by the enormous four-engined Focke-Wulf Condors was, for a time, a serious problem, but by installing a number of catapult-launched Hurricane fighter aircraft on merchantmen within a convoy, this danger was to some extent eliminated. It was considered that the loss of a Hurricane each time (the pilot baling out when he ran out of fuel, to be picked up by escort

vessels) was fair exchange for shooting down a Condor, probably the eyes of a U-Boat wolf-pack. Later, when escort carriers (converted merchant ships) accompanied convoys, the danger of Condor reconnaissance was ended. The first escort carrier, the *Empire Audacity*, converted from a captured German ship used for carrying bananas, earned this class of small aircraft carrier the nickname, 'Banana Boat'.

Improved ASDIC (the detection of submerged U-Boats by bouncing back sound signals from their hulls) led to more accurate depth-charge attacks by convoy escort vessels, fast corvettes and frigates. The 'Hedgehog' appeared, a mortar that threw 24 small depth-bombs in a wide arc ahead of the attacking ship. This was followed by the fearsome 'Squid', which fired three full-size depth-charges ahead of the ship. When aircraft were fitted with radar and carried adaptable depth-charges, undersea warfare became a far more dangerous undertaking – only the highly experienced or cautious U-Boat commanders survived.

The German surface raiders on whom the Kriegsmarine had relied so heavily were never really much of a success. When the *Deutschland* made her run back to Kiel after sinking less than 8,000 tons (8,120 tonnes) of Allied shipping, the Kriegsmarine created a diversion by ordering the two battle-cruisers *Scharnhorst* and *Gneisenau* to make a run from Wilhelmshaven into northern waters. Immediately six British battleships, two aircraft carriers, 12 cruisers and innum-

A German U-Boat in the Channel.

erable destroyers began a search, but it was left to an armed merchant cruiser, the *Rawalpindi*, to discover the German vessels off Iceland. Without hesitation, having first got off a radio message, she bravely went into the attack. Her 6-inch (15-cm) guns were never a match for the 11-inch (28-cm) guns of the battle-cruisers, but she gallantly fought on, ablaze from stem to stern, until her last gun was silenced. With the British heavy units closing in, the *Scharnhorst* and *Gneisenau* were forced to make for their home base, with every chance of being intercepted and mauled by a much more powerful British squadron. Fortunately for them, blinding rainstorms

and heavy seas came to their aid, and they were able to reach Wilhelmshaven unde-tected after only six days at sea and with just the *Rawalpindi* to their credit.

Battle of the River Plate

Meanwhile the *Graf Spee* had left the Indian Ocean for the South Atlantic in-tending to raid shipping from the west coast of Africa to South America. Between 27 November and 7 December she sank the liner *Doric Star*, the 8,000-ton (8,100-tonne) *Tairoa* and the *Streonshaln*, 900 miles (1,440 km) east of Rio de Janeiro. Her last victim, carrying 6,000 tons (6,100

tonnes) of Argentine beef to Britain, managed to radio her last position before going down; she also identified her attacker as a 'pocket-battleship', mistakenly naming her the *Admiral Scheer*. But that made no difference; 3,000 miles (4,800 km) away in the Falklands, Commodore Harwood's cruiser division picked up the signal, and correctly anticipating that Langsdorf intended to raid the valuable flow of shipping in the River Plate area, headed north at full speed to cut him off. Assuming the *Graf Spee* would cruise at 15 knots, her most economical speed, Harwood's navigator calculated that they should come up with her sometime in the afternoon of 12 December 1939.

Actually it was the following morning at 0616 hours that the *Graf Spee*'s look-outs reported ships approaching. Within seconds they were identified as enemy cruisers – three of them. Alarm bells rang throughout the raider as her crew rushed to battle stations. The six 11-inch (28-cm) guns swung on target, the range and direction were fed into the gunnery computers and the 'pocket-battleship' was ready to open fire. It would seem that there was little to fear from the 8-inch (20-cm) guns of the armoured cruiser *Exeter* and 6-inch (15-cm) guns of the light cruisers *Ajax* and *Achilles*; Langsdorf gave the order to fire at 19,500 yards (17,800 m), well beyond their range. He was confident that he could deal with them without sustaining any serious damage to his ship. Although his gunners had never fought a naval action before, they were battle-trained and should register hits in excellent visibility.

Commodore Harwood, however, had no intention of being picked off piecemeal so his cruisers came into attack from widely divergent bearings. At first the German gunnery officer, taken unawares, split his main armament between the British ships. This uncertainty resulted in sloppy firing. After a few minutes he swung the whole of his 11-inch (28-cm) fire power onto the *Exeter* and, at 0624 hours, obtained hits which destroyed her bridge and put one of her after turrets out of action; two further flashes marked the end of her forward

turrets. With only one turret of the British armoured cruiser still firing, the *Graf Spee* brought her main armament to bear on the *Ajax* which had closed the range to 8,000 yards (7,300 m) and her eight 6-inch (15-cm) guns to concentrate on the *Achilles*. At 0738 hours, with the range down to 7,000 yards (6,400 m), Langsdorf turned the *Graf Spee* towards the two light cruisers and, easily evading a torpedo attack from the *Ajax*, knocked out her after turrets. His situation becoming more hopeless each minute, Harwood ordered a withdrawal under cover of a smoke screen, intending to take up the attack again after dark. To his surprise the enemy did not take up the chase but set course for the River Plate. Ordering the badly damaged *Exeter* back to the Falklands, he followed with the two light cruisers, carefully staying beyond the range of the deadly 11-inch (28-cm) guns.

Even before the battle started the *Exeter*'s radio was crackling over the air, giving the time and position of the engagement and revealing the identity of the enemy. Reinforcements were converging from every direction. The remaining cruiser of Harwood's squadron, *Cumberland*, which was steaming up from the Falklands, would be the first to arrive that night. The

The British cruisers go in during the Battle of the River Plate.

battleship *Renown*, three cruisers and the aircraft carrier *Ark Royal* were on their way, but would take at least five days. The net was closing in on the raider.

At 0050 hours on 14 December, the *Graf Spee* dropped anchor in Montevideo harbour. Unless Captain Langsdorf could prove serious damage to his ship, wounded crew in need of medical attention or shortage of fuel and food, he would only be allowed to remain in the Uruguayan port for 24 hours before his ship was interned. On the evening of his arrival, a Uruguayan Navy Technical Commission reported that the *Graf Spee* had sustained 27 shell holes, none of a serious nature; some damage had been sustained by the galleys; and 36 members of the crew had been killed during the action. The German *Chargé d'Affaires*, basing his request on the findings of a technical expert flown from Germany, asked that the *Graf Spee* be allowed to remain in Montevideo for two weeks. Uruguay – neutral, but unfriendly –

granted her 72 hours. Actually two weeks would have better suited the British cruisers prowling off the mouth of the river.

By 16 December Langsdorf, realizing that he would be unable to avoid the heavy British units rapidly closing in, radioed Berlin for instructions. Orders arrived at 0300 hours the following day, directly from Hitler: the *Graf Spee* was to be scuttled. That evening a skeleton crew took the 'pocket-battleship' out of the river, and six miles (10 km) southwest of Montevideo, streaming smoke after heavy explosions, she slipped under the calm waters of the estuary. Three days later Kapitän zur See Langsdorf was found lying on an old Imperial German naval ensign in a Montevideo hotel. He had committed suicide, leaving a note for the German Ambassador, 'I alone am responsible for the scuttling of the *Admiral Graf Spee*. I am happy for my death to wipe out anything that may have dishonoured the flag.'

Further German raiders who made their

The scuttling of the Graf Spee.

way into the Atlantic – the *Hipper*, *Scharnhorst*, *Gneisenau* and *Admiral Scheer* – met with varying success. The *Scheer* sank five of the 36 ships that made up convoy AX84. The tally would have been higher but for the gallant action of Captain Fegan, commander of the armed merchant cruiser *Jervis Bay*. Giving orders for the convoy to scatter, he steered his ship, guns blazing, straight for the German ship. The outcome was a foregone conclusion, but it took the *Admiral Scheer* three hours to sink the *Jervis Bay*. During those three hours most of the convoy escaped but it was time bought at the expense of fearful sacrifice. Between 22 January and 22 March 1940, the *Scharnhorst* and *Gneisenau* accounted for 116,000 (117,860 tonnes) of merchant shipping before returning to their base at Brest; the *Hipper* sent 13 ships to the bottom. Growing British patrols were making it increasingly difficult for German raiders to operate successfully, and Grossadmiral Raeder's brilliant plan, 'Rheinübung', was doomed.

'Sink the *Bismarck*'

The original *Rheinübung* plan committed the brand-new battleships *Bismarck* and *Tirpitz*, the battle-cruiser *Gneisenau* and the heavy cruiser *Prinz Eugen*, to a surprise break-out into the wastes of the Atlantic. There they would not only wreak untold damage, but it would take the best part of the British Home Fleet to search for them. In the event, when the task force set out, it consisted of the *Bismarck* and *Prinz Eugen* only, a 'teaspoon force' according to its commander, Admiral Lütjens. The *Gneisenau* was damaged and the *Tirpitz* was not yet battle ready. As they left the port of Gotenhafen in the Baltic, in the dawn light of 20 May 1941, the *Bismarck*'s captain, Kapitän zur See Lindemann, listened with horror as the ship's bandmaster struck up 'Muss i denn'. This tune was traditionally played aboard battleships embarking on a long cruise – half the illicit transmitters in Polish Gotenhafen would

The German warship, bows under in a heavy sea.

*The German battleship
Bismarck sets out on her ill-
fated mission.*

already be tapping out the news to London.

Any remaining element of surprise was
finally shattered when they were sighted
going through the Kattegat by the Swedish
cruiser *Gotland*; a British sympathizer in
Swedish intelligence immediately informed
the Admiralty. It came as no surprise to
Lindemann when the *Bismarck* and her
attendant cruiser were circled by a photo-
reconnaissance Spitfire as they lay-to off
Bergen. Ruefully Admiral Lütjens thought
that he might just as well have radioed the
Admiralty himself, as he turned his two
ships north towards the narrow Denmark
Strait above Iceland. Only the latest
weather report of fog, heavy rain and snow
squalls would see him safely into the Atlantic now.

The mighty 52,000-ton (52,800-tonne)
Bismarck, the most powerful fighting ship
afloat, in company with the *Prinz Eugen*,
ploughed through the heavy seas, nosing
her way through fog and snow squalls at 15
knots. They made the Denmark Strait
without being sighted: less than two miles
(3 km) to starboard lay polar pack ice; to
port, minefields stretched to the coast of
Iceland. At 1922 hours, the alarm bells
shrilled – the radar had picked up a bleep: a
surface vessel was approaching on the port
bow. The *Bismarck*'s main armament
moved on target. Minutes later a three-
funnelled cruiser broke from the fog and
was quickly identified as a British *Norfolk*
class heavy cruiser – it was, in fact, the
Suffolk. Thirty seconds later the *Bismarck*'s
15-inch (38-cm) guns opened up, throwing
up great columns of water as their shells

straddled the cruiser, which was already in
a fast, tight turn, making smoke as she fled
for the safety of the fog bank. Too late. An
intercepted radio message, decoded by the
'B-Dienst' team, read, 'One battleship, one
cruiser in sight at 20°. Range seven nautical miles, course 240°.' The need for
caution gone, Lütjens gave the order for
full speed ahead and the two ships smashed
through the heaving seas at close on 30
knots.

The *Prinz Eugen* took station ahead; the
sensitive forward radar on the *Bismarck* had
been put out of action by the jar of her 15-
inch (38-cm) guns. The two German vessels had a good chance of disappearing into
the North Atlantic once they cleared the
Denmark Strait, but now there were *two*
radar echoes astern – the *Suffolk* had been
joined by the *Norfolk*, her sister ship.
Unable to shake off the shadowing cruisers,
Lütjens pressed on hoping to outrun any
capital ships sent to intercept him. He had
no means of knowing that the battleship
Prince of Wales and the battle-cruiser *Hood*
– the 'Mighty Hood', terror of Kriegsmarine war games – were steaming full
ahead to cut him off.

The dawn of 24 May broke bright and
clear. Alarm bells announced the sighting
of two heavy cruisers, but as the smoke
trails drew closer, they were confirmed as
two capital ships. The four turrets of
Bismarck's 15-inch (38-cm) guns swung
towards the enemy as the optical range-
finders and directors fed the range and
direction into the fore and aft gunnery
computer rooms. Ballistic instructions were

relayed to the turrets, the 'lock-ready-shoot' indicators showed the guns on target. At 23,000 yards (21,000 m) the heavy armament fired on the *Hood*; it was 0555 hours. Six minutes later, a plunging salvo from the *Bismarck* scored a direct hit; one shell, penetrating the too-thin deck armour of the *Hood*, went off in her after ammunition room, detonating 100 tons (102 tonnes) of high explosive. A gigantic orange fireball soared up between the masts, tearing the ship apart; huge sheets of metal flew out from a pall of brown smoke; a 15-inch (38-cm) turret cart-wheeled through the air – there were only three survivors out of a crew of 1,419. The *Prince of Wales*, also hit and with her bridge shattered, broke off the engagement.

Ignoring the pleas of Kapitän zur See Lindemann to give chase, Admiral Lütjens gave the order to turn south and run for St. Nazaire, thereby sending the *Prinz Eugen* into the Atlantic alone. The *Bismarck* had been hit three times. One shell had opened up the bows which caused her to ship 2,000 tons (2,030 tonnes) of sea water and gave the ship a list of 3 degrees. Another shell had ripped into her fuel tanks, leaving a tell-tale oil slick as 1,000 tons (1,020 tonnes) of fuel leaked out. The Admiral, more politically aware than his Captain, realized that the British must throw in everything to avenge the *Hood*. He was right. The battleship *King George V*, the battle-cruiser *Repulse* and the aircraft carrier *Victorious* were well on their way from Scapa Flow. 'H-Force', consisting of the battle-cruiser *Renown* and the aircraft carrier *Ark Royal*, accompanied by a heavy cruiser force, were steaming north from Gibraltar.

Then Lütjens made a fatal mistake. Obsessed with the quality of the radar aboard the British cruisers, he gave up trying to elude them, and sent off two radio signals to the German Naval Group Command West in Paris. In fact, he had shaken off the shadowing cruisers, and the Scapa Flow force, crossing his course astern, were heading into the Atlantic, 150 miles (240 km) north, too far away to catch up with the *Bismarck* before she reached St. Nazaire. The following morning the German battleship was still steaming south at 28 knots, now only 690 miles (1,104 km) from the French port. The only hope of stopping her now was the torpedo aircraft of the *Ark Royal* coming up from the south. Although Lütjen's radio signals had given away his position, the British had still been unable to make contact with the *Bismarck*.

Then the luck changed. At 1030 hours a Coastal Command Catalina sighted the German battleship, and when it was relieved from its task of shadowing by a wheeled aircraft, the *Bismarck*'s crew knew at once that there was an aircraft carrier in

The Prinz Eugen *fires during sea trials.*

the area. The day dragged on without an
attack being launched, and as twilight
began to fall, hopes began to rise – darkness
would certainly see them safe. By the
following morning they would be well
within range of the shore-based Luftwaffe
bombers standing by to give them cover.
(A sortie of Swordfish had indeed taken off
at 1450 hours, but they had attacked the
heavy cruiser *Sheffield*, mistaking her for
the *Bismarck*. Fortunately not one of the
torpedoes hit.) The anticipated attack
finally came at 2055 hours; 16 Swordfish,
ancient 'Stringbags', lumbered in at
100 mph (160 km/h) through the growing
twilight. Fifteen dropped their 'fish' but all
missed; incredibly none of the aircraft had
been hit by the wall of flak being thrown up
by the *Bismarck*. The last aircraft came in
from the stern, too low and too close for
the anti-aircraft gunners to depress their
guns to bear on it. As one torpedo hit the
rudders and jammed them, the *Bismarck*
swung 12 degrees to starboard in a circle.
Desperate attempts made to correct her
course were of no avail; she settled on a
northern course which took her towards
the oncoming force from Scapa Flow. The
next morning, after numerous unsuccessful
torpedo attacks by destroyers throughout
the night, she was yawing at 7 knots
towards the British capital ships – a sitting
target. Adolf Hitler's radio message, 'I
thank you in the name of the entire
German People', did nothing to raise the
feeling of impending doom. At 0827 hours
the British ships opened up at 25,000 yards
(23,000 m), rapidly closing to the 8-inch
(20-cm) gun range of the heavy cruisers.
Salvo after salvo crashed into the German
battleship, but still she fought back, until,
a battered hulk, she was torpedoed by the
cruiser *Dorset* at close range. The Germans
claimed that even then she had to be
scuttled. Finally, at 1039 hours, the *Bismarck* slid beneath the waves, her ensign

still proudly flying. Of her crew of 2,200,
only 115 survived. It had taken 2,876
shells and 39 torpedoes to sink her.

The sinking of the *Bismarck* saw the end
of commercial raiding by German surface
warships. German armed merchant cruisers
continued to operate in the Western
Pacific and Indian Oceans, however,
sinking 586,602 tons (595,988 tonnes)
of merchant shipping before they were
destroyed.

Although he had only four veteran
battleships at his command (two had
fought at Jutland), Admiral Sir Andrew
Cunningham, commander of the British
Mediterranean Fleet, played havoc with
the Italian Navy which was rated the fifth
most powerful in the world. His success
was, in the main, due to the exploits of his
carrier-borne aircraft. On the night of 10
November 1940, two waves of Swordfish
attacked and inflicted considerable damage
on an Italian fleet at their base at Taranto.
For the loss of two aircraft, the battleship
Conte de Cavour had been destroyed and
two others put out of commission for six
months.

In March of the following year, a powerful Italian squadron consisting of the
41,000-ton (41,660 tonnes) battleship *Vittoria Veneto*, six armoured cruisers and 11
destroyers, sailed for Crete to destroy a
British troop convoy in the area. Immediately, the old battleships *Warspite*, *Barham*
and *Valiant* left Alexandria in Egypt to
intercept. On the afternoon of the 28
March, having been damaged in a torpedo
attack carried out by Swordfish and Alba-
cores, the *Vittorio Veneto* turned for home
with her escort, making 19 knots towards
Taranto. A second attack, off Matapan at
sunset, by Albacore torpedo bombers from
the *Formidable*, crippled the heavy cruiser
Pola, which was left wallowing helplessly.
Once he realized the *Pola* was no longer
with his fleet, the Italian commander,

Admiral Iachino, unaware of the approaching British battle squadron (the Italians at that time had no radar), sent back Vice-Admiral Cattaneo with two heavy cruisers and four destroyers to assist her. Faced with the oncoming battleships, the Italian cruisers had no chance. In three minutes 15-inch (38-cm) salvoes left the cruisers *Zara* and *Fiume* sinking; the *Pola* was also sent to the bottom, along with two destroyers.

Maiali

Smarting under the humiliation of two resounding naval defeats, the Italians planned to exact their revenge in December 1941 by carrying out one of the most daring operations of the war. They intended to sink two of the three British battleships still remaining in the Mediterranean where they lay in Alexandria harbour – the *Queen Elizabeth* and *Valiant*. The *Warspite* had left the area and they were not to know that the other one, the *Barham*, had already been sunk by a German U-Boat.

As early as the First World War, the Italian Navy had been experimenting with midget submarines and other underwater assault techniques. By 1939 they had perfected the use of 'maiali' (pigs), manned torpedoes with detachable warheads, driven by frogmen. These had been introduced by two marine engineer lieutenants, Tesei and Toschi, during the Abyssinian campaign. Crewed by two frogmen, the 'siluro a lenta corsa', or S.L.C. (slow-running torpedo), was 17 ft (5.2 m) long, 18 inches (46 cm) in diameter and carried a 660-lb (300-kg) warhead – enough to rip the bottom out of a battleship. Silent electric motors drove them through the water at a speed of 2 to 3 knots, with a range of ten miles (16 km). The *maiali* were designed to work at a maximum depth of 77 ft (23.5 m). Below that the thin metal of the craft buckled. The frogmen each wore a Davis Underwater Escape Apparatus, which recycled oxygen. They were fitted with two diving tanks, steered by means of a control column and magnetic compass, and had a tool-box containing compressed-air net-lifters, net-cutters and clamps. The *maiali*, although dangerous to operate, were never seen as suicide weapons; the frogmen always had a chance to escape – the suicide torpedo came later when Japan entered the war. Erroneously termed 'human torpedo', the *maiali* were later copied by the Royal Navy who called them 'Chariots'.

In the main, though, the British and German navies concentrated on building

HMS Ark Royal.

and developing midget submarines which could be launched close to their targets by parent submarines. The Royal Navy had a number of 'X-Craft', four-man midget submarines, in commission by 1943. They were designed to penetrate the Norwegian fjords to attack German surface ships. They, like the *maiali*, were fitted with detachable warheads. The German midget submarines, on the other hand, carried torpedoes and were mainly designed for coastal defence in the event of an attempted invasion. In September 1943 six X-Craft attacked the battleship *Tirpitz* in Altenfjord, and although their explosive warheads did not sink her, they caused enough damage for the warship to be moved south for repairs, which brought her within bomber range of the R.A.F.

The exploits of two Italian seamen, Paolucci and Rosseti, who in 1918 succeeded in attaching an underwater charge to the Austrian battleship *Viribus Unitis* and sinking her, inspired the formation of the M.A.S. in 1940. The 10th Flotilla M.A.S. (*Motoscafanti sommergibili* – motor-torpedo-boats) was set up to build and experiment with various types of small assault craft, the most successful of which were the *maiali*. After a number of disappointing attempts that ended disastrously for *maiali* crews, they at last sank two ships

in the harbour at Gibraltar. Encouraged by this, and insensed by the outrage of Matapan, the M.A.S. planned a daring and seemingly suicidal attack on the British naval base at Alexandria.

As the Italian submarine *Scire* slipped away from her base on the Greek island of Leros, her commander, Captain Count Julio Borghese, was very much aware that Greek agents would already be radioing his departure to the British. If the *Scire* was out, with the distinctive *maiali* containers built on to her deck, it could mean one thing only: an attack on Alexandria harbour. Twice such an attempt had been made, ending with the destruction of both submarines and their entire crews. So it was a nervous commander who eased *Scire* to the surface, 6 miles (10 km) off the Egyptian coast at 2000 hours on 18 December 1941. It was a still, pitch-black night, the muddy water gently lapping over the deck of the submarine; a distant glow marked the position of the British naval base. The attack had been planned to coincide with the Nile flood which would muddy the water for miles beyond the mouth of the river, making detection from the air all but impossible.

Six nightmarish figures, clad in rubberized canvas suits and goggles and with a Davis apparatus strapped to their chests,

The Bismarck *as sighted from a Catalina, from a painting by Norman Wilkinson.*

Left: Italian maiali, the 'human torpedoes', used with such devastating success at Alexandria.

clambered down the conning-tower ladder and hauled out and mounted their *maiali*. The attack group leader, 24-year-old Lieutenant-Captain Luigi de la Penne, and his diver, Leading-seaman Emilio Bianchi, had the battleship *Valiant* as their target. Captain Antonio Marceglia and Spartaco Schergat were to sink the *Queen Elizabeth*, and Captain Vincenzio Martelotta and Mario Marino were to destroy an unidentified aircraft carrier. As they turned their painfully slow craft towards the mole, Borghese was already taking the *Scire* down; he would rendezvous off Rosetta to pick them up – if they made it.

After nearly four hours in the bitterly cold water, the frogmen arrived shivering at the anti-submarine boom, having narrowly escaped being blown out of the water by the 22-lb (10-kg) bombs of a guard ship. Such guard ships dropped a haphazard line of bombs to deter frogmen. The three heavy anti-submarine nets had no gaps in them and de la Penne was loath to use the noisy compressed-air net-cutters – in any event, the nets were almost certainly wired for sound. When attempts to swim their *maiali* over the nets proved unsuccessful, it seemed that the mission had failed. Then, on the stroke of midnight, the powerful lights that illuminated the sandbanks marking the deep channel into the harbour went on; a boom ship dragged open the nets and four destroyers nosed their way in. An instant decision and the Italians were alongside the destroyers, a bare few feet from their hulls, being pushed under by the

wash. Choking and spluttering, they came to the surface – they had been unable to wear their masks because reflections from the goggle lenses would have given them away – they were in.

The order for 'liberty of manoeuvre' was given and the group split up to attack. De la Penne and Bianchi made for the *Valiant*, her vast bulk silhouetted by the bright quayside lights under which a number of merchantmen were unloading their cargo – the battleship was less than a mile (1,600 m) away. A half-hour's cruise through the oily, flotsam-strewn water and they had reached the *Valiant*'s anti-submarine net, a rope contrivance lined with steel balls which clattered together in the slight swell. Despite the noise they made hauling the *maiale* over the net, there was no sign of activity aboard the warship. Swiftly they submerged, aiming for the *Valiant*'s keel; with a dull thud they hit the hull of the battleship. Bianchi leapt off to

Below: Leaving a maiale on the sea bed in order to attach the warhead.

attach the warhead wire to the port side of the ship. The *maiale* slowly sank to the bottom, spun round, then slithered to a stop as its propellers became choked with the slimy ooze. Chest-deep in liquid mud, de la Penne desperately tried to haul his craft closer to the battleship's keel; Bianchi, suffering from lack of oxygen, had fainted and floated to the surface. De la Penne was alone. For an hour he struggled with the *maiale*, dragging it inch by inch under the centre of the keel. At one point, blinded by the sweat pouring down his face, he attempted to clear his mask but only succeeded in filling it with water. Unable to see or breathe, he was forced to gulp down the stinking harbour water. At last the warhead was positioned under the centre of the *Valiant*, directly below her ammunition locker, and the fuses set. Sick and fainting, de le Penne floated to the surface only to be greeted by rifle fire from the battleship. Frenziedly he scrambled up the ship's buoy, only to find his diver, Bianchi, already crouching there.

To their relief, the two Italians were taken for parachutists and were hurried ashore to be questioned by Commander Crabbe, who recognized de la Penne. (Crabbe, himself a renowned frogman, was to disappear mysteriously some years after the war, while diving under a brand-new Soviet cruiser on a courtesy visit to Portsmouth harbour.) Immediately the Italians were taken back to the *Valiant*, questioned and, by a cruel stroke of fate, housed in the ammunition locker under which lay the fused warhead. Demanding to be taken to the captain, de la Penne informed him that his ship was about to go up but, refusing to reveal the position of the warhead, he was taken back to the ammunition locker – however, Bianchi had gone; he was alone. Over the Tannoy broadcasting system, he could hear the order, 'Stand by to abandon ship. Stand by to abandon ship', blaring out – only a skeleton crew was left aboard. With barely minutes to go before the explosion, he began to pray – very quickly. He was still praying when the flash came – a deafening roar – then he passed out. He regained consciousness to the stench of high explosive fumes. Miraculously the hatch of the locker had been blown off and so he scrambled to the upper deck, to a scene of panic and confusion.

As he staggered aft, overjoyed at being alive, the sun came up behind the *Queen Elizabeth*. There was a sudden roar and the battleship lifted out of the water – Marceglia and Schergat had succeeded. Marceglia and Schergat reached the Old Pier which had been specified by Italian Intelligence, and made their way to Rosetta only to be arrested when they tried to cash the British bank notes with which they had been provided and which were invalid in Egypt. Finding that the aircraft carrier had already sailed, the third team slung its warhead beneath the stern of a 7,750-ton (7,870-tonne) oil tanker, the *Sagona*. But the alarm had been given and Martelotta and Marino were picked up as they crawled exhausted up the steps of the Old Pier.

After close interrogation, the six Italians were taken off to a British Prisoner of War Camp in Palestine. Between them they had struck a crippling blow – the Royal Navy was now without a single capital ship in the Mediterranean, and would be for many months to come. Both the *Valiant* and *Queen Elizabeth* had settled to the bottom of Alexandria harbour, their upper decks a foot or so above the surface of the water.

Pearl Harbor

The success of the Royal Navy's torpedo bombers at Taranto had not gone unnoticed in the Far East. A pilot himself, Admiral Isonekei Yamamoto, Commander-in-Chief of the Combined Fleet of the Imperial Japanese Navy, had long been a staunch advocate of naval aviation, and saw it as the means of achieving Japan's ambitions in Southeast Asia. Here, in

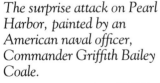

The surprise attack on Pearl Harbor, painted by an American naval officer, Commander Griffith Bailey Coale.

Japanese aircraft warm up on the flight-deck of the Kiryu .

Southeast Asia, were all the raw materials Japan needed if she were to be self-sufficient and independent of Western nations for her very existence: tin and rubber from Malaya; oil, nickel, lead, coal and phosphates from the East Indies; iron from the Philippines; and rice from Burma and Indo-China. The stumbling block to the achievement of these ambitions was the United States of America, in particular the U.S. Pacific Fleet at its base in Pearl Harbor, Hawaii. The Japanese Imperial General Staff were aware that should Japanese armies sweep south into Asia, the United States forces were bound to intervene, despite their strong isolationist policy towards the European war.

The introduction of the Two-Ocean Naval Expansion Act by the U.S.A., after France had fallen to the Germans, finally swayed any remaining Japanese Army and Navy leaders who were averse to going to war with the United States. The Act called for the construction of seven battleships, 18 aircraft carriers, 27 cruisers, 115 destroyers and 42 submarines by 1944, at a cost of $4,000,000,000. When added to the 358 major warships already in commission and the 130 on the stocks, it would make Japan's hope of fighting a defensive naval engagement in the Western Pacific impossible. Based on the theory that a fleet lost ten per cent of its effectiveness with every 1,000 miles (1,600 km) it operated from its base, and on the fact that the U.S.

Navy was already committed in the Atlantic, Japanese naval planners calculated a 10:7 advantage to the Americans. These appeared more than advantageous odds for the Japanese Fleet, concentrated in one place, to fight a defensive battle among the Carolines and Marianas and thereby force the Americans to recognize a negotiated peace. The Two-Ocean Act, which would give the U.S. Navy a 10:3 advantage, altered all that. Japan's only hope was to attack the U.S. Pacific Fleet before the building programme got under way, when the ratio would be most advantageous to her, sometime in late 1941 or early 1942.

The mounting success of the Axis Powers in Europe encouraged the Imperial Navy General Staff to draw up a startling plan by March 1941, for a lightning, unheralded, carrier attack on Pearl Harbor. Historically such attacks had succeeded for Japan against the superior naval forces of Russia and China at the turn of the century, when localized Japanese superiority had forced her enemies to sue for peace. In both instances, surprise offensive operations had won the day.

The architect of the surprise attack on Pearl Harbor was Admiral Yamamoto, assisted by Vice-Admiral Onishi. (The latter was an even more fervent advocate of naval aviation, who was later to introduce the 'Kamikaze' suicide attacks.) The detailed planning fell to Commander Minoru Genda and a small staff. Originally

Diagram of the Japanese
attack on Pearl Harbor.

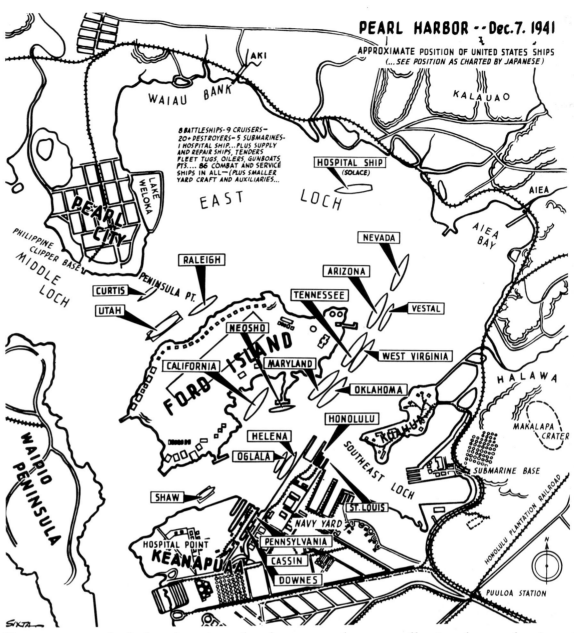

PEARL HARBOR -- Dec.7. 1941

APPROXIMATE POSITION OF UNITED STATES SHIPS
(...SEE POSITION AS CHARTED BY JAPANESE)

AKI

WAIAU BANK

WAIPIO PENINSULA

MIDDLE LOCH

PHILIPPINE CLIPPER BASE

PEARL CITY

LAKE WELOKA

EAST LOCH

8 BATTLESHIPS-9 CRUISERS-
20+ DESTROYERS-5 SUBMARINES-
1 HOSPITAL SHIP...PLUS SUPPLY
AND REPAIR SHIPS, TENDERS
FLEET TUGS, OILERS, GUNBOATS
PTS.... 86 COMBAT AND SERVICE
SHIPS IN ALL—(PLUS SMALLER
YARD CRAFT AND AUXILIARIES...

HOSPITAL SHIP
(SOLACE)

KALAUAO

AIEA

AIEA BAY

NEVADA

ARIZONA

VESTAL

RALEIGH

CURTIS

PENINSULA PT.

UTAH

NEOSHO

CALIFORNIA

FORD ISLAND

MARYLAND

TENNESSEE

WEST VIRGINIA

OKLAHOMA

HONOLULU

HELENA

OGLALA

SHAW

HOSPITAL POINT

KEANAPUA

NAVY YARD

PENNSYLVANIA

CASSIN

DOWNES

ST. LOUIS

SOUTHEAST LOCH

SUBMARINE BASE

HALAWA

MAKALAPA CRATER

HONOLULU PLANTATION RAILROAD

PUULOA STATION

SIXTA

Yamamoto marked the American battleships as the main target, but Genda
reasoned that if they really believed in the
effectiveness of carrier-borne attack, then
the U.S. aircraft carriers must be their
principal objective. With traditional
thoroughness the Japanese set about solv-
ing the problems of such an operation: first,
how to get 450 naval planes within striking
distance without being detected; second,
how to sink capital ships in such an
enclosed space.

Normally Japanese torpedo attacks were
delivered from around 250 ft (76.2 m) at
150 mph (240 km/h); the torpedo plunged
to 14 fathoms before it took an upward
course. This would be out of the question
in the restricted space of Pearl Harbor with
its eight fathoms of water. Genda, Naval
Attaché in London at the time of the
Taranto attack which had also been delivered in eight fathoms of water, had carefully studied the Fleet Air Arm techniques,
and now applied them to his training
schedule. It was agreed that torpedo attacks

were the most effective, but as the American capital ships were moored in two lines,
it would be impossible to attack the inner
line in this manner. They would be attacked by high-altitude 'pattern-bombing'
and dive bombing. To achieve total surprise, the Japanese Fleet would have to sail
for 11 days before issuing a Declaration of
War, in order to arrive at an attacking
distance of 230 miles (368 km). Any merchantmen from Britain, Holland, France
and the U.S. encountered would be sunk
and the ships of other nations would have
their radios put out of action. Should the
worsening negotiations between Japan and
the U.S. prove successful at the eleventh
hour, the commander of the attack force,
Vice-Admiral Chuichi Nagumo, would be
informed in enough time to enable him to
turn his fleet and return to Japan.

On 26 November 1941 the Task Force
put to sea from Tankan Bay in the remote
Kurile Islands: four fleet aircraft carriers
and two light fleet carriers, housing a total
of 450 aircraft; also two battleships; three

cruisers; and nine destroyers. Their course was planned to avoid normal shipping lanes, sailing between the Aleutians and Midway Island, out of range of patrols from either place. They would almost certainly meet some rough weather, but on this route there would be less chance of being detected, a situation further enhanced by enforced radio silence. The calculated odds that only seven days in the month would be fine enough for refuelling at sea were high, but they were odds that had to be accepted; in any event, they turned in favour of the Japanese. The American reply to the Japanese proposals proved unsatisfactory to the War Junta in the Japanese Cabinet, so the decision to go to war was taken on 1 December 1941. On 3 December Yamamoto radioed Naguma, 'Niitaka yama nobore' ('Climb Mount Niitaka') – this was the agreed signal to attack at sunrise at 0750 hours on Monday 8 December (1320 hours on Sunday 7 December, Washington time). Japanese ambassador Nomura had been instructed to hand Secretary of State Cordell Hull a Declaration of War at a meeting requested for 1300 hours, 20 minutes before the attack. As it turned out, Nomura was not received until 1420 hours by which time the attack was well under-

way and Cordell Hull had already received a radio message from the Commander-in-Chief of the U.S. Pacific Fleet, Admiral Kemmel, 'Air attack on Pearl Harbor. This is no exercise'.

About 230 miles (368 km) north of Pearl Harbor, Nagumo's carriers turned into the wind for the take-off; the first wave of 183 aircraft flew off. H-Hour for Pearl Harbor was set at 0750 hours. At 0740 hours strike leader Commander Mitsuo Fuchida fired a 'Black Dragon' flare. Flying at 10,000 ft (3,050 m), the torpedo bombers broke off to lead the attack. Below them lay, nose-to-tail, seven battleships at their moorings. Fuchida transmitted the victory signal 'Tora, Tora, Tora' at 0753, just before the first bombs fell. But to Naguma and Genda, it could never be a complete victory. When he had learned the previous night that there were no aircraft carriers in Pearl Harbor, Nagumo had hesitated to implement the attack.

The Americans were caught completely unawares, their battleships unprotected by torpedo nets, their anti-aircraft defences at stand-by. A last-chance radar report at 0706 which claimed to have established contact with a large number of aircraft closing at 150 knots was ignored in the

View of Pearl Harbor taken from one of the incoming Japanese aircraft.

A photograph of the attack taken from the submarine base at Pearl Harbor.

belief that they were a group of B-17s being flown in that morning from California. Within minutes the U.S. airfields were virtually obliterated; of the 394 aircraft assembled, only a handful managed to get off the ground and most of those were destroyed on take-off or while gaining height. In all, 188 aircraft were destroyed in the attacks. At 0758 hours the first torpedoes crashed into the helpless battleships. It was not until the second wave of 170 Japanese aircraft appeared that American AA flak became effective, but by then most of the damage had been done. By 1000 hours it was all over. For the loss of 29 naval planes, Nagumo had sunk or put out of commission 18 warships including eight battleships, wiped out 80 per cent of the aircraft on Oahu, and killed or wounded 3,681 American personnel.

Vice-Admiral Nagumo had every reason to be pleased with the outcome of the operation, but he saw long-term disaster in the escape of the American aircraft carriers – and he was right. The value of carrier-borne aircraft attack had been hammered home to Washington in no uncertain manner, and left with few front-line battleships, the United States Navy rebuilt its tactical formation around the Fast Carrier Task Group concept, a concept that was eventually to defeat the Imperial Japanese Navy.

Battle of Midway

Following Pearl Harbor, the Japanese High Command became obsessed with acquiring oil, hardly listening to Admiral Yamamoto's plea for a long-term strategic plan. A brilliant stream of successes – Wake Island, the Philippines, Malaya and Singapore and the Dutch East Indies – gave Japan all the oil she needed. The British battleship *Prince of Wales* and battle-cruiser *Repulse* were sunk by torpedo aircraft, Hong Kong had surrendered and the disastrous Battle of the Java Sea had left the way open to an invasion of Ceylon and Australia. Already the Imperial Army had entered Burma. The main Japanese problem appeared to be her future strategy: should Japan turn her attention to Ceylon or to Australia or should she strike westwards towards India to join up with her Axis partners in the Middle East or should she try to take Pearl Harbor and destroy the U.S. Pacific Fleet? The latter option would necessitate the same element of surprise as had already been achieved once before at Pearl Harbor, but this was not possible with Midway Island acting as a long-distance outpost to the base. However, this gave Yamamoto a chance. The capture of Midway would provide a highly desirable air base against the increasing activity of American aircraft carriers; it would deny them an advance submarine fuelling base and act as a jumping-off point to capturing Pearl Harbor. Yamamoto, however, also saw an attack on Midway as the bait to draw out the U.S. Pacific Fleet and destroy it; he was convinced that failure to do so in 1942 would lose Japan the war.

At the beginning of May an Imperial directive was issued ordering Yamamoto, as Commander-in-Chief of the Combined Fleet, to 'Carry out the occupation of Midway Island and key points in the Aleutians, in co-operation with the Army.' Operation MI was underway, and a vast fleet, divided into five major tactical groups, assembled in Japanese waters.

Group I
Battle-Fleet – Admiral Yamamoto
6 Battleships including the mammoth *Yamato* in which he flew his flag
1 Light Fleet Carrier *Hosho*
3 Light Cruisers
21 Destroyers
2 Seaplane Carriers transporting midget submarines

Group II
First Carrier Assault Group – Vice-Admiral Nagumo
4 Aircraft Carriers
2 Battleships
3 Cruisers
12 Destroyers

Group III
Midway Invasion Force – Vice-Admiral Kondo
2 Battleships
9 Cruisers
1 Light Fleet Carrier
22 Destroyers
12 Troop Transports

Group IV
North Fleet (Aleutians) – Vice-Admiral Hosogaya
2 Aircraft carriers
4 Cruisers
9 Destroyers
1 Troop Transport

Group V
Submarine Screen Group – Vice-Admiral Komatsu
15 Submarines

The number of aircraft was about 700

The Americans had only 3 aircraft carriers, 13 cruisers, 29 destroyers, 19 submarines and 342 aircraft with which to face the immense Japanese fleet. Should the two come within heavy gun range, there could be only one outcome – the U.S. Pacific Fleet would be annihilated. However, Admiral Chester Nimitz, who had replaced Admiral Kemmel as C-in-C Pacific Fleet, held three trump cards; first, he had 119 aircraft based on Midway Island, an unsinkable aircraft carrier; second, having broken the Japanese naval code, he knew exactly what Admiral Yamamoto intended; and third, the Japanese Admiral had no idea that there were American carriers in the area because a misleading report from Tokyo had put them in the region of the Solomons. As far as Yamamoto's intelligence reports were concerned, he would be facing 750 marines, 24 flying boats, 12 bombers and 20 fighters on Midway. The invasion force under Vice-Admiral Kondo was carrying 5,000 Japanese assault troops. The stage was set for an entirely new concept of naval warfare.

A drawing, in the traditional Japanese manner, of mechanics working on aircraft aboard a carrier.

Hellcats lined up on the flight-deck of an American carrier in the Pacific.

STRENGTHS OF FLEETS

	Japanese	American
Battleships	11	Nil
Aircraft Carriers	8(700 aircraft)	3(223 aircraft)
Cruisers	22	13
Destroyers	65	28
Submarines	23	19
Shore-based Aircraft	Nil	119 on Midway.

As he knew Yamamoto's intentions, Admiral Nimitz was not deceived by Vice-Admiral Hosogaya's diversionary attack on the Aleutians, instead he concentrated on locating the enemy's Midway force.

In the pre-dawn darkness of 4 June 1942, 250 miles (400 km) northwest of Midway, the Japanese pilots scrambled up to the flight-decks of their carriers and were greeted by the roar of aircraft engines warming up and the shouts of the ships' crews lining the decks. Nagumo himself had briefed them ending with the words, 'Although the enemy is lacking in fighting spirit, he will probably come out to attack during our invasion'. It was still dark when the *Akagi*'s floodlights came on and wave after wave of aircraft took off to shouts of '*Banzai*' from the assembled crews. Nagumo had no reason to believe that there were American carriers in the area, but he was inclined to be cautious and held back half the aircraft and his best pilots to meet a possible counterattack. He also ordered off seven reconnaissance planes for an air search but the fortunes of war were definitely against the Japanese at this point. Two were delayed for 30 minutes by catapult trouble, another was forced to return through engine trouble and the remainder turned back halfway through their search because of poor visibility – the course of at least two would have taken them directly over the oncoming American carriers.

Having detected the incoming Japanese aircraft by radar at 0553 hours, every U.S. plane was airborne by 0600 hours – the bombers and Catalinas to keep away, the fighters to gain height and attack. The 21 Buffalos and six Wildcats were no match for the 'Humps', an improved version of the original 'Zero'. Dreadfully outnumbered, only 12 returned to base and seven of those were so badly damaged that they never flew again. Japanese bombers plastered the airfield and installations, but their aiming was made erratic by intensely accurate anti-aircraft fire; ten of them were shot down. At 0700 hours the bomber group under Lieutenant Tomonaga signalled that a second strike would be necessary.

A number of bombing sorties by B-26s (Flying Fortresses), Grumman Avengers,

Marauders and Douglas Dauntless bombers from Midway proved unsuccessful. Not a single Japanese ship was hit and, without fighter escort, the bombers were cut to pieces; 18 were shot down and many that made it back to base never flew again. Tomonaga's call for a second bombing attack on Midway hurried Nagumo into making a fatal decision. The aircraft on the carrier *Kaga* had been loaded with torpedoes for an anti-ship strike; the Japanese Admiral now ordered these to be changed for bombs. They were taken below to the hanger decks where mechanics and armourers worked frantically to exchange torpedoes for bombs. It was in the middle of this, the deck littered with bombs and torpedoes, that a report came through that there was an American surface strike force in the vicinity. Incredibly enough, it was first reported as a cruiser force but, at 0830 hours, the presence of aircraft carriers was confirmed. By then 68 dive bombers, 29 torpedo aircraft and 20 fighters were beginning their 200-mile (320-km) flight from American TF.16 (Task Force 16), which included the *Hornet* and *Enterprise* under

the command of Rear-Admiral Spraunce. TF.17 under Rear-Admiral Fletcher with the carrier *Yorktown* and her 75 aircraft was a further hour astern.

The arming process was reversed aboard the *Kaga* as the crew hurried to re-arm with torpedoes. Further confusion hit the Japanese carrier as the aircraft from the Midway strike force came in to land. Thus it was 0915 hours before a flustered Nagumo was able to turn to face the enemy. The first American assault was beaten off with a fearful loss of American aircraft; it appeared that American naval pilots were no match for the battle-experienced Japanese pilots. His fleet unscathed, Nagumo moved the heavy carriers north for his own strike; the *Akagi* and *Soryu* were 5 miles (8 km) apart, followed by the *Kaga* and *Hiryu*, 2 miles (3 km) astern. It was at this point that the dive bombers from the *Yorktown* arrived overhead, supported by the reformed aircraft from the *Hornet* and *Enterprise*. Captain Fuchida aboard the *Akagi* later wrote, 'Dark objects were already falling – bombs, and straight at me. . . . There came an explosion, a blinding flash

Overleaf: Swordfish torpedo attack, from a painting by the author.

The Japanese aircraft carrier Zuiho *being attacked by strike planes from USS* Enterprise.

USS Yorktown *goes down during the Battle of Midway.*

Opposite top: Japanese ships avoiding attack by strike planes of the U.S. Navy.

Opposite bottom: A Japanese Kamikaze pilot aims his 'Zero' at the USS Missouri.

from a direct hit, then a second explosion more violent than the first.' The second wave of American aircraft exacted a terrible revenge for the massacre of the U.S. pilots in the first attack. Inside four minutes the *Akagi* had been hit three times. One 1,000-lb (450-kg) bomb penetrated the flight-deck and exploded among 40 armed and fuelled aircraft parked at-the-ready below. Within 15 minutes Nagumo transferred his flag to a light cruiser – the *Akagi* was a roaring inferno. At much the same time the *Kaga* was hit in a number of places; she also had bombs explode in her hanger deck among combat-ready aircraft, and was soon ablaze. Dive bombers from the *Yorktown* attacked the *Soryu*, catching her ready for take-off, her aircraft lined up on the flight-deck, none of them yet airborne. Hit numerous times, she too was set ablaze from stem to stern. Later she was sunk by torpedoes from the American submarine *Nautilus*. It took only five minutes for the dominance of the Imperial Japanese Navy in the Pacific, which had lasted almost six months, to be utterly destroyed.

However, there was still the *Hiryu*. Resolving to sell herself dearly, she flew off 18 'Val' dive bombers escorted by a handful of 'Zeros' – her target was the *Yorktown*. Even though the Japanese suffered heavy losses, the first strike from the *Hiryu* set the *Yorktown* on fire; the second strike of ten 'Kate' torpedo bombers completely crippled the American carrier, leaving her listing so badly that she was abandoned as lost. She was finally sunk some days later by a Japanese submarine. The *Hiryu* survived until the following day when, once again,

the vulnerability of large surface ships to attack from the air was demonstrated. Left a rapidly burning hulk, the *Hiryu* was finally sent to the bottom by torpedoes from one of her own destroyers.

After a token shelling of Midway to 'save face', Yamamoto withdrew his main force, having lost the heavy cruiser *Mikuma*. The Japanese successes in the Pacific were finished. She had lost four of her frontline carriers, all 256 of her aircraft and, perhaps even more important, half of her experienced air crews. The 16-inch (41-cm) guns of her capital ships had been quite useless – the enemy had never even been sighted. The Americans, on the other hand, although they lost 100 aircraft, recovered most of their pilots. The Battle of Midway was the turning point of the war in the Pacific, and although it dragged on, during which time both the mammoth *Yamato* and *Musashi* were sunk by aircraft attack, the outcome for the Imperial Japanese Navy was never really in doubt.

Suicide tactics were tried as a last resort, including 'human torpedoes' and 'kamikaze' attacks by aircraft and manned bombs, but the results hardly justified the loss of fanatically brave men and aircraft, and certainly had no effect on the outcome of the war. For 1,228 aircraft expended and 298 manned bombs, the Japanese claimed 81 enemy ships sunk and 195 damaged; the actual figures were 34 vessels sunk and 288 damaged. During the summer of 1945, the atomic bombs dropped on Hiroshima and Nagasaki ended the war but opened up a fearful new concept of warfare which was to revolutionize future naval strategy.

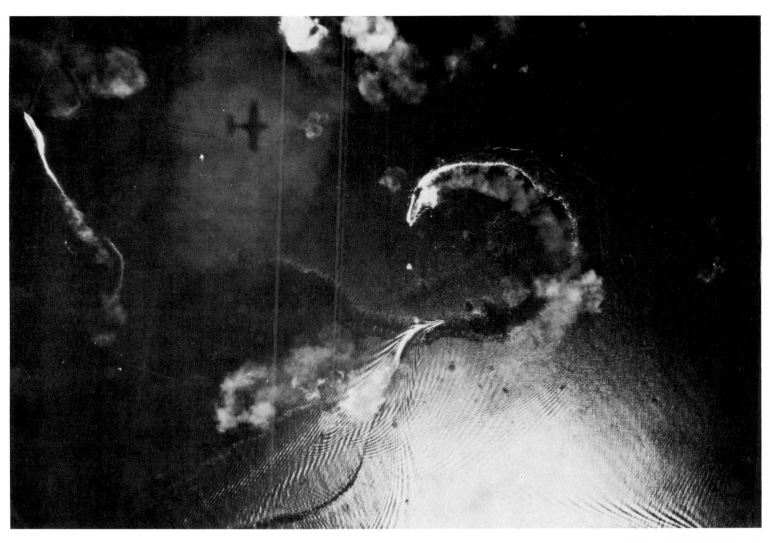

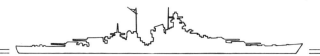

Modern Sea Warfare

By the end of the Second World War even the most entrenched champion of the big-gun ship had been forced to admit that aircraft had proved to be the single most important factor in the victory at sea. The mightiest, most heavily armoured battle-ships had succumbed to attacks from the air, and the aircraft carrier ruled supreme. True, the 72,800-ton (74,000-tonne) *Musashi* with her massive AA fire power had absorbed 20 torpedoes, 17 hits by armour-piercing bombs and suffered 15 near-misses before she finally went under, but in the end, aircraft sunk her. The loss of life when a battleship went under was usually enormous; the *Musashi* lost 1,039 of her complement of 2,400; the *Yamato* more than 3,000; only three men were saved from the *Hood's* crew of 1,419 and 115 from the *Bismarck's* 2,200.

The Twilight of the Battleship

Nonetheless, it was on the quarterdeck of the battleship USS *Missouri* that the Japan-ese signed the surrender terms. Naval per-sonnel were reluctant to see the end of the once-proud floating fortresses that had reigned as the epitomy of naval power since the Armada. Britain built the *Vanguard* in 1944, but not being completed until 1946, she never saw action – although her 15-inch (38-cm) guns had, having first been used on the battle cruisers *Glorious* and *Courageous* in the First World War. She displaced 42,500 tons (43,200 tonnes) and was designed and built to withstand every form of attack – on the surface, below it, or from the air. These qualities, how-ever, were never put to the test; after a brief service with the fleet, she followed her earlier sister battleships to the breaker's yard. The Americans, reluctant to scrap all their 57,450-ton (58,400-tonne), 16-inch (41-cm) battleships, either relegated them to a 'mothball fleet', cocooned in silver-grey plastic, or turned them into national monuments. Other plans, at one stage or another, were put forward to convert them into missile ships, oil tankers or replenish-ment ships, but all these schemes fell through on the grounds of cost.

Battleships did, however, give one final twitch, before giving way to the aircraft carrier. In the age of the guided-missile, nuclear warhead and fast, supersonic air-craft, it was discovered that it was cheaper and more efficient to carry out shore bom-bardment from a battleship. In conse-quence, the United States took the 57,450-ton (58,400-tonne) *New Jersey* out of mothballs and, after a re-conversion costing $21,000,000, put her into action in Vietnam in 1968, where she fired 5,688 16-inch (41-cm) shells, more than seven times as many as she fired during the Second World War.

Before the end of the Second World War, it was obvious to many that the irreconcilable ideological differences be-tween the Soviet Union and the West would widen rather than narrow. As it turned out, the nations of the world split into two mutually antagonistic camps. On the one side behind the 'Iron Curtain' was the U.S.S.R. and her Communist satel-lites; on the other were the Western demo-cracies. At the end of all previous wars national economic exhaustion had forced nations into a policy of disarmament, but this pattern was reversed after the Second World War. The hoped-for disarmament programme, in fact, turned into a substan-tial arms race. To counter Soviet ag-gression, the U.S.A., Britain, France and other Western powers signed the North Atlantic Treaty which called for the setting up of a common NATO defence force. The Soviets, for their part, built up their forces, fearing aggression from the West. Having always been regarded primarily as a land-based threat, the Soviets began to enlarge their navy in a dramatic fashion, concentrating on the submarine. The Western nations, on the other hand, led by the U.S., discarded the battleship as a major naval strike weapon and turned to the development of bigger and better aircraft carriers.

Both the United States and Britain were reluctant to relinquish the superiority they had gained in naval aviation by the end of the Second World War. The U.S. had

USS New Jersey fires her 16-inch guns after her re-fitting in 1968.

Opposite: Preparing the catapult for an aircraft launch aboard USS Independence.

Opposite bottom: Launching an Exocet missile.

41,000 naval aircraft; Britain had 1,336 planes which were divided among 52 aircraft carriers into more than 70 strike and fighter squadrons. Both had ambitious carrier-building programmes in hand, but these were later curtailed as other events took over. The arrival of jet-propelled aircraft, larger and heavier than their predecessors, posed innumerable problems for the carrier designers. The vastly increased speed of aircraft called for longer flight-decks; their increased weight called for stronger ones; and their increased size meant that fewer could be stowed. All was set for a radical change in the design of aircraft carriers to cope with the higher take-off and landing speeds required, when a number of innovations cancelled out these problems. The first of these innovations was the angled flight-deck which allowed aircraft with fast landing speeds the chance to throttle up and go round for another attempt in the case of misjudgement. This was followed by the steam catapult. Drawing power from the ship's boilers, these catapults were powerful enough to launch the heaviest of naval aircraft. Deck-landing at speed was made safer by the mirror landing sight (MLS) which superseded the batman. Projecting a beam of white light from a curved mirror along the flight-path of the aircraft, it allowed the pilot, by keeping the beam centralized between two horizontal green lights, to come in at the correct height and

Below: The USS Antietan and USS Wisconsin refuelling at sea during the Korean war.

direction. Finally, the introduction of the Hawker Siddeley Kestral in 1966, which was later developed into the Hawker Harrier, reduced the need for long flight-decks. The attributes of the vertical/short take-off and landing (V/STOL) aircraft cannot be over-estimated. Such aircraft proved their worth in the Falklands campaign.

Guided Missiles

Following the end of the Second World War, both the Eastern Bloc and the Western powers had seen their increased naval programmes in terms of conventional warfare, but two innovations had emerged from the war that were to change all that. Small rockets were nothing new in sea warfare by 1944, and the Germans went a step further with the development of a medium-range rocket, the V2. With research the V2 could have become a devastatingly accurate weapon. The second and even more deadly discovery was the harnessing of atomic fission. The devastation wreaked at Hiroshima and Nagasaki had demonstrated only too clearly the power of a nuclear explosion. In the East and the West scientists were quick to appreciate that a marriage of the two 'ideas' would create a weapon that could cause untold havoc at a range of thousands of miles. At the end of the war, German scientists, who led the field in guided-missile development, were eagerly snapped up by both

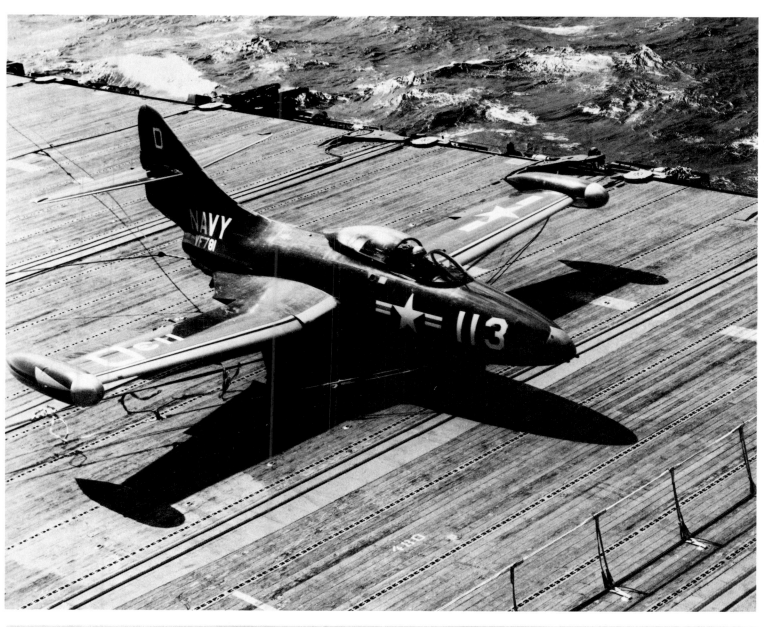

sides to develop surface-to-surface, surface-to-air and air-to-surface missiles, guided by radar.

In 1958 the Soviets produced the world's first guided-missile ships. The *Kildin* class destroyers were capable of delivering a guided missile with either a conventional or a nuclear warhead, homing it onto its target over a distance of 100 miles (160 km). By 1961 this was increased to a range of 250 miles (400 km). As radar beams were unable to bend, a missile was effectively reduced to horizon range, unless corrected by an intermediate aircraft or ship which could re-'fix' its target. These intermediate stages were a weak link that could be taken out by the target itself. Western navies, with strong carrier forces

able to deliver telling blows from the air, followed a different route in their development of missiles. Primarily concerned with warding off missiles delivered from long-range aircraft (the Tu20 'Bear' with a range of 9,000 miles/14,400 km could guide a missile as big as a fighter aircraft, the AS.3. 'Kangeroo', a distance of 300 miles/480 km), the West concentrated on developing surface-to-air missiles linked to sophisticated surveillance systems.

Guided missiles and homing torpedoes rapidly replaced the 'big-gun' as the main armament in warships and did away with the need for large capital ships. Usually travelling at near-supersonic speeds (or above) and guided by radar, radio or television control, such devastating weapons put

Opposite: Preparing the catapult for an aircraft launch aboard USS Independence.

Below: A battery of Seawolf missiles.

aircraft or a ship, were introduced to take out enemy vessels and fast bomber aircraft. The Ikara is a long-range anti-submarine missile equipped with an accoustical torpedo.

The Mammoth Carriers

The development of the aircraft carrier continued to play a major part in American naval policy, though many other navies considered her too large and vulnerable a target for attack by close-range missiles; her aircraft also were equally vulnerable to new target-seeking anti-aircraft weapons. As the U.S.S.R. concentrated her efforts on building up a powerful submarine fleet, Western navies began to construct special anti-submarine craft, and a number of U.S. Navy carriers were equipped for AS (anti-submarine) duties. Still believing in the large-carrier concept, the Americans began to put a number of super-carriers into commission. But these vessels were no longer to be regarded as attack forces against an enemy fleet, but instead were to be seen as a means of gaining political aims by showing a massive localized offshore strength. The *Forrestal*, completed in 1955, was a 59,000-tonner (59,900 tonnes) with a 1,039-ft (317-m) angled flight-deck and a speed of 33 knots; it housed 70 aircraft, and among them were Douglas A3C Skywarriors, the largest-ever carrier-borne aircraft, capable of carrying a 1,200-lb (545-kg) nuclear bombload. Even bigger carriers followed; the 76,000-ton (77,200-tonnes) *Enterprise* in 1961, followed by the 82,000-ton (83,300-tonnes) *Nimitz* in 1975. But by then ship propulsion had entered the nuclear age.

The Suez operation of 1956 highlighted a new strategic concept in the use of aircraft carriers. Each carrier became a mobile naval task force, able to deal with limited wars or 'brush fires', as they were termed. Carriers were converted to enable them to embark an entire Royal Marine Commando Unit together with its arms, equipment and vehicles, all of which could be put ashore by helicopter. When President Nasser of Egypt denied Israel entry to the Suez Canal and war broke out between the two countries, Britain and France intervened with a joint ultimatum, which, when it was ignored, prompted them to plan an amphibious operation. Executed without the benefit of a land base, it turned out to be a model operation. The aircraft from the six carriers involved eliminated Egyptian air opposition and allowed them

Above: The operations room aboard the 22-class frigate HMS Broadsword.

Opposite: The American navy pursued a policy of the giant aircraft carrier.

large ships at risk and called for the development of anti-missile missiles to take them out. The Exocet, a 1,433-lb (651-kg) missile with a 352-lb (160-kg) warhead, capable of near-supersonic speed and with a range of 32 to 43 miles (51 to 69 km), can be fired from a ship or Super Etendard aircraft. Travelling as it does, 6 to 10 ft (1.8 to 3.0 m) above the surface of the sea, it is difficult to detect by shipboard radar. The range and bearing of the target are fed into the missile's guidance system before it is launched, and then it homes onto the target by radar. Close-range surface-to-air missiles such as Seawolf, which reach supersonic speeds (Mach.2.) and have fully automatic radar control and guidance, were developed to combat the Exocet-type missile. After a number of initial teething problems, they proved extremely effective in this role during the Falklands campaign. Smaller guided missiles with a shorter range, which can be fired either from an

A strike aircraft reflected in the visor of a crewman aboard USS Saratoga.

to send in three Royal Marine Commandos to establish a bridgehead for a large-scale Anglo-French parachute landing. The third Commando, which was flown in by helicopter, created a precedent that has since been developed into a successful method of dealing with 'brush fires'. Although a textbook action, the carriers emerging with considerable credit, world opinion brought about a cease-fire and a United Nations Force took over. Many lessons had been learned and the Royal Navy built a specialist AS (Anti-Submarine)/Commando Carrier, HMS *Hermes*, which was completed in 1959. Displacing 28,500 tons (29,000 tonnes), she was 744 ft (227 m) long with a speed of 30 knots, and carried 50 helicopters: Sea King helicopters armed with homing torpedoes for her AS role; Wessex and Gazelles for her commando role. In addition to a ship's company of 980, there was accommodation for a Royal Marine Commando of 750 officers and men, together with equipment and vehicles.

The Expanding Soviet Navy

The Soviet Navy, although it had a powerful submarine fleet, had lagged behind the NATO countries in terms of all-purpose surface craft, and it went into the Cuban 'adventure' without the warships to back it up. Once the United States became aware of Khrushchev's intention to base medium-range ballistic missiles on Cuba, the Americans rapidly blockaded the sea approaches to the island, her carriers *Enterprise* and *Independence* shadowing the Russian freighters and warships, her AS and escort vessels dogging the Soviet submarines. Faced with a head-on conflict, the Soviet Union had little choice but to back down; her missile-laden freighters turned for home. More than anything this brought home to the Kremlin the need for an all-purpose navy. Therefore, from 1962 onwards, there was a vast and speedy expansion in the number and type of surface warships as well as submarines. The 5,000-ton (5,080-tonne) *Kashin* class guided-missile destroyers were followed by the 5,700-ton (5,800-tonne) *Kynda* class and then by the *Kresta 1s*, which saw the addition of a helicopter pad. The *Moskva*, one of two AS carriers housing 18 helicopters, appeared in 1967. These 18,000-ton (18,300-tonne) hybrids, following the lead set by the Japanese *Ise* conversions of the Second World War, were cruiser forward and carrier aft, and were capable of a maximum speed of over 30 knots. Unlike many navies, the Soviet fleet sided with the U.S.A. in recognizing the need for large aircraft carriers, and in 1976 the 40,000-ton (40,640-tonne) *Kiev* was completed. With a length of 934 ft (285 m) and a maximum speed of over 30 knots, she was capable of operating both helicopters and V/STOL aircraft.

Fast Frigates and Destroyers

With the giant battleship and armoured cruiser having been replaced by much smaller warships, which, however, still carried the same punch, many naval strategists began to doubt the future of the massive carriers. In view of the increasing sophistication of weapon development, they make a large, tempting target, particularly for underwater attack. To back up their submarine strike force, which could deliver ballistic missile attacks – conventional and nuclear – from the sea bed over a range of 2,000 miles (3,200 km), the world's navies turned to building smaller, more highly versatile ships. At first existing cruisers were converted for missile attack and re-equipped with rapid-firing, radar-controlled guns which were fully automated for a 'hands off' system of firing.

In 1962 the first of a new type of 5,000-ton (5,080-tonne), purpose-built super destroyer began to take its place in the navies of the world. These super-destroyers were armed with ship-to-air and close-range guided weapons, as well as radar-controlled guns, their steam turbines could be boosted by gas turbines for fast acceleration, and they could travel at well above 30 knots.

The role of anti-submarine warfare has grown in proportion to the rapid expansion of the Soviet submarine fleet and there is an increasing demand for small, fast, but powerfully armed, vessels. The modern frigate is, in its own way, as graceful as her forerunner of Nelson's day, but is far more

Below: The Soviet warship Kiev.

Bottom: The Russian helicopter assault ship Moskva.

United States guided-missile warships on station.

costly to run (an estimated £3,300,000 a year not including her helicopter). Displacing around 2,500 tons (2,540 tonnes), frigates have taken over the role of the old-time destroyers, the 'maids of all work'. The Royal Navy's 2,815-ton (2,860-tonne) *Amazon* class frigate was designed to protect convoys and other naval forces against attack by surface ships, submarines, aircraft and missiles, and has a speed of more than 30 knots. Her fully computerized, automated weapon systems carry the punch of a heavy cruiser.

Because it has a centralized storeroom complex supplying replaceable parts by vertical hoist, sophisticated action information equipment and easily operated gas turbine engines, the normal complement of a ship of this size has been reduced from 513 to 171 which allows more accommodation space to be allotted to the ship's company.

Although armed for an all-round defence capability, the Royal Navy 3,556-ton (3,613-tonne) *Broadsword* class frigate was primarily designed for an anti-submarine role and was the first to be built around an all-missile armament. Armed with Exocet and Seawolf missiles and six AS torpedo tubes, she also carries two Lynx anti-submarine helicopters.

Experience in Battle

Until the Falklands campaign, experience of the behaviour of complex, automated weapon and surveillance systems was gained by simulated war games and exercises. To carry out an amphibious operation, 8,000 miles (12,800 km) away in the South Atlantic in an area which is often battered by tumultuous seas, called for immaculate logistics, and it is to the credit of the planners that replenishment, repairs and maintenance were implemented with clock-work precision, allowing small latitude for mishaps. Sadly, at the very

PRINCIPAL ARMAMENT OF AN *Amazon* CLASS FRIGATE

One 4.5-inch (11.4-cm) Vickers Mark 8 automatic gun – capable of delivering up to 30 rounds a minute (fired either by manual control, or a 'hands off' method, leaving the tracking and decision to fire entirely to the computer)

Exocet missiles – surface-to-surface

Seacat missiles – surface-to-air, surface-to-surface.

Two triple anti-submarine torpedo tubes (firing homing torpedoes)

One Westland Lynx multi-purpose helicopter, carrying either six air-to-surface guided missiles, or two anti-submarine torpedoes.

HMS Amazon, *first of the 21-class frigates.*

beginning, the need was demonstrated for a long-range, radar-equipped surveillance aircraft, able to send back information of a fast-approaching enemy. This omission was the main contributory factor to the loss of the destroyer *Sheffield*, and put the other ships of the fleet at risk, until other precautions were taken to transmit early warning of an enemy attack. The two carriers *Hermes* and *Invincible*, designated AS/Commander Carrier and AS Cruiser respectively, flying helicopters and V/STOL Harriers, were unable to operate the larger surveillance aircraft required.

During the actual landings, the sensitive radar-controlled automated missile systems were confused by radar clutter reflected from the hills, some of which were less than a mile away. Visual look-outs came into their own, and, together with the gunners of the 40-mm, 20-mm, and LMGs (Light Machine Guns), on occasion fought a Second World War type of aircraft engagement. It is difficult to say how much was learned from the Falklands operation, but there can be little doubt that designers and naval strategists have taken a long, hard look at a number of aspects of current warship design.

Even before the Second World War had ended, Allied submarine experts were moving into German shipyards to get their

hands on the advanced, experimental U-Boats under construction there. In particular, they were interested in the Walther propulsion system, which seemed to offer vastly higher underwater speeds. The Soviets certainly experimented with Walther engines, but how far they got with them before discarding the idea has never been revealed. The British built two Walther-powered boats – known as the 'blondes' in reference to their peroxide fuel. They did little more than demonstrate the insoluble drawbacks of the system, and were finally taken out of commission, much to the relief of their crews – explosions had been reported and there had been a leak of noxious fumes aboard. The U.S. Navy showed no interest for it had a better card up its sleeve – nuclear fission.

The Nuclear Submarine

In a search for higher underwater speeds, the Type XXI U-Boat was carefully studied, and the new post-Second World War submarines began to take on a more streamlined silhouette and to possess a greater battery capacity. To eliminate underwater drag the designers dispensed with the deck gun; the cluttered conning tower with its platforms and periscope standards gave way to a streamlined fin; and the schnorchel

underwater breathing equipment became an accepted addition. As the quality of sonar and ASDIC became more sensitive, the Americans began experimenting with 'Hunter-killers', a new concept in anti-submarine warfare. They reasoned that a submarine could be developed into an effective anti-submarine weapon by virtue of the fact that both operated under the same conditions. The introduction of silent-running motors made this an attractive proposition, but the main problem that still remained was the inability to maintain high underwater speeds for any length of time. Once her batteries ran out, a submarine was forced to surface to re-charge them. This problem was solved in the most dramatic fashion; after some costly experiment, the Americans finally perfected the first water-cooled nuclear reactor in 1952.

By 1955 they had installed a nuclear power plant in USS *Nautilus*, a 3,530-ton (3,586-tonne) submarine with a three-decked hull 324 ft (99 m) long – a fearful new underwater menace had been created.

In some ways its propulsion system was a step backwards to the era of the steam submarine. The heavily shielded (to pre-vent the escape of radiation) nuclear reac-tor converted water into steam to drive two twin-shaft geared steam turbines; this system gave the submarine an underwater speed of over 20 knots. The main differ-ence between a nuclear reactor and a conventional steam boiler is that heat generated within a reactor has no need to draw oxygen from the air. This, together with the use of 'scrubbers' which remove toxic gases and recycle clean air, allows the modern nuclear submarine to stay sub-merged for over three months. The *Nautilus*, at first, used Uranium 235 to fuel her reactors, but when she was refuelled two years later, this was replaced by en-riched Uranium, now the standard fuel for nuclear-propulsion. By logging over 80,000 nautical miles submerged on a single fuel-ling, she achieved the potential dream of submariners of the past. Her success paved the way for the wide expansion of the nuclear submarine, and her subsequent

A Soviet Echo *class submarine in a heavy swell.*

successors have reached incredible reported underwater speeds, some in excess of 35 knots.

Later, the Americans, concerned with the threat of a possible Soviet nuclear attack with ballistic missiles, set up a seaward early warning radar 'picket line' using surface ships and large nuclear submarines. One of these picket submarines, the 6,000-ton (6,100-tonne) *Triton*, powered by two nuclear reactors, actually circumnavigated the world, submerged, in February 1960, a distance of 41,500 miles (66,400 km) at an average speed of 18 knots. The addition of the Polaris missile to a nuclear-powered submarine produced the ultimate, most horrendous naval weapon ever conceived. At a cost of $3,500,000,000, the U.S. Navy produced a missile, whose destructive power was virtually equal to that of all the bombs dropped during the Second World War. As each nuclear submarine is armed with 16 such missiles, the destructive force of a Polaris and Poseidon (its successor which carries twice the payload is capable of delivering missiles to three separate targets) submarine fleet defeats the imagination.

Able to lie motionless on the sea bed for months on end, a Polaris submarine can fire a missile from underwater up to 2,000 miles (3,200 km), pin-pointing it on target by sophisticated guidance systems. As the furthest point on land is only 1,700 miles (2,720 km) from the sea, every city in the world is within range. At the first awareness of the Polaris, the Soviets pushed forward a crash-development programme to keep up with the nuclear arms race, followed closely by Great Britain.

An Ultimate Weapon?

At the moment there appears to be no means of detecting a nuclear submarine lying on the sea bed, which would indicate little likelihood of countermeasures in the foreseeable future. The direction that naval strategy will ultimately follow is anyone's guess. With American and NATO Polaris submarines ringing the Soviet Union, and Soviet Polaris submarines lying on the sea bed around the United States, the world has a nuclear stand-off. Should, however, East or West discover a method of detecting these motionless monsters – what then?

Above: A nuclear ballistic missile submarine, USS Woodrow Wilson.

Overleaf: The launch of a Trident missile from a U.S. Navy submarine.

Index